W9-BAL-192

THINK Unix

JON LASSER

Think Unix

Jon Lasser

International Standard Book Number: 0-7897-2376-x

Library of Congress Catalog Card Number: 00-100690

Printed in the United States of America

First Printing: July, 2000

02   01   00   4   3   2

Trademarks

Warning and Disclaimer

Associate Publisher
Tracy Dunkelberger

Acquisitions Editor
Katie Purdum

Development Editor
Hugh Vandivier

Managing Editor
Thomas F. Hayes

Project Editor
Tonya Simpson

Copy Editors
Kay Hoskin
Mike Dietsch

Indexer
Kelly Castell

Proofreader
Benjamin Berg

Technical Editors
Andy Johnston
Scott Orr

Team Coordinator
Vicki Harding

Interior Designer
Maureen McCarty

Cover Designer
Anne Jones

Production
Darin Crone

Contents

About the Author

Jon Lasser lives in Baltimore, Maryland, with his wife, Kathleen, and their three cats. Professionally, Jon juggles Unix systems administration along with both writing and speaking about Unix systems administration. He is also lead coordinator for the Bastille Linux Project, which aims to simplify security on Linux systems.

Dedication

For Kathleen, who knows it's for her anyway.

Acknowledgments

As much as authors might wish otherwise, writing a book is not a solitary endeavor. Above all, I have to thank Kathleen, who washed more than her share of dishes and supported me in countless other ways while I wrote this book. Thanks also to the rest of my family for encouragement, for support, and for maintaining a certain level of excitement about the project.

Thanks go to everyone at Macmillan, especially Katie and Hugh. Thanks, Katie, for pushing me to finish up the book proposal. Thanks to my technical reviewers, Scott and Andy. Thanks, Andy, for long discussions about how one might write a good intro to Unix book.

Many friends contributed to the process in their own special ways. Special thanks go to Karen, for her perspective on design, and to Steve, Shawn, and Jay for asking the right questions.

Thanks to all of my co-workers at UMBC, for tolerating week-long absences throughout this book, for general support, and for always pushing me to deepen my own Unix knowledge.

Finally, thanks to the Tuesday night crew at The Brewer's Art and the Thursday Night Bolton Hill Walkers' Patrol, for helping to keep me sane.

Tell Us What You Think!

As the reader of this book, *you* are our most important critic and commentator. We value your opinion and want to know what we're doing right, what we could do better, what areas you'd like to see us publish in, and any other words of wisdom you're willing to pass our way.

As an associate publisher for Que, I welcome your comments. You can fax, email, or write me directly to let me know what you did or didn't like about this book—as well as what we can do to make our books stronger.

Please note that I cannot help you with technical problems related to the topic of this book, and that due to the high volume of mail I receive, I might not be able to reply to every message.

When you write, please be sure to include this book's title and author as well as your name and phone or fax number. I will carefully review your comments and share them with the author and editors who worked on the book.

Fax: 317-581-4666

Email: quetechnical@macmillanusa.com

Mail: Associate Publisher
         Que
         201 West 103rd Street
         Indianapolis, IN 46290 USA

Introduction

About This Book

So here you are, standing in the bookstore, flipping through this book, trying to decide whether *Think Unix* is for you. Fortunately, you decided to read this part of the book, so I can answer your question directly.

Is This Book For You?

First of all, this book is intended for people with some computer experience. If you've never used a PC or Macintosh, there are probably better places for you to start than this book. I don't start at the beginning. I assume you have an idea of what a file is; what a folder or subdirectory is; where to find the keyboard, monitor, and mouse; and how to turn your computer on. Furthermore, this book is written for people who aren't deathly afraid of trying new things and for people who occasionally make educated guesses about how the whole darned thing works.

This isn't the kind of book that tells you to enter your username at the `login:` prompt and your password at the `password:` prompt. (If you don't know this, I'm telling you now: Enter your username at the `login:` prompt and your password at the `password:` prompt.)

On the other hand, this book is written for people who have never used Unix. Experienced users might learn something but should probably look elsewhere. This book has no information about systems administration, for example, though I hope that it provides a good foundation for such knowledge.

This book is written for people who read closely. This is a short book, and I don't waste much space. The examples are chock-full of useful information, even if it might not be directly relevant. For example, in the first chapter where I discuss reading documentation, I use the man page for logout. That's the only place logout is discussed. If you skip the examples, you might not know how to log out of your system!

Because it's a short book, I've had to cut some things out. There's very little discussion of the "Unix culture." (Yes, there is such a thing, and it's what made the Internet great.) I will mention it in passing, however, when it actually affects how the system works. Furthermore, I don't cover applications: I don't discuss mail readers, news readers, Web browsers, spreadsheets, or word processors. What I say does have a bearing on how these programs operate on Unix, or at least how they should operate. (Many of these products clearly display their PC or Macintosh heritage, however, and don't act as Unix programs ought to act.)

Another feature of this book is that it's full of practice problems. Although nothing can substitute for actual hands-on experience, practice problems give you a way to judge your understanding of a topic and to decide whether you need to reread the section or chapter or even ask a friend for help. I strongly recommend that, if you know a Unix guru already, you bribe her with large quantities of chocolate, tea, cheese, or her favorite alcoholic beverage. Many Unix people are microbrew fanatics. (Disclaimer: I'm a professional Unix guru, and I like both good chocolate and good beer, so I might be a bit biased on this point.)

Finally, if you don't have a sense of humor, this book might not be for you. If you didn't crack a smile once during this entire section, we might not get along. (You didn't have to find every joke funny, of course, but the others in this book fall along these general lines.) I use funny command and filenames, sometimes to make a point but also to keep it interesting for myself.

This Book's Approach

Unix is distinguished from operating systems such as Windows and Mac OS in that it is "deep": beyond the surface user interface lies a wealth of functionality and power rivaled by few other systems. The price of this richness is that there's a lot to learn.

Because of this depth, this book's approach to Unix is a high-level conceptual view. Many computer books, especially ones about Unix, take what I consider to be a "phrasebook" approach. That is, they go about teaching a large number of individual commands, often with a somewhat useful classification scheme—for example, "commands dealing with directories" or "commands dealing with files." It's as though these books were tourists' phrasebooks, helping foreigners journey through a place that they can't even hope to understand.

By contrast, this book's approach is more like that of a foreign-language textbook: Rather than concentrating on prepackaged statements, you will learn to think and speak Unix. By that, I mean that you will learn to solve problems the way that Unix was designed to do things, rather than just muddling through. You will learn the logical structure of the operating system—its grammar, if you will. My goal isn't simply to get you comfortable with navigating the Unix command prompt, but also to let you feel at home while learning new commands not discussed in this book and, most importantly, combining multiple commands to achieve particular goals.

In that vein, the entire first chapter of *Think Unix* is dedicated to Unix documentation. Learning to look up the answers is necessary if you want to become a proficient user of the operating system. Because of this attention, *Think Unix* doesn't burden you with an appendix describing several hundred Unix commands. Instead, you will learn to look to the system itself for that information.

Because Unix is a deep system, it's possible to learn it a little bit at a time. Usually, what you don't know doesn't interfere with what you're doing. Learn enough to navigate comfortably, and return later to learn more. In writing this book, I've discovered things about Unix I didn't know, and I've been using Unix professionally for six years.

There are disadvantages to this book's approach to learning Unix. Foremost among them is the absence of necessary knowledge at any given point in the learning process. This is the result of any linear approach to learning a complex system: It's rarely possible to start from nothing and proceed based only on what is already known, especially if the practical is discussed before all of the theoretical learning is finished. Of course, nobody wants to read 200 pages of theory before learning anything useful, so sometimes you might need to plow ahead without completely understanding everything. You may wish to mark these sections and return to them later, or you might simply wish to give the book more than one reading if you've never used Unix before. Any well-written book should reward multiple readings.

Reference Platform

The reference platform—that is, the type of machine on which the examples are tested and from which their output is displayed—is a Linux machine with GNU tools. When referencing the Korn Shell I use pdksh, and for the C Shell I use tcsh. In short, I use my home machine: a Red Hat Linux 6.1 box with Bash 1.14 as the default shell. (The *shell* is the program that interprets the command line and allows the user to interact with the system. Many shells are available on Unix systems.)

This choice of platform is not because Linux in general, or Red Hat Linux in particular, is "better" than any other version of Unix. Instead, it's a popular and easy-to-obtain distribution with adequate commercial support and boxed sets available at many retail outlets. If you don't already have some form of Unix on your home PC, I recommend starting with the most recent release of whichever distribution the nearest Linux guru recommends. (I recommend Linux over other Unix versions for home PCs because there are a larger number of Linux experts than experts in FreeBSD, NetBSD, or OpenBSD. Furthermore, recent Linux distributions have installation processes much simpler than the installers for other Unix versions. Both of these traits are important to new users. Still, if your local guru recommends one of the BSD versions instead, feel free to give that a try.)

Sometimes, to make a point, or because there is significant divergence between different flavors of Unix (yes, the many versions of Unix are known as *flavors*), I demonstrate a particular command on one of the many other flavors of Unix. When I do this, I mention the specific version I use so that you know what to expect. Because they're what I use at work, I'll tend to provide contrasting examples from Solaris 2.6 and Irix 6.5. Again, this isn't intended to imply any sort of superiority, merely availability.

An Ultra-Super-Brief History of Unix

One reason why Unix is a deep operating system, in the sense I referred to earlier in this introduction, is that it has a history. Unix is just about 30 years old, depending on how you count, and its predecessors are several years older than that. At this point, the Macintosh OS is about 15 years old and Windows somewhat younger. (Windows, of course, used to—and in some cases still does—run on top of MS-DOS, but that's a particularly shallow operating system, in terms of the services it provides.)

One advantage of living in the modern age is computers that are much faster than we really need them to be and that possess more memory and disk storage than we should know how to fill. I'm certainly not going to get into specifics here because if I do that future generations will laugh at how slow our computers were and how insignificant their storage. Similarly, I won't tell you how slow computers were in 1969, when Unix was born, and I won't tell you how little memory and disk space they had.

If I did, you would almost certainly laugh, and you probably wouldn't believe me anyway. If you're still reading this in the bookstore, you'd probably think that I was either stupid or lying to you, and as a result you might not buy this book. If you've already bought the book, if you're reading it in a library, or if you've borrowed a friend's copy, I still won't tell you, because then you might not *read* the book, and I wouldn't like that one bit.

Suffice it to say, these were *very*, and I do mean *very*, small computers.

In fact, the computer on which Unix was born (a PDP-7, if you must know) was small even for its day. The people who wrote it (Ken Thompson and Dennis Ritchie, among many others) did so after being moved off the Multics project, which ran on much larger computers. Because of their limited resources, Unix programs had to be small. Unlike most modern applications on Windows or Macintosh, you didn't have a single program that did a whole bunch of things—like, for example, a typical WYSIWYG word processor—but many smaller programs, each of which did one thing. One goal was to have small programs so that they could fit into memory. Disk space was at such a premium that everything was as small as possible, including program names. It was (and is) a common Unix convention to remove the vowels from a command's name to save space. It also happens to save a fair amount of typing if you use the system much.

The decisions made in the first several years of development have shaped the Unix approach to problem solving. The main consequence is the idea of small programs, each with limited functionality, which can be put together in various combinations to produce results. This philosophy is often known as the "toolbox approach," and understanding this is key to my suggestion that Unix can be learned as a language.

Because there are a multitude of small commands, and the idea is to put these commands together to get what you want, you need a way to connect them. This book is about those connections: what they are, how they work, and how to string several commands together into Unix sentences. After you learn to put sentences together and you start putting together whole paragraphs' worth of commands, you have begun to *Think Unix*.

I

Unix Concepts

1

Unix
Documentation

I've always been of the opinion that it's more important to be able to figure things out as you go along than to know a whole bunch of things when you begin. As such, the most important thing you can learn is *how* to learn. This chapter is all about Unix documentation, and thus how you can teach yourself.

Man pages (an abbreviation of "manual pages") are, more or less, the standard documentation on Unix systems. They were the first form of online documentation on Unix and are still the most common type. Newer formats, such as GNU Info and Web pages, are becoming more important, but even these formats tend to share several conventions with classic Unix man pages.

A few words of warning are in order.

Words of Warning

Man pages were originally written by Unix developers for Unix developers, and they still tend to be written by programmers, which implies that they're written *for* programmers as well. (How many programmers do you know who can speak to normal people? That's pretty close to the number of programmers who can write for normal people as well.) Furthermore, because writing documentation is a boring, time-consuming process (and much less fun than programming—at least if you're a programmer), the documentation often comes last...if it comes at all.

As a result, a fair number of programs are in various stages of *undocumentation*. Some programs have man pages that are too cryptic for the average user. More programs have man pages that are out of date. Other man pages are simply incorrect, and a shocking number of programs are almost entirely undocumented. Furthermore, third-party software often comes with its own documentation (man pages or otherwise) that is wildly nonstandard—if the software's author bothers with documentation at all.

That said, you need to learn how to read man pages. Poor documentation is still the best place to start when it's the only game in town. Although you can get by for a short while without learning this stuff, by doing so you're asking for trouble. Or at least you're asking your Unix guru more questions than he'll be happy answering. The most frequent guru response to many user questions is RTFM: *Read The "Fine" Manual.* (Well, most gurus mentally substitute a different word for *fine*, but you get the idea.)

Reading Man Pages

To understand man pages, you have to see them first. The first command you must learn is man, which is the standard tool used to read man pages. There are other, perhaps better, tools, but man is still the most important. In its simplest form, you can display a man page by typing `man` *`ManPageIWantToRead`* at your prompt.

Perhaps the second most important command to learn is `logout`, because if you don't sign off of the system when you are finished, anybody else can read your files and send mail as you. This is a common problem on multiuser machines, especially at shared workstations or in computer labs at universities. Often, malicious people will send embarrassing or insulting mail from a machine where the legitimate user has forgotten to log out. This, obviously, won't do, so pretend you logged in to a Unix box and typed the one command your guru told you: `man logout`. Something quite like the following might come up on your screen:[1]

```
LOGOUT(1) Unix Users Guide

NAME
logout - exit from a login shell

SYNOPSIS
logout

DESCRIPTION
Terminates the current login shell and ends the associated session.

SEE ALSO
login(1)
```

The first thing to notice about this man page is its header. You should note that it includes the name of the program, a number in parentheses after the program name (the manual section), and the name of the notional manual that "contains" the page. (Of course, man pages aren't real pages bound in a real book, so in reality no manual physically contains the page.)

Below this header, you should notice that the man page is divided into several elements. Some of these segments, such as the name, the synopsis, and the description, should be present in every man page. Others, such as *see also* might not be present on a given page.

The name segment contains not only the name of the command, as one would assume, but also a very brief description of the purpose of the command. This is because the name is easily searchable, as you'll soon see. The description provided here might not be helpful to beginning users (or at all!), but any search capabilities are better than none.

---

1. Actually, I was rather disturbed to find that the Linux man page for *logout* is totally useless for normal people and that Irix doesn't even have a man page for this. Of course, there's a perfectly logical deep technical reason, but it's still a bad idea. Shame on all you developers. The man page you actually see for *logout* is based both on the Solaris man page and my own knowledge of the system. Actually, most of the man pages you'll see in this chapter are composites of several man pages, stripped-down pages used to illustrate a point, or both. Look at the real pages on your system to see the full functionality of these commands.

Although it's not obvious in this case, the synopsis is the most critical portion of the man page: It shows all the modifiers that can be applied to the command. In the case of logout, there are no modifiers: The only thing you can do is type **logout**. The synopsis has a special, well-defined syntax that I will examine more closely.

The description might or might not be useful. Remember that these pages were written by programmers, who generally can't remember what it was like to be a novice even when they try. In this case, between the name of the command and both the short and long descriptions, it should be possible to puzzle out what the command does.

The name, synopsis, and description are present on nearly every man page. Other common parts include a files portion, which lists files used or referenced by the command, and an authors field, which lists the names and often the email addresses of the responsible parties. Sometimes you'll see a bugs section, which lists known problems with the command. Occasionally there will be a history, which might explain why things were done the way they were done or perhaps describe how this command is different from the older version of the command.

The man page for logout also contains a see also segment, which points at the page for login. Note that, as in the header, there is a parenthesized number. Man pages are grouped into numbered sections, each with its own purpose.

Manual Sections

The Unix manual is divided   into ten sections. These are numbered one through nine, plus a section named "n." For nonprogrammers, the important sections are one and six. Section one contains what are broadly defined as *user command*s, such as *logout*, *login*, and *passwd*. Section six provides the documentation for a number of *games*. (In fact, many games have their man pages in the first manual section, but this is one of the many instances of sloppy documentation I warned you about earlier.) Section four or five, depending   on what flavor of Unix you have installed, contains descriptions of configuration *file formats*, such as mail reader configurations. You might find these useful when you want to know how to configure a particular application or service.

Programmers might be interested   in sections two and three of the manual, which contain *system calls* and *subroutines*, respectively. Other manual sections differ between Unix flavors but are generally reserved for system-level commands and information.

Terminology: Arguments and Options

Before I can talk about syntax, I need to spend a moment discussing *arguments* and *options*. An argument is something entered at the end of the command line, generally the name of a file or some text on which the command will act:

```
[ jon@frogbog jon ]$ command YesItIs NoItIsnt
```

The piece at the beginning, up to the dollar sign, is the command prompt as I have it set on my system at home. (jon is my username, frogbog is the name of the machine, and jon is also the directory I'm sitting in.) I'm running a command named command that has two arguments, YesItIs and NoItIsnt. Perhaps those arguments are the names of files in my directory.

An option is something entered on the command line, generally between the name of the command and its arguments. An option generally alters the functionality of the program, telling it to behave in a way other than its default. Options are usually prefaced with one or two hyphens:

```
[ jon@frogbog jon ]$ command --red --blue YesItIs NoItIsnt
```

red and blue are options, perhaps changing the color of text in the output of the command. They are both long options, whole words prefaced by two hyphens. Long options are new to the Unix world, relatively speaking. You can tell that they're new because they favor descriptive power over brevity. Some Unix people hate long options for precisely this reason.

Short options are generally prefaced with a single hyphen, and many programs allow them to be grouped together. Assuming it supported short options as well as long options and allowed options to be grouped together, the command could be typed **command -r -b YesItIs NoItIsnt** or **command -rb YesItIs NoItIsnt**. Short options are plentiful in the Unix world, and many programs with long options support short options that do the same thing, to make everyone happy.

Syntax

The synopsis lists all the different forms of the command being examined. Now look at a slightly more complicated synopsis, as well as part of its description:

SYNOPSIS

        passwd [-l] [-u [-f]] [-d] [-S] [username]

DESCRIPTION

The *passwd* command is used to update a user's password.

-l This option allows a system administrator to lock the specified user's account.

-u This is the reverse of -l -- it will unlock the account password by removing the ! prefix. This option is available to root only. By default passwd will refuse to create a passwordless account (it will not unlock an account that has only "!" as a password). The force option -f will override this protection.

```
-d This is a quick way to disable a password for an account. It
will set the named account passwordless. Available to root only.

-S This will output a short information screen about the status of
the password for a given account. Available to root user only.
```

In a command synopsis, *bracketed arguments and options are optional*.[2] Thus passwd has several possible options: `-l`, `-d`, and `-S`. What is that last group of options, `[-u [-f]]`? It's optional, that's for certain, but inside that there's another optional piece: `-f` is not a valid option unless `-u` is used as well. But none of these options is actually available to users other than the system administrator. (Why am I examining them, you ask? Because you need to learn to read man pages, that's why.)

You should also note that the optional argument *username* is a variable: You are not expected to literally put the word *username* at the end of the passwd command. Instead, *username* is a placeholder for your data. Perhaps you want to change your friend Bob's password; in that case, you could type **passwd bob** and, if you were logged in as the system administrator, the system would prompt you for Bob's new password.[3] If Alice asked you to change her password, you could type **passwd alice** to change her password. The only time you might type **passwd username** is if you actually had a user whose account name was username, but you'd probably do that only if you were being deliberately silly, or if you were writing up examples in a computer book.

In general, variables are set apart in man pages by a change in emphasis: They are underlined, boldface, italicized, or a different color, depending on your system configuration. However, because the people who wrote up the man pages aren't perfect, or because they haven't read this chapter, sometimes variable options and arguments look precisely like the surrounding text. In general, this should be made clear in the description portion of the man page. Careful reading is often rewarded.

Besides brackets, there are two more common modifiers for options and arguments. An ellipsis (known to less uppity folk as "three periods") signifies multiple arguments of the same or similar form. For example, the command

```
cat file [...]
```

displays at least one file but can show any number of files.[4]

A vertical bar (known in the Unix world as a *pipe*) signifies exclusive choices. For example, the rm command syntax looks like this:

```
rm [-f|-i] file [...]
```

---

2. Yes, mandatory options are possible. Why do you ask?

3. Assuming, of course, that Bob's account name is bob. If Bob's username were fred, you would type **passwd fred** instead.

4. Actually, *cat* doesn't need *any* arguments, but as I said earlier, some of these examples have been radically simplified.

It removes files with either the -f argument or the -i argument, but not both. New users might want to remove files with the -i argument, which confirms the deletion of each file before actually removing it. The -f option, by contrast, forces a removal, without asking, of a file. (This is the default behavior on Unix.)

More Pages to Read

The best way to learn is by doing. Some subjects are best learned with constant, repetitive practice. In this spirit, this section contains a pair of fairly typical man pages broken down and interpreted. If you're sure you know what you're doing, I suggest that you skip to the practice problems in the next section. If you don't do well with those, come back and try these.

echo

```
ECHO(1)                          FSF                      ECHO(1)


NAME
        echo - display a line of text

SYNOPSIS
        echo [OPTION]... [STRING]...

DESCRIPTION
        Echo the STRING(s) to standard output.

        -n      do not output the trailing newline

        -e      enable interpretation of the backslash-escaped
                characters listed below

        -E      disable interpretation of those sequences in
                STRINGs

        -help display this help and exit (should be alone)
        -version
                output version information and exit (should be
                alone)

        Without -E, the following sequences are recognized and
        interpolated:

\NNN the character whose ASCII code is NNN (octal)
\\ backslash
\a alert (BEL)
\b backspace
```

```
\c suppress trailing newline
\f form feed
\n new line
\r carriage return
\t horizontal tab
\v vertical tab
```

REPORTING BUGS
        Report bugs to bug-sh-utils@gnu.org

SEE ALSO
        The full documentation for echo is maintained as a Texinfo
        manual. If the *info* and *echo* programs are properly
        installed at your site, the command

                info echo

        should give you access to the complete manual.

COPYRIGHT
        Copyright © 1999 Free Software Foundation, Inc.
        This is free software; see the source for copying condi
        tions. There is NO warranty; not even for MERCHANTABILITY
        or FITNESS FOR A PARTICULAR PURPOSE.

The header and name sections of this page are self-explanatory. The synopsis, unfortunately, collapses all the options into a single [OPTION]..., which makes it difficult to determine what combinations of options are valid. For example, it's clear, after you read the description, that the -e and -E options are mutually exclusive. Furthermore, it appears that -e is the default, but the description never makes this entirely clear.

The [STRING]... is the line of text to display. A *string* is geek speak for a line of text. Now try it out:

```
[ jon@frogbog jon ]$ echo Test Message
Test Message
```

Yes, it certainly seems to display a line of text. Now try one of the special codes (the man page uses the fancy phrase "backslash-escaped characters," but you know what they mean[5]) listed on the page:

```
[ jon@frogbog jon ]$ echo Test Message\n
Test Messagen
```

---

5. And if you don't, don't worry about it. You can see in the example, and if it still doesn't make sense, I'll discuss it again in Chapter 7. Feel free to skim this part.

That didn't work, isn't that strange? The reason is that the shell, the program we are in when we log on to the system and that interprets the command line, converts the backslashes for you.[6] As you would with the echo command, you must escape the backslash, like so:

```
[ jon@frogbog jon ]$ echo Test Message\\n
Test Message\n
```

That didn't work either! Perhaps this interpretation of the man page is incorrect, and -E is the default, not -e. Now try that:

```
[ jon@frogbog jon ]$ echo -e Test Message\\n
Test Message
```

(If you can't see, there's an extra blank line after the test message.) That worked, despite the system's best efforts to confuse us.

One of the primary reasons people read man pages is to determine the syntax of the command. Although it might be trivial in this example that the page was unclear regarding the defaults, it's often not trivial, and you might well be reduced to this sort of trial-by-error to figure out what the command really does. As far as the backslash escape issue, I will cover that again later in more detail, and if that part went by too fast, don't worry. This also shows, however, that sometimes what you don't know can interfere with what you do know. Most of the time, however, it doesn't, and you can blithely ignore those things you can't figure out.

cal

```
CAL(1) Unix Reference Manual

NAME
cal - displays a calendar

SYNOPSIS
cal [-mjy] [month [year]]

DESCRIPTION

Cal displays a simple calendar. If arguments are not specified,
the current month is displayed. The options are as follows:

-m Display monday as the first day of the week

-j Display julian dates (days one-based, numbered from January 1)

-y Display a calendar for the current year.
```

---

6. For more about shells, see Chapter 6.

A single parameter specifies the year (1 - 9999) to be displayed;
note the year must be fully specified: "cal 89" will *not* display
a calendar for 1989. Two parameters denote the month (1 - 12) and
year. If no parameters are specified, the current month's calendar
is displayed.

A year starts on Jan 1.

The Gregorian Reformation is assumed to have occurred in 1752 on
the 3rd of September. Ten days following that date were eliminated
by the reformation, so the calendar for that month is a bit unusual.

HISTORY
A cal appeared in Version 6 AT&T UNIX.

The header and the name are fairly self-explanatory: cal is a user utility that displays
a calendar. The history is present, but not particularly informative. (Hey, it's a history; what do you want?)

The synopsis shows what looks to be a single option, -mjy, but if you read the
description, it is clear that these are three separate options. What's going on here?
With many utilities, short options can be grouped together on the command line
with a single hyphen. (Obviously, this wouldn't work particularly well for long
options, which is probably why you can't do it.) On at least one utility you can
group options together without a hyphen, but that's an exception I'll talk about
later.

The description seems simple enough, but if you look closely, there seems to be a
conflict between the synopsis and the description. Now have another look:

SYNOPSIS
cal [-mjy] [month [year]]

DESCRIPTION
.
.
.
-j Display julian dates (days one-based, numbered from January 1)

-y Display a calendar for the current year.

A single parameter specifies the year (1 - 9999) to be displayed;
note the year must be fully specified: "cal 89" will not display
a calendar for 1989. Two parameters denote the month (1 - 12) and
year. If no parameters are specified, the current month's calendar
is displayed.

A year starts on Jan 1.

If you look at the arguments on the cal command line, it seems that a single argument would be the month and two arguments would be the month and the year. The description, however, suggests that only one argument (they use the word *parameter*, but it's the same thing in the end, isn't it?) would represent a year.

This is clearly a case where the page is either confusing or misleading, depending on who you are and how you read. Now try the command both ways and see what happens:

```
[ jon@frogbog jon ] cal 12
```

```
                    12

        January              February                March
Su Mo Tu We Th Fr Sa    Su Mo Tu We Th Fr Sa    Su Mo Tu We Th Fr Sa
               1  2        1  2  3  4  5  6           1  2  3  4  5
 3  4  5  6  7  8  9     7  8  9 10 11 12 13     6  7  8  9 10 11 12
10 11 12 13 14 15 16    14 15 16 17 18 19 20    13 14 15 16 17 18 19
17 18 19 20 21 22 23    21 22 23 24 25 26 27    20 21 22 23 24 25 26
24 25 26 27 28 29 30    28 29                   27 28 29 30 31
31
 .
 .
 .

        October              November               December
Su Mo Tu We Th Fr Sa    Su Mo Tu We Th Fr Sa    Su Mo Tu We Th Fr Sa
                  1        1  2  3  4  5              1  2  3
 2  3  4  5  6  7  8     6  7  8  9 10 11 12     4  5  6  7  8  9 10
 9 10 11 12 13 14 15    13 14 15 16 17 18 19    11 12 13 14 15 16 17
16 17 18 19 20 21 22    20 21 22 23 24 25 26    18 19 20 21 22 23 24
23 24 25 26 27 28 29    27 28 29 30             25 26 27 28 29 30 31
30 31
```

So that's what the year 12 looked like; I didn't know that my birthday was on a Thursday that year. Now try again. This time I want to see September 1752, because the note at the end of the description looks interesting:

```
[ jon@frogbog jon ] cal 9 1752
```

```
   September 1752
Su Mo Tu We Th Fr Sa
       1  2 14 15 16
17 18 19 20 21 22 23
24 25 26 27 28 29 30
```

That doesn't agree with the man page either, does it? If the page author intended to say, "ten days beginning with the third of September," that's not right because in that case the thirteenth would be on the calendar; if the page author intended to say "ten days after the third of September," then the third of September *would* be on the calendar. The only interpretation that makes sense is "the third of September, and ten days following."

At any rate, the bug is probably (and I do emphasize *probably*) not in the software, because that's the sort of detail that Unix geeks dwell on; the documentation, it seems, is another story entirely. This is also demonstrated in that the synopsis clearly should read as follows:

```
SYNOPSIS
cal [-mjy] [[month] year]
```

Reader beware.

Practice Problems

1. Given the following synopsis, how many people does the imaginary command dinner require as arguments? How many arguments can you use?

    ```
    SYNOPSIS
    dinner [-d|-t] host hostess [ guest ... ]
    ```

2. Given the following synopsis, which options are optional and which are mandatory?

    ```
    SYNOPSIS
    lunch [--in|--out] --cuisine=cuisine count
    ```

3. Create a man page synopsis for television. Television takes only one option, either off (--off) or on (--on). All other features of television are handled by its graphical user interface.

4. Create a man page synopsis for ice cream. Ice cream takes one or more flavors as arguments and mutually exclusive short options for either a cup or a cone. Use a u to represent a cup and o to represent a cone.

5. Create a man page synopsis for a telephone call. Telephone takes mutually exclusive options for handset or speakerphone, and either a seven- or ten-digit phone number. Ten-digit phone numbers might optionally be prefixed by the numeral one. Optionally, hyphens might be placed after the one, after the area code, and after the telephone exchange. Use the letter N to represent a single digit, h to represent a handset, and s to represent a speakerphone.

Documentation Hide-and-Go-Seek

Although understanding man pages is critical to reading Unix documentation, other informative files might be strewn all about the computer and the Internet as

well. We're going on a short tour of some of the places all the information you
need might be hidden. Of course, much of this documentation uses the same
command synopsis format as man pages, so you haven't wasted your time by learning how to read them. I promise, knowing how to read man pages is the number
one underrated Unix skill; finding the documentation you need is the number two
underrated Unix skill.

Some Unix users say that man pages are helpful only if you already know what
you're looking for. Although it certainly doesn't hurt to know the name of the
command you're after, there is another way: apropos or man -k. Some systems have
one, some systems have the other, and some systems even have both. If your system
has both, they tend to work identically. In the following, I use apropos, but man -k
would work identically on systems that don't have an apropos command.

To use the apropos command, simply run it with an appropriate keyword for what
you would like information on. If I wanted information on documentation, I
might type the following:

```
[ jon@frogbog jon ] apropos documentation
perldoc (1) - Look up Perl documentation in pod format.
perlpod (1) - plain old documentation
perltoc (1) - perl documentation table of contents
```

That's not exactly what I was looking for, so I'd try a different keyword:

```
[ jon@frogbog jon ] apropos manual
man (1) - format and display the on-line manual pages
man2html (1) - format a manual page in html manuals with -mdoc
perlxs (1) - XS language reference manual
whereis (1) - locate the binary, source, and manual page files
for a command
xman (1x) - Manual page display program for the X Window System
```

There we go! Not only can I find the documentation for the man command, but
I've found xman, so that I can read man pages in X, and man2html, so that I can convert manual pages to HTML. Note that apropos searches only the short description given in the Name portion of the man page.[7]

The whatis command is a complement to the apropos command: You provide the
command name, and it provides the short description. If I saw reference to the
passwd command and I wanted to know what it did, I might type the following:

```
[ jon@frogbog jon ]$ whatis passwd
passwd (1) - update a user's authentication tokens(s)
passwd (5) - password file
```

---

7. Furthermore, *apropos* uses a prebuilt database to speed up these searches. If your sysadmin has been
lax in her or his duties, that database might be out of date. (If you *are* the admin, you can rebuild the
database with *makewhatis*. *makewhatis* lives in different places on different systems; check your manual for more details.)

That would certainly provide a quick idea of what the passwd command does. Note that whatis searches all manual sections unless otherwise specified.

One final way for you to search man pages is man -K. (That's a capital *K*, not a lowercase *k*.) man -K searches not only the short description, but the entire text of every man page that it can find on your system. This can take a very long time, especially on systems with many man pages or slow disks, but sometimes it's the only way to find the information you're searching for.

If you choose to use the xman command to view man pages in your X Window System, you can read the documentation in a nice, proportional font. It has a search feature that enables you to search the current page or via apropos, though not via man -K, and you might have multiple pages displayed at once. Unfortunately, one very nice feature that is missing in xman is the capability to click through to another page in the See Also portion of the man page or to click any of the pages returned by an apropos search. Nevertheless, reasonably proficient Unix users can thoroughly customize xman, and it might be worth a look.

GNU Info is another very common format for software documentation, especially for GNU project software.[8] GNU Info is a hypertext system, essentially similar to the World Wide Web. Generally, each system has a central directory of all GNU Info pages on the system, and you can search your current page.

The standard tool to read GNU Info documentation is info. It runs in a standard text console, so you can just type **info** from a terminal session to start it up. It has built-in help and a tutorial, so it should be relatively easy to navigate despite its somewhat less-than-intuitive navigation keystrokes.[9] To see a specific *node* (that's the GNU Info terminology equivalent to a man page or Web page), you can type **info commandname**.

Of course, many people write up large portions of their documentation in plain-text, which has the advantage of being easy to write and simple to read without complex tools. The three most common ways to read ASCII text are cat, more, and less. Each of them can be run simply with the command name followed by the name of the file.

cat is the simplest of the three: It simply outputs the text to the screen. This is fine for short files, but longer files might scroll off the screen or even out of your backscroll buffer, if you have one. more displays the text one page at a time, prompting you to press a key after each screen.

---

8. The GNU project is a group of people who have cloned most of the standard Unix tools. Linux uses GNU tools, and many administrators build the GNU tools on their systems in order to have standardized tools available everywhere. (Other administrators claim that GNU tools are inferior to native tools and refuse to build them. This is an essentially religious conflict, sort of like Mac versus Windows. Unix is full of religious conflicts; that's part of being a deep system with a culture that has accreted around it.)

9. Less-than-intuitive for me, at least.

Some old Unix systems have a command called pg that does basically the same thing, but a little bit differently. Other, newer, Unix systems might have a command called pg that doesn't help you read man pages. more is generally considered to be at least as flexible as pg, at least in its more recent incarnations. (As there are with Windows and Mac programs, there are different versions of various Unix programs. These Unix programs, however, can be as much as 30 years old.) Generally, I'd recommend staying away from pg unless you really know what you're doing.

The most advanced (and hence the most complicated) plaintext reader available on most systems is less. It lets you to scroll forward and backward in your text file, and even has all sorts of search capabilities built in. The spacebar progresses through the document page-by-page, whereas the b key pages through the document in reverse. (On some systems, the PageUp and PageDown keys have been mapped to the same function.) To quit less, just use the letter q. The letter h brings up a help menu listing all the keys, and the man page is fairly complete if you're interested in using some of the advanced features of less.

Where are these text files you might want to read? Scattered in directories throughout the system, no doubt. Often, programs downloaded from the Internet have README files or other text documentation along with the program itself. Many administrators leave these files in the directory where the files were put, often /usr/doc, /usr/src, /usr/local, or /usr/local/src. Many Linux systems put the documentation for individual programs in /usr/doc/; each program has a separate subdirectory named by package name and version number, such as /usr/doc/gzip-1.2.4. (If you don't understand these directory names, don't worry; I discuss directories in Chapter 2.)

Given the popularity of the Internet, it seems inevitable that many programmers have put their documentation on the World Wide Web or even in HTML files stored locally on your system. The best way to find this documentation is often your favorite Web directory (Yahoo! is still my favorite) or search engine (Google is what I use for searching). A well-written query should result in finding the documentation you need if it's on the Internet. (If it's stored locally on your system, HTML documentation is likely to be in the same sorts of places as plain-text manuals.)

It's best to read this documentation with your favorite Web browser, if you have one. If you're stuck in a text console, the best (and quite nearly only!) text-based Web browser on Unix is lynx. lynx can be run without any options to begin browsing the Web, or with the name of a locally accessible file.

In the same vein, a great deal of information about Unix software is available on the Internet. Often the best resource for information on a given program or environment is the FAQ, the Frequently Asked Questions list for a given piece of software. Traditionally, the FAQ has been posted to the appropriate newsgroup for the software on a regular basis, in the hopes that people would read the FAQ rather than ask the same questions over and over again. (Unfortunately, it tends not to work quite that way, but it's much more convenient to tell people to read the FAQ than it is to answer the question in full each time it's asked.) These days the FAQ is often posted on a Web page in addition to, or sometimes instead of, being sent to the newsgroup on a monthly basis.

As long as I'm on the topic, newsgroups are often a good source of information specific to a given software package. Newsgroups are arranged in a tree, by subject. Linux newsgroups are listed under `comp.os.linux` and include `comp.os.linux.announce` (announcements regarding Linux software), `comp.os.linux.hardware` (for questions related to hardware), `comp.os.linux.advocacy` (for discussions regarding ways to convince people to switch or to improve the image of Linux in the wider world), and so on. Most Unix groups are in the `comp.os.unix` hierarchy; many of these groups have FAQs.

Because of the large volume of spam posted to Usenet (a situation that has improved somewhat at present), and because of the smaller breadth of topic, many software packages have mailing lists. Mailing lists are like newsgroups, only the messages go straight into your mailbox rather than forcing you to go to them on Usenet. These lists are generally referenced on the relevant software package's Web page, and often have publicly accessible archives as well. I highly recommend that you search the archives before sending mail to the list, so you don't annoy the list readers with questions that have already been answered. Those people are your tech support, and it's in your best interest to reduce the work they need to do to help you out. (If you do that, you can often get better help from experienced users than you can from official customer support; if you don't do that, you probably won't get help from anyone.)

If you use Netscape to browse the Web or read email, you can also use it to read Usenet newsgroups. (The exact way to do this depends significantly on what version of Netscape you use.) Console-based newsreaders include `tin`, `trn`, `slrn`, and literally dozens of others. `tin` and `slrn` are generally considered simpler to use, but that sentiment is hardly universal. `xrn` is one newsreader for X, but I don't even know anyone who uses that rather than Netscape or a terminal-based newsreader.

If GNOME or KDE is installed on your system, you have other options for reading documentation. The `gnome-help-browser` is a Web browser that reads several formats besides HTML. It reads the (nonstandard) GNOME help format (though this seems relatively unused at this point), GNU Info files, and standard Unix man pages. Reading GNU Info files in a Web browser–like format is sensible and quite useful; furthermore, when reading man pages, other listed man pages are clickable links! This makes jumping among a set of related pages much simpler. Although `gnome-help-browser` has a built-in `whatis` command, it has neither `apropos` nor a more general search tool. This absence hurts what would otherwise be the single most complete documentation reader for Unix.

kdehelp is fundamentally similar to gnome-help-browser, only with a search function. You can read man pages, KDE's HTML-based documentation, and GNU Info files. It makes pretty little clickable links, and it uses colors and font changes for emphasis. You can search the documentation you're currently looking at, and you can search KDE's HTML-based documentation, man pages, or both. (As of this writing, GNU Info files can't yet be searched.) It's not especially different from gnome-help-browser, but your system might have only one or the other, if it has either.

Platform-Specific Documentation

Back in the 1980s, each commercial Unix vendor did its best to "differentiate" its flavor from all the other Unix flavors. (The customers, of course, just wanted a Unix that worked right, but nobody really asked them.) One consequence of this battle is that even today each vendor has at least one nonstandard documentation format available with special flavor-specific supplemental information in this format. It's helpful to have some idea of what these are and where to find them, but don't take this whirlwind tour as the final word. This is one instance where it's especially helpful to check your system's official documentation, if you know where your admin put it.

These days, the World Wide Web is rapidly becoming the standard place to find Unix documentation, though some vendors still resist. I can't cover every Unix platform in this section, so I'll cover some common flavors. Furthermore, companies have a bad habit of moving files around their Web sites, so individual URLs might be out of date. As always, ask your system administrator or your vendor for more information.

Linux

Fortunately, Linux began to become successful at about the same time the World Wide Web did, so just about all Linux-specific documentation is available on the Web.[10] All official Linux documentation is available in several different file formats— including HTML, PostScript, plain text, and DVI[11]—as well as the source files used to produce all these other formats. All this documentation is part of the Linux Documentation Project (LDP). The LDP homepage is at http://linuxdoc.org/ and has links to both manuals and *HOWTOs*.

---

10. This is more and more true of other Unix vendors, as you'll see; the customers are finally beginning to get what they want.

11. The native output of the TeX typesetting program, a powerful typesetting system that runs on many Unix machines.

HOWTOs are where most of the useful Linux documentation is kept: These files are often produced not by the people who wrote the software but by typical users who have simply documented how they solved their own problems. The good news about these files is that they provide useful, direct information on solving problems without all the theoretical claptrap that clogs up books such as this one. The bad news is that they don't always work the same on your system as they did on the author's system, and they often lack the theoretical framework necessary to make sense of adapting these procedures for your system. Furthermore, a fair number of HOWTOs are outdated or not particularly complete; the HOWTO maintainers are all volunteers who are just trying to help out the community and share their knowledge.

HOWTOs come in two sizes: regular and mini. Mini-HOWTOs are simply shorter than regular ones, and might come only in plaintext or HTML. They're generally structured rather like typical computer manuals, only dedicated to a single topic; most are in the range of one to several dozen pages, though some are several hundred pages long. In addition to being available on the Web, many systems enable you to install them locally.[12]

Solaris

Sun, too, has seen the light, and all current documentation is now available on the World Wide Web at `http://docs.sun.com/` including Solaris 2.4, newer operating systems, and all UltraSparc hardware. The old Sun4 hardware architecture manuals don't appear to be on the Web at this time. Most manuals can be printed via Adobe PDF files, the collection is well-organized, and search features seem to work well. Unless you have older Sun products, I'd strongly recommend sticking to the Web-based documentation because it seems better than older Sun online documentation.

AIX

Like Sun and Linux, most current AIX documentation is available from IBM on the Web. The main page is at `http://www.rs6000.ibm.com/library/` and the manuals that come with the system are available at `http://www.rs6000.ibm.com/resource/hardware_docs/index.html` in both HTML and PDF format. The search engine is moderately good but not uniformly excellent, and I found the site somewhat less intuitive than Sun's.

---

12. On Red Hat Linux systems, they should be located in `/usr/doc/HOWTO` if you installed them. Most other Linux systems should have them in a similar location.

IRIX

SGI's Web offering of documentation is at `http://techpubs.sgi.com/` and is improving rapidly. Manuals are available for all supported operating systems (Irix 5.3 and 6.2–6.5 at the time of this writing) as are all the hardware books. Manuals are, by and large, available only in PDF format, but all man pages are on the system in HTML, as are all the release notes.

SGI includes extensive documentation in their release notes for many programs. These notes can be viewed at their Web site or via their `relnotes` (1) program. SGI has always excelled at online documentation, and all product manuals are generally available via the `insight` (1) graphical manual viewer. Search capabilities are pretty good both with `insight` and the Web site, though the system's `relnotes` aren't mass searchable.

Suggested Exercises

Suggested exercises differ from practice problems in that they have no answers in the back of the book. Suggested exercises have no universally valid answers, and might involve getting up from your keyboard.

1. At the terminal prompt, type **info** and see if this starts GNU Info. If it does, follow the tutorial instructions displayed on your screen and learn to navigate `info` documentation.

2. Find a large file on your system. Try examining it with `cat`, `more`, and `less`. (If `less` is not installed on your system, you will get an error message. Don't worry, this won't hurt anything.)

3. If you can navigate the X Window System, start `xman` and browse through some of the available man pages. Next, try typing **gnome-help-browser** and see if it's installed on your system. Try navigating some documentation with this browser. Repeat the process with **kdehelp** if it's installed on your system. See if you have a clear preference for one of these applications over the others.

4. Look for your Unix vendor's Web site and look for documentation related to your Unix flavor. In particular, look for manuals that provide information other than that given in man pages.

5. Locate the manuals that came with your Unix system. If you use Unix in an institutional environment, find out whether a publicly accessible set of manuals is available.

Files and
Processes

If you've been watching closely, you might have noticed that I've already begun to discuss files. If you've been watching *exceptionally* closely, you might have even caught me discussing processes. I didn't mean to, I promise. I meant to save it all for this chapter. Of course, because one of the points of running an operating system is to manipulate files and processes, discussing Unix without discussing them has been quite difficult. Well, I can talk about them now, and because they're a pre-requisite—thought you finished with prereqs in college, didn't you?—for dealing with the rest of Unix, we'd better get started.

Files

If you've dealt with a computer before, chances are you've dealt with files. You might have called them "documents" or even "applications," but those are just names for special types of files. Every system sees files a little bit differently, but Unix sees them in a very simple way: *Unix considers all files as streams of byte*s. Unix also considers almost everything to be a file; I'll talk about that later in this chapter.

Exegesis: What's a File?

That seems deceptively simple, so let's perform a little bit of exegesis on that state-ment. (You thought you were finished with exegesis in college too, didn't you?[1]) By *Unix*, what are we discussing? The operating system, surely. But I don't simply mean the set of system calls that developers use to write Unix programs. (Developers call this set of specifications for how to write programs an API: an Application Program Interface.) I don't even mean simply the set of programs common to all Unix systems. I also mean that the vast majority of Unix applica-tions look at files this way.[2]

When I say that files look to Unix like "streams" of bytes, I'm saying that the data stored in files appears to be sequential: one byte after another for the entire length of the file. Searches on files can be (with some restrictions, as we'll later see) for-ward or backward, never sideways, measured in bytes.[3] Whether your CPU is 32 or 64 bits, Unix measures distance in files in sets of eight bits.

---

1. ...or grad school, for some of you.

2. This discussion also raises the question of what an operating system is. Some claim that an operating system is a piece of software that mediates access to disk space and memory, along with arbitrating between whatever programs are running. Others feel that the term also encompasses some applications with basic functionality required for comfortable use of the system.

3. A byte, for those of you who might be unfamiliar with the term, is a computer representation of a single Latin-alphabet character or a number between 0 and 255, precisely eight bits long. A bit is the most fundamental unit of computer memory, representing a single one or zero. Modern computers tend to operate on 32-bit long numbers, though some newer systems operate on 64-bit numbers, and some older systems operate on 16-bit numbers. The first generation of home PCs, as a rule, operated on eight-bit numbers. This is important in that some CPUs handle the bytes that make up 16- or 32-bit words in different orders: some put the larger part first (these systems are called big-endian), and some put the smaller part first (these are called, not too surprisingly, little-endian). This doesn't begin to affect you until you start building software from the source and wonder why sometimes things are bro-ken, but this seemed as good a point as any to mention it.

This has the distinct advantage of working perfectly for text files: Advance the file by one unit, and you will inevitably be one character farther in the file.[4]

Of course, I said that "Unix considers all files as streams of bytes," not that Unix considers all files *only* as streams of bytes. That's because programs can overlay some sort of structure on that data by refusing to operate on files which are not formatted the way that the program expects them to be formatted. Your word processor only reads files that it thinks look like word processing documents; anything else and it'll tell you it can't open the file.

Most Unix utilities, however, look at files only as streams of bytes. A perfect example is cat, which reads whatever files it's told to and prints them out. (cat is short for *concatenate*, because it prints them out one after another. That's concatenating them, inasmuch as you can concatenate bytes.)

Say Elvis has a file named tao.txt[5] that contains a short list of Chinese philosophers and writers and he wants to look at the file:

```
[ elvis@frogbog elvis ]$ cat tao.txt
Lao Tzu
Chuang Tzu
K'ung Tzu
Meng Tzu
Wang Bi
```

This is fairly straightforward: The authors are listed as they appear in the file. Each character is read from the file, and this stream of bytes is placed on the screen in the same order. Now say Elvis has a second file with some Western philosophers named things.txt and he wants to look at both sets of names:

```
[ elvis@frogbog elvis ]$ cat tao.txt things.txt
Lao Tzu
Chuang Tzu
K'ung Tzu
Meng Tzu
Wang Bi
Socrates
Plato
Aristotle
Heraclitus
Plotinus
```

---

4. This isn't true with files written in non-Latin alphabet encodings, but it is true of standard ASCII text files.

5. The file which can be named isn't the true file.

Of course, if he had typed `cat things.txt tao.txt`, the output would have read

```
Socrates
Plato
Aristotle
Heraclitus
Plotinus
Lao Tzu
Chuang Tzu
K'ung Tzu
Meng Tzu
Wang Bi
```

The files, after all, are just streams of bytes. The `cat` command just concatenates two files or two streams of bytes. When the order of the files is reversed, so is the order in which they are printed. Sequential data is, well, sequential.

Filenames

You might have noticed that both filenames end with `.txt`. If you're used to Windows this probably didn't surprise you because most Windows filenames have an *extensio*n. (Heck, old DOS machines had only eight characters for a filename and three more for the extension.) Unlike Windows boxes, but like Macs, the extensions are more or less optional. The system doesn't use them for anything important; they're present mostly for the user's convenience. Why did Elvis bother to end these filenames with `.txt`? Because it's useful for him to know how to read a file. You're not bound to these rules, but people make these conventions because they are useful. Some Unix programs force you to use specific extensions, but most of the time these defaults can be overridden.

Unix filenames are more flexible than those on Windows or Mac: They can be several hundred characters long on most modern Unix systems and can contain any character except a forward slash. Personally, I recommend sticking to letters, numbers, periods, hyphens, and underscores. Most other characters have special meanings and must be escaped with backslashes, as in our exploration of the `echo` in Chapter 1. Some older Unix systems have further limitations on filenames; check your manual.

Filenames are also case sensitive: Capital and lowercase letters are treated differently. `ThisFile` is different from `thisfile`. When filenames are sorted, uppercase letters appear before lowercase letters. Files that contain important information, such as README files or other documentation, often begin with capital letters so that they are easy to find.

Digression: Unix as a Multiuser Operating System

Nearly since its inception, Unix has been a multitasking, multiuser operating system; it has been designed for simultaneous use by more than one person at a time. A book oriented toward PCs or Macs would tell you now that this was because hardware was expensive, and multiuser use was a way of spreading out that expensive investment. Furthermore, that sort of book would tell you, on an interactive system (where users interact with the computer in real-time rather than send a bunch of punch cards down to a machine room and get back output sometime later) it's rare that a single user saturates the machine's capacity, so having multiple users on a system at once is much more efficient.

Of course, this isn't a Mac- or PC-oriented book, so I don't have to tell you that. Instead, I can tell you that multiuser systems have much wider applicability than single-user systems. In families, for example, it would be nice for Mom's financial records to be stored safely away from Junior's homework, and it would be nice if Junior in turn couldn't read Sis's diary. And it would be nice if each of them could have their own icons on their own desktops, without messing up Dad's filing system. Only a multiuser system can do all that effectively.

As far as multitasking goes, that's now fairly common (if poorly implemented) in the PC world, for precisely the same reason as it exists in the Unix world. Additionally, in a heavily networked world, it's nice if you can send out Web pages or copy files over the network while you're word processing. Or, in the server world, a computer can be a Web server, file server, and mail server all at the same time.

An effective multiuser system, obviously, needs separate areas for each person's files and settings and a way to distinguish who's who. The latter, the authentication mechanism, is why Unix asks you for your username and password before you can use the system. Separate areas for files and settings exist for each user in a separate directory (or folder, for Mac users) called a *home directory*.[6] When you log in, the default place where your files are stored is your home directory.

Now Back to Our Show

Now Elvis has logged in to his Unix box, and he'd like to see his list of Western philosophers, but he can't remember what he called it. He *does* remember that it's in his home directory, so he can just take a look:

```
[ elvis@frogbog elvis]$ ls
Desktop Mail README ThisFile tao.txt things.txt thisfile
```

6. In the Unix world, settings are always stored in files (and almost always in plaintext!), so this is redundant but perhaps helpful for PC or Mac users.

Hmmm, is it things.txt? Let's take a look:

```
[ elvis@frogbog elvis]$ cat things.txt
Socrates
Plato
Aristotle
Heraclitus
Plotinus
```

Yup, that's it. But what if he knows that the file ends in .txt and he wants to see only those files?

Wildcards

Wouldn't it be nice for Elvis to see only the files whose names end in .txt? This being Unix, he can:

```
[ elvis@frogbog elvis]$ ls *.txt
tao.txt things.txt
```

That asterisk (*) is a wildcard. As in a good old-fashioned game of poker, a wild-card is something that matches anything. If twos are wild, a two can stand in for anything; just so, an asterisk stands in for anything.[7] Also as in a poker hand, you can have any number of wildcards: *i* would match Mail, ThisFile, things.txt, and thisfile. It wouldn't match Desktop, README, or tao.txt.

Unlike in a poker hand, an asterisk can stand for any number of things at once: The asterisk in *.txt replaces tao in one instance and things in another. Unix uses a question mark to stand in for any single character: ?his?ile would match both ThisFile and thisfile, but it wouldn't match ThisIsntAFile. Also unlike poker, * can match nothing at all: This* would not only match ThisFile and ThisOtherFile, but also This. A question mark, by contrast, requires that something be present in the space reserved by that wildcard.

Unix has one last commonly used wildcard: Square brackets can be replaced only by whatever characters are within those brackets. [Tt]his[Ff]ile would match only ThisFile and thisfile. (It would also match thisFile and Thisfile, if those files existed in this directory.) One additional complication is that two characters separated by a hyphen can be replaced by any character in that range of ASCII characters. This[A-Z]ile would match ThisFile, ThisMile, ThisBile, and 23 others.

---

7. For some reason, wildcard matching is also known on Unix as *globbing*. Perhaps the image is of a sticky mass of files all stuck together on one point, that being the wildcard.

For the sake of intellectual uniformity, consider a range of characters separated by a hyphen as a single character. If you can do this, it's clear that [A-Za-z] matches all uppercase and lowercase letters and that [0-9A-Za-z] matches all letters and numbers.[8] This[0-9A-Za-z]ile would match This0ile, This9ile, ThisFile, Thisqile, and anything else with a single letter or number in place of [0-9A-Za-z].

Practice Problems

1. Which of the following is not a valid Unix filename:
   - firstfile.txt
   - FIRSTFILE.TXT
   - first file
   - first/file
   - first!file

2. What would be the appropriate command line to view the contents of a file named stupid_answer.txt?

3. How would I list all files whose names begin with the lowercase letters *g*, *h*, and *p*?

4. How would I list all files whose names begin with lowercase *g*, have any three characters following that, and end with *tly.txt*?

5. Which of the following filenames are matched by [A-G]*ing.?xt?

   - Gagging.text
   - Bing.xt
   - AGing.txt
   - ing.ext
   - Going.nxt

---

8. ASCII characters are listed on a chart in a specific numerical pattern, determined at the dawn of the personal computer age in accordance with certain bit-level numerological properties in order to make certain low-level computing tasks simpler. Numbers are contiguous with each other, capital letters are contiguous with each other, and lowercase letters are contiguous with each other, but other characters fill in gaps between numbers, uppercase letters, and lowercase letters. Thus the range of ASCII A–z includes not only upper and lowercase letters, but several additional symbols as well.

Directories

Even if you use wildcards to sort through files quickly, using a single directory to store files would become difficult after only a short time.[9] To combat this difficulty, the *subdirectory* was invented. (A subdirectory is the equivalent of a folder on Mac OS.) Elvis already has a couple of subdirectories in his home directory:

```
[ elvis@frogbog elvis ]$ ls -F
Desktop/ Mail/ README ThisFile tao.txt things.txt thisfile
```

The -F option to ls adds a special character to certain types of files to distinguish them: / distinguishes a directory, * marks an executable file (a program, in other words), and @ marks a symbolic link (which I won't discuss until later).[10] Desktop and Mail are directories. Desktop was created by the operating system to hold information for certain GUI-based programs, and Mail was created to hold Elvis's email.

Wouldn't it be nice for Elvis to have a directory in which to keep his songs? He sure thinks so:

```
[ elvis@frogbog elvis ]$ mkdir songs
[ elvis@frogbog elvis ]$ ls
Desktop Mail README ThisFile songs tao.txt things.txt thisfile
[ elvis@frogbog elvis ]$ cd songs
[ elvis@frogbog songs ]$ ls
[ elvis@frogbog songs ]$
```

One thing worth noting is that Unix programs tend to be the strong-but-silent type (more James Dean than Elvis), and if a command is successful it returns the minimum necessary output. Thus, the mkdir command (to make the directory) and the cd command (to switch into that directory) don't return any output.

If Elvis had tried to cd into a directory that didn't exist, he would have seen an error message:

```
[ elvis@frogbog songs ]$ cd old-songs
bash: old-songs: No such file or directory
```

---

9. Of course, there's the story of the Macintosh user who had every file she ever created right there on her desktop. That desktop was so thoroughly covered with overlapping files that her co-workers just thought she had ugly desktop wallpaper. How she found the documents she wanted, I'll never understand…

10. Of course, *ls* has all sorts of useful options; you might want to check the man page.

The error might be somewhat cryptic, but it should be possible to extract an understanding of why the command failed.[11]

The most important thing to note about creating and moving into directories is that directory structure is fundamentally hierarchical: Except for the very first directory, each directory is inside another directory. Elvis has three subdirectories in his home directory, and each of those can have any number of directories or files inside it. One Unix program available on the Internet named tree draws a map of the files and directories "underneath" the current directory:

```
[ elvis@frogbog elvis ]$ tree -d
.
|- Desktop
|    |- Autostart
|    |- Templates
|    '- Trash
|- Mail
'- songs
```

In addition the Desktop, Mail, and songs directories, Elvis has three additional sub-directories inside the Desktop directory. (These were also created by the system or at least by the system administrator.)

Absolute and Relative Paths

If Elvis were sitting at the prompt in his home directory, those directories could be identified as Desktop/Autostart, Desktop/Templates, and Desktop/Trash. Because the forward slash (/) is used as a directory separator, slashes in filenames can't be used. Were Elvis already in the Desktop directory, those directories could be identified simply as Autostart, Templates, and Trash. The name of a file or directory can be given relative to your current location in the directory tree.

There must, of course, be some absolute point from which all directories on a given system can be located.[12] Logically speaking, that point is the directory that contains all the other directories on a system. On Unix, this point is called the *root directory*, and all files on the system lie somewhere inside the root directory or its subdirectories. Fittingly enough, the symbol for the root directory is a single

---

11. One piece of Unix folklore that has been passed around for well over a decade, however, is a list of malformed commands that produce amusing error messages. Sadly, few of those joke commands produce the same amusing output today. Even sadder is that the new error messages are often no more helpful than the old ones.

12. ...unless, of course, somebody implemented a completely relativistic filesystem. As far as I know, no such filing system exists.

forward slash. To give an absolute path to a file or directory, it must have a leading slash, representing the root directory, and then every directory between that and the one you're interested in. The `Desktop/Autostart` directory (a path relative to Elvis's home directory) might have an absolute path of `/home/elvis/Desktop/Autostart` or (generally on a larger system) `/users/e/elvis/Desktop/Autostart`.

Think of the root directory on Unix as you would the Macintosh desktop, where all the different disks on the system each look like a file folder. (On Unix, actually, all disks are mounted by the system administrator in a particular subdirectory, but that might be at any level in the system, not just directly under the root directory.) On PCs it's somewhat different because each drive has its own root directory, but play along for a minute and pretend that each drive letter is a filename in an imaginary root directory. (It's a stretch, but I promise you the concepts are logically equivalent.)

As with both PCs and Macs, filenames must be unique *within a given subdirectory*, but those same filenames can be used at other points the filesystem: I can have a file named `test` in my home directory, and I could have a file named `test` in any subdirectory in that home directory. (Heck, if I wanted to, I could even have a file named `test` in a directory named `test`, but that might get confusing. Of course, I do it anyway.)

On Unix, each directory has a parent directory: `/home/elvis/Desktop`'s parent directory is `/home/elvis`, and its home directory is `/home`. Of course, that's only helpful for dealing with absolute paths. How could you use this concept of a parent directory with relative paths?

The answer is surprising, perhaps, but also elegant: Each directory has a directory inside it that is really its parent directory. The parent directory's name is two periods (`..`). Thus `/home/elvis` can be referred to as `/home/elvis/desktop/..`, though of course that's not really any more useful than just typing `/home/elvis`. What is useful is being able to `cd ..` to move up a directory level or even being able to use `ls ../songs` when you're sitting in your mail directory. Because it has no parent directory, the root directory's `..` directory points to itself.

Another special subdirectory has only a single period for a name and is present in each directory on the system. This represents that very directory in which it sits. `/home/elvis/./` is exactly the same as `/home/elvis/`. This is a little more useful if you consider that, when you're in `/home/elvis`, `/home/elvis/Desktop` is `./Desktop`. After all, we can refer to that directory by the still-shorter `Desktop`, right?

The single-dot directory is actually useful when copying or moving files from one directory to another. The move command (`mv`) and the copy command (`cp`) each take two (or more) arguments: a *source* or multiple sources and a *destination*. The source is just that, the original that is to be either moved or copied, and the destination is the place where the file or files end up.

Elvis is tired of his philosophers and wants to file them away. He wants a directory named `arc` to be his archive, and he wants to move `tao.txt` and `things.txt` into that directory. There are several ways he can do this, but typically he'd do the following:

```
[ elvis@frogbog elvis ]$ mkdir arc
[ elvis@frogbog elvis ]$ mv tao.txt things.txt arc
```

By doing this, he's moving two files into a relative-path directory. Now let's say Elvis changes his mind and wants to move the files back into his home directory. He could always use mv arc/tao.txt arc/things.txt /home/elvis, but with a single-dot directory (and judicious use of wildcards), he can use mv arc/t*.txt . Without that single dot as a placeholder, he'd end up overwriting things.txt with the contents of tao.txt. arc/t*.txt would expand, producing the command mv arc/tao.txt arc/things.txt, certainly not what Elvis wanted.

Another efficient way for Elvis to move his files back is as follows:

```
[ elvis@frogbog elvis ]$ cd arc
[ elvis@frogbog arc ]$ mv *.txt ..
[ elvis@frogbog arc ]$ cd ..
```

At this point, however, you're probably more concerned with why Unix lets you do stupid and dangerous things like overwriting your files when you so obviously intend to copy them. The answer is twofold: First, Unix is still just a computer program, and we've all been taught that computers do only what we tell them to do. The corollary that has become apparent as more software becomes automated is that when they try to guess what we want them to do, they still don't do the right thing. On top of that, they become less predictable, and hence less useful as tools under our control. Second, Unix always gives you enough rope to hang yourself and then some, because if it didn't, it wouldn't be either powerful enough or flexible enough to suit its users. Trust me on this one for now. I know that it sounds both arrogant and reckless, but it's also one of the deep truths of computing, at least as we know it today.

Copying works more-or-less identically to moving files: You simply cp *.txt .. to make an additional copy of the .txt files in the current directory in this directory's parent directory. The cp and mv commands take somewhat different option flags, but that's why we have man pages. Furthermore, it's worth noting that Unix doesn't have a separate rename command: You just mv files within the current directory. If Elvis wants to change the name of things.txt to west.txt, he can simply use mv things.txt west.txt—an elegant if not necessarily intuitive solution.

"But wait," I hear you asking, "I don't see . or .. when I ls my home directory! What gives?"

On Unix, any filename beginning with a period is hidden: It doesn't show up in a standard ls of a directory. In order to see *dotfiles*, Elvis needs to use the -a option to ls:

```
[ elvis@frogbog elvis ]$ ls -a

.            .bash_history   .kde     Mail      tao.txt
..           .bash_logout    .kderc   README    things.txt
```

```
.Xauthority  .bash_profile  .screenrc  ThisFile  thisfile
.Xdefaults   .bashrc        Desktop    songs
```

There they are, along with another handful of files put there by the system when the account was created.

One More Special Directory: ~

One more special directory worth learning is ~, which refers to your home direc-tory.[13] ~ acts as a directory name like any other: You can cp from or to ~ just as you can from . or .. or /home/elvis. There's an additional trick, though: Any user can use ~elvis to refer to Elvis's home directory, and any user can use ~jon to refer to my directory.

Practice Problems

The following practice problems are a single sequence of commands. Begin each command from where the last one left off. (Assume you are in the same directory, with the same directory structure.)

6. Make a directory in your home directory called chapter-2.

7. Change into your chapter-2 directory.

8. Make a directory inside chapter-2 named test-1 and another one inside chap-ter-2 named test-2.

9. Change into the test-2 directory.

10. From test-2, remove the test-1 directory.

11. Try to remove test-2 from within that directory. What happens?

12. Change into your home directory.

13. If test-2 still exists, remove it. Remove the chapter-2 directory as well.

Permissions and Ownership

Because Unix was designed to support many users, the question naturally arises as to how to know who can see what files. The first, and simplest, answer would be simply to permit users to examine only their own files. This, of course, would make it difficult if not impossible to share, creating great difficulties in collaborative environments and would cause a string of other problems: Why can't I run ls? Because the system created it, not you, is only the most obvious example of such problems.

---

13. Some very old systems don't support the use of ~ to represent the home directory. That's because the default shell on these systems is the Bourne shell, which also lacks other useful features. Ask your system administrator if the ksh or bash shells are available if you'd like to use this feature. (I discuss shells in Chapter 6.)

Users and Groups

Unix uses a three-part system to determine file access: There's what you, as the file owner, are allowed to do; there's what the group is allowed to do; and there's what other people are allowed to do. Let's see what Elvis's permissions look like:

```
[ elvis@frogbog elvis ]$ ls -l

total 36
drwxr-xr-x    5 elvis     users        4096 Dec  9 21:55 Desktop
drwxr-xr-x    2 elvis     users        4096 Dec  9 22:00 Mail
-rw-r--r--    1 elvis     users          36 Dec  9 22:00 README
-rw-r--r--    1 elvis     users          22 Dec  9 21:59 ThisFile
drwxr-xr-x    2 elvis     users        4096 Dec 12 19:57 arc
drwxr-xr-x    2 elvis     users        4096 Dec 10 00:40 songs
-rw-r--r--    1 elvis     users          46 Dec 12 19:52 tao.txt
-rw-r--r--    1 elvis     users          21 Dec  9 21:59 thisfile
-rw-r--r--    1 elvis     users          45 Dec 12 19:52 west.txt
```

As long as we're here, let's break down exactly what's being displayed. First, we have a ten-character-long string of letters and hyphens. This is the representation of permissions, which I'll break down in a minute. The second item is a number, usually a single digit. This is the number of *hard links* to that directory. I'll discuss this later in this chapter. The third thing is the username of the file owner, and the fourth is the name of the file's group. The fifth column is a number representing the size of the file, in bytes. The sixth contains the date and time of last modification for the file, and the final column shows the filename.

Every user on the system has a username and a number that is associated with that user.[14] This number is generally referred to as the *UID*, short for *user ID*. If a user has been deleted but for some reason her or his files remain, the username is replaced with that user's UID. Similarly, if a group is deleted but still owns files, the *GID* (group number) shows up instead of a name in the group field. There are also other circumstances when the system can't correlate the name and the number, but it should be a relatively rare occurrence.

As a user, you can't change the owner of your files: This would open up some serious security holes on the system. Only root can chown files, but if she or he makes a mistake, you can now ask root to chown the files to you. As a user, you can chgrp a file to a different group of which you are a member. That is, given that Elvis is a member of a group named users and a group named elvis, he can chgrp elvis west.txt or chgrp users west.txt, but because he's not a member of the group beatles, he can't chgrp beatles west.txt.[15] A user can belong to any number of groups. Generally (though this varies somewhat by flavor), files created belong to the group to which the directory belongs. On most modern Unix variants, the

---

14. Actually, as far as the system's concerned, you're really just a number. The name is there because humans aren't really good at memorizing huge lists of numbers, but most of the time you can pretend that the name's the thing.

15. Nor would they want him to, I'm sure.

group that owns files is whatever group is listed as your primary group by the system in the /etc/passwd file and can be changed via the newgrp command. On these systems, Elvis can chgrp users if he'd like his files to belong to the users group, or he can chgrp elvis if he'd like his files to belong to the elvis group.

Reading Permissions

So, what were those funny strings of letters and hyphens at the beginning of each long directory listing? I already said that they represented the permissions of the file, but that's not especially helpful. The ten characters of that string represent the permission bits for each file.[16] The first character is separate, and the last nine are three very similar groups of three characters. I'll explain each of these in turn.

If you look back to Elvis's long listing of his directory, you'll see that most of the files simply have a hyphen as the first character, whereas several possess a d in this field. The more astute reader might note that the files with a d in that first field all happen to be directories. There's a good reason for this: The first permissions character denotes whether that file is a special file of one sort or another.

What's a special file? It's either something that isn't really a file (in the sense of a sequential stream of bytes on a disk) but that Unix treats as a file, such as a disk or a video display, or something that is really a file, but that is treated differently. A directory, by necessity, is a stream of bytes on disk, but that d means that it's treated differently. I'll talk about other sorts of special files later in this chapter.

The next three characters represent what the user who owns the file can do with it. From left to right, these permissions are *read*, *write*, and *execute*. Read permission is just that—the capability to see the contents of a file. Write permission implies not only the right to change the contents of a file, but also to delete it. If I do not possess write permission to a file, rm not_permitted.txt fails.

Execute permission determines whether the file is also a command that can be run on the system. Because Unix sees everything as a file, all commands are stored in files that can be created, modified, and deleted like any other file. The computer then needs a way to tell what can and can't be run. The execute bit does this.[17]

Another important reason you need to worry about whether a file is executable is that some programs are designed to be run only by the system administrator: These programs can modify the computer's configuration or be dangerous in some other way. Because Unix enables you to specify permissions for the owner, the group, and other users, the execute bit enables the administrator to restrict the use of dangerous programs.

---

16. Yes, they do actually represent individual ones and zeros. I'll return to this later.

17. On Unix, many programs are simply text files that contain lists of commands. These files are called *scripts*. We'll talk more about scripts later, but suffice it to say, a user might well want to turn a normal file into an executable.

Directories treat the execute permission differently. If a directory does not have execute permissions, that user (or group, or other users on the system) can't cd into that directory and can't look at information about the files in that directory. (You can usually find the names of the files, however.) Even if you have permissions for the files in that directory, you generally can't look at them. (This varies somewhat by platform.)

The second set of three characters is the group permissions (read, write, and execute, in that order), and the final set of three characters is what other users on the system are permitted to do with that file. Because of security concerns (either due to other users on your system or due to pervasive networks such as the Internet), giving write access to other users is highly discouraged.

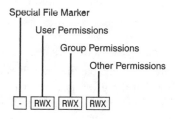

Figure 2.1

Permission bits from an ls -1 display.

Changing Permissions

Great, you can now read the permissions in the directory listing, but what can you do with them? Let's say that Elvis wants to make his directory readable only by himself. He can chmod go-rwx ~/songs: That means remove the read, write, and execute permissions for the group and others on the system. If Elvis decides to let Nashville artists take a look at his material but not change it (and there's a group nashville on the system), he can first chgrp nashville songs and then chmod g+r songs.

If Elvis does this, however, he'll find that (at least on some platforms) members of group nashville can't look at them. Oops! With a simple chmod g+x songs, the problem is solved:

```
[ elvis@frogbog elvis ]$ ls -1
total 36
drwxr-xr-x   5 elvis    users      4096 Dec  9 21:55 Desktop
drwxr-xr-x   2 elvis    users      4096 Dec  9 22:00 Mail
-rw-r--r--   1 elvis    users        36 Dec  9 22:00 README
-rw-r--r--   1 elvis    users        22 Dec  9 21:59 ThisFile
drwxr-xr-x   2 elvis    users      4096 Dec 12 19:57 arc
```

```
drwxr-x---   2 elvis    nashvill     4096 Dec 15 14:21 songs
-rw-r--r--   1 elvis    users          46 Dec 12 19:52 tao.txt
-rw-r--r--   1 elvis    users          21 Dec  9 21:59 thisfile
-rw-r--r--   1 elvis    users          45 Dec 12 19:52 west.txt
```

Special Permissions

In addition to the read, write, and execute bits, there exist special permissions used by the system to determine how and when to suspend the normal permission rules. Any thorough understanding of Unix requires an understanding of the *setuid*, *setgid*, and *sticky* bits. For normal system users, only a general understanding of these is necessary, and this discussion is thus brief. Good documentation on this subject exists elsewhere for budding system administrators and programmers.

setuid

The setuid bit applies only to executable files and directories. In the case of executable programs, it means that the given program runs as though the file owner were running it. That is, xhextris, a variant on Tetris, has the following permissions on my system:

```
-rwsr-xr-x 1 games games 32516 May 18 1999 /usr/X11R6/bin/xhextris
```

There's a pseudo-user called games on the system, which can't be logged in to and has no home directory. When the xhextris program executes, it can read and write to files that only the games pseudo-user would normally be permitted. In this case, there's a high-score file stored on the system writable only by that user. When Elvis runs the game, the system acts as though he were the user games, and thus is able to store the high-score file. To set the setuid bit on a file, you can tell chmod to give it mode u+s. (You can think of this as uid set, though this isn't technically accurate.)

setgid

The setgid bit, which stands for "set group id," works almost identically to setuid, except that the system acts as though the user's group is that of the given file. If xhextris had setgid games instead of setuid games, the high score would be writable to any directory owned by the *group* games. It is used by the system administrator in ways fundamentally similar to the setuid permission.

When applied to directories on Linux, Irix, and Solaris (and probably most other POSIX-compliant Unix flavors as well), setgid bit means that new files are given the parent directory's group rather than the user's primary or current group. This can be useful for, say, a directory for fonts built by (and for) a given program. Any user might generate the fonts via a setgid command that writes to a setgid directory. Setgid on directories varies by platform; check your documentation. To set the setgid bit, you can tell chmod to use g+s (gid set).

sticky

Although a file in a group or world-writable directory without the sticky bit can be deleted by anyone with write permission for that directory (user, group, or other), a file in a directory with the sticky bit set can be deleted only by either the file's owner or root. This is particularly useful for creating temporary directories or scratch space that can be used by anyone without one's files being deleted by others. You can set permission +t in chmod to give something the sticky bit.

Numeric Permissions

Like almost everything else on Unix, permissions have a number associated with them. It's generally considered that permissions are a group of four digits, each between 0 and 7. Each of those digits represents a group of three permissions, each of which is a yes/no answer. From left to right, those digits represent special permissions, user permissions, group permissions, and other permissions.

Digression: Computer Math

It's okay to skip this section if you don't care about the math behind the permission numbers, but I wouldn't include it here if I didn't think it was at least interesting and probably useful at some point. If you understand what I mean when I tell you that permissions are in octal, not hex, you can also probably skip this section safely.

Most current computers work in *hexadecimal:* base 16 math. Hex, as it's commonly known, is convenient because it's equal to precisely four bits. Four is a good number of bits because it's a power of two, and this permits you to have words that are also powers of two, and it makes your standard eight-bit byte exactly two hexadecimal digits.

Permissions work, by contrast, in *octal:* base-eight math. That's equal to exactly three bits. Many older computers worked in octal, which didn't have the beautiful mathematical properties of hex but had the advantage of being simpler to convert mentally between octal and binary—that's base two for you non-math people who've slogged through this paragraph (good going!)—and the added advantage of not needing numbers beyond nine.

Octal counts from 0 to 7 per digit, and the next number is 10, which translates to eight in a standard decimal math. Hex counts from 0 to F per digit, and the next number is 10, which is 16 in decimal. That's right: the letters *A* through *F* are digits in hex, representing decimal values from 10 through 15. If you spend a lot of time working with computers, you might eventually learn to translate between binary, hex, and decimal, but even then you never spend much time these days with octal, which, if you think about it, is really just hex with a leading zero bit.

Of course, if you're reading this section, I should probably explain that one, too: in base two, each bit is either a one or a zero. But as you learned when you did "place value" in math, a digit has different values as you move left within a number. In normal base-10 arithmetic, a three in the "ones place" is just three, but in the "tens place," it's 30, and in the "ten-thousands place," it's 30,000. You just multiply your digit by the value of the place.

In binary as in decimal, the rightmost digit is the ones place, and each place is worth your base times the previous place's value. For decimal, that's one, ten-times-one (ten), ten-times-ten (one hundred), ten-times-one-hundred (one thousand), and so on. For binary, that's one, two-times-one (two), two-times-two (four), two-times-four (eight), and so on.

Finally, you add up the multiplied-out values of each digit to find the total value of the number. In decimal, 4,004 is four-times-one-thousand plus four-times-one, which is in fact four-thousand-four. In binary, 1001 is one-times-eight plus one, which is nine. The maximum hex digit is 1111: one-times-eight plus one-times-four plus one-times-two plus one, which is 15 in decimal, or F in hex. The maximum octal number is 111, which is one-times-four plus one-times-two plus one, or 7.

One final note, before we return to more immediately useful material, is that there's an easy shortcut from binary to hex or octal. Because each place's value in binary can be multiplied by only zero or one, the values of each place with a one can simply be added together. Now you'll understand why all the permission bits are worth one, two, or four apiece and can simply be added together.

So, About Those Permission Bits...

Most programs reading permission bits expect four digits, though often only three are given. Shorter numbers are filled in with leading zeros: 222 is treated as 0222, and 5 is treated as 0005. The three rightmost digits are, as I previously mentioned, user (owner) permissions, group permissions, and other permissions, from left to right.

Each of these digits is calculated in the following manner: read permission has a value of 4, write permission has a value of 2, and execute permission has a value of 1. Simply add these values together, and you've got that permission value. Read, write, and execute would be 7; read and write without execute would be 6; and no permission to do anything at all would be 0. Read, write, and execute for the file owner, with read and execute for the group, and nothing at all for anyone else would be 750. Read and write for the user and group, but only read for others would be 664.

The special permissions are 4 for setuid, 2 for setgid, and 1 for sticky. This digit is prepended to the three-digit numeric permission: a temporary directory with sticky read, write, and execute permission for everyone would be mode 1777. A setuid root directory writable by nobody else would be 4700. You can use chmod to set numeric permissions directly, as in chmod 1777 /tmp.

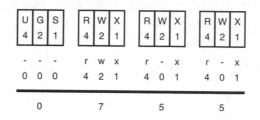

Figure 2.2

Converting named to numeric permissions

umask

In addition to a more precise use of chmod, numeric permissions are used with the umask command, which sets the default permissions. More precisely, it "masks" the default permissions: The umask value is subtracted from the maximum possible settings.[18] umask deals only with the three-digit permission, not the full-fledged four-digit value. A umask of 002 or 022 is most commonly the default. 022, subtracted from 777, is 755: read, write, and execute for the user, read and execute for the group and others. 002 from 777 is 775: read, write, and execute for the user and group, read and execute for others. I tend to set my umask to 077: read, write, and execute for myself, and nothing for my group or others. (Of course, when working on a group project I set my umask to 007: My group and I can read, write, or execute anything, but others can't do anything with our files.)

You should note that the umask assumes that the execute bit on the file will be set. All umasks are subtracted from 777 rather than 666, and those extra ones are subtracted later, if necessary.

Practice Problems

The following problems are hypothetical. Unless appropriate users and groups exist on your system, and unless you have appropriate permissions, it is impossible to execute these commands.

---

18. Actually, the permission bits are XORed with the maximum possible settings, if you're a computer science type.

14. What command would be used to change the owner of a file in the current directory named not-possible.txt to trinity?

15. You need to give the entire group matrix access to the file no-spoon.txt. Make sure that they have write access to the file.

The following problems should be possible to execute, though it might be difficult to test your results. I will provide permission bits from an ls -l, though I will not include the rest of the display. To create the file too-many-hyphens, simply run the command touch too-many-hyphens.

16. chmod 664 too-many-hyphens. What can users, not yourself and not in your group, do to this file?

17. Using named permissions, remove your group's permission to write to too-many-hyphens without removing their ability to read the file.

18. Use numeric permissions to change the permissions on too-many-hyphens so that nobody can read, write, or execute it, including yourself.

19. Now try removing the file. What does your system do? If you are unable to delete the file, change the permissions so that you can do so, and then remove the file.

Special Files

Because Unix sees almost everything as a file, there are some things that aren't files but that exist somewhere underneath the root directory. These are special files. Every special file is a marker on the disk pointing either to something else on the disk or to something else entirely.

Links

Links are the type of special file most commonly needed by typical users. Links let two filenames refer to the same actual file or directory on disk, and they come in two varieties: *hard links* and *soft links*. Before we can adequately discuss either sort of link, however, we must take a quick look at how files are stored on disk.

How Directories Really Work

If you think about it, there are only two ways a directory on disk could work: It either must literally *contain* files or *point to* files that are stored elsewhere. The former case would be as chapters are to a book: Files would be stored in sequence within the directory and a table of contents could be built from this data. Clearly, this would be large and slow, and changing the contents of the directory would involve moving large chunks of data around in rapid succession. Instead, if a directory only pointed to files, it would be the table of contents. Removing a chapter would only require that its name be crossed out and the page count altered.

On Unix, the second approach is much closer to how directories work: A subdirectory is a list of files, with a pointer to the actual file. Because the files aren't stored sequentially on disk, deleting a file requires only removing its name from the directory in which it's stored and marking as free the portions of disk that it used.

Hard Links

A *hard link* is simply an additional pointer to the same file on the disk as another one. Actually, even the original file is a hard link to the data. All links are considered equal, and a file is deleted only when all the hard links to that block of data are removed.

When a file is modified, the data changes in all hard-linked files, but when a file is deleted, a hard link to that data remains. Hard links are useful for making sure that files used by more than one project are available so long as any one of those projects is in use. For example, the original outline for this book was in my `docs/unixbook/proposal` directory, but when I started working on the actual book, I found it convenient to access from my `docs/unixbook/thinkunix` directory. Because I knew that I might remove the proposal directory before the book was complete, I made a hard link of my outline. From the `docs/unixbook/thinkunix` directory, I simply typed `ln ../proposal/subject-outline.txt .` (note my use of relative paths to make this easier to type, and that the period is the current directory). Most Unix utilities are smart enough to keep the same filename if you move, copy, or link to a directory rather than to a file.

In fact, the most common use of hard links is by the system. (Remember the . and .. directories?). Each of those is a hard link to the appropriate place. If you refer way back to the section "Users and Groups," earlier in this chapter, you'll see the "hard links" count directly following the file permissions of each directory entry. Each directory has a hard link count of at least two: one for the directory in its parent directory and one for the identity link within the subdirectory. For every subdirectory within that directory, add one hard link for the link back up to the parent directory.

Hard links have one serious problem: Each disk partition has its own numbering scheme for *inodes*, the disk blocks that contain information about the specific file or directory and that are (at least as far as the system is concerned) part of the file. As such, hard links are possible only between files on a given partition: You can't make a hard link from a file on your root filesystem to your home filesystem.

Soft Links

Soft links are the solution to this problem: Instead of pointing to an inode, soft links simply point to the filename. This has both advantages and disadvantages: The obvious advantage is that you can have soft links (also known as *symbolic links* or *symlinks*) across filesystems. The primary disadvantage is that you can be left with *dangling links*, symbolic links that point to absent files. The file being pointed to has been deleted for some reason or perhaps was never created.

Symbolic links are indicated, in a directory listing, with an l as the first character of the file permissions. The permissions on a symbolic link don't refer to what you can do to the file: Only root or the owner of the symbolic link can delete it and anyone can follow it, but you must have permissions to read, write, or execute the file referenced by the symlink.

Symlinks can be either absolute or relative. If I'm the system administrator, it might be convenient to have /usr/opt point to /opt, but it might be more convenient for /etc/rmt to point to ../sbin/rmt in case my filesystem is not mounted where I expect it to be.

I have found it convenient to have a thinkunix directory in my home directory that points to my docs/unixbook/thinkunix directory, so I made a symlink:

```
ln -s docs/unixbook/thinkunix
```

I could just as easily have made a hard link, however, in this particular case. Most people prefer soft links to hard links because there is no consideration as to filesystem boundaries, but in most cases either sort will do.

Practice Problems

Make a file called here by running the command

```
echo nothing > here
```

before doing the following questions.

20. Make a hard link to here named there.

21. chmod 000 here and chmod 600 there. Why can you cat there and not cat here, given that these are in fact the same file?

22. rm here. Can you still look at the contents of there? Why or why not?

23. Make a symbolic link from there to a file named everywhere.

24. rm there. Can you still look at the contents of everywhere? Why or why not? rm everywhere when you are finished.

Devices

Unix sees virtually every device attached to your CPU as a file. This includes (at least) your mouse, your disks, your memory (on most systems), your terminal (if you're using a physical terminal, and even your console on many others), your Ethernet card (again, on most systems), any modems you might have, your sound card, and so on. Most of these "files" reside in the /dev directory.

Devices come in two major flavors, *character devices* and *block devices*. In a long listing of the /dev directory, character devices have a c as the first character of the permissions, whereas block devices have (not surprisingly) a b in that field.

Block devices are intended to be read in *blocks*: a group of bytes all at once. The number of bytes read at a time is the *block size*. Many devices have a block size of 512 bytes, though disks can have a significantly larger block size (4,096 bytes or even more). Block devices are most often used for less interactive devices. You generally don't notice that the system holds on to your data until you have a certain number of bytes before writing to disk, an operation known as *buffering*. If you *flush* a block device, to force the system to write out data right at that moment, it generally pads the data with blank characters up until the end of the block.

Character devices, by contrast, are files that are meant to be read a single character at a time. Devices that are more interactive and require the appearance of better performance or devices that can't guarantee data in a timely fashion are generally character devices. Typical examples are mice, because you certainly wouldn't want to wait for a certain amount of movement before the system became aware of it, and modems, because you want to receive and transmit data as you have it and not wait for 512-byte chunks.[19] Some character devices aren't really devices because they don't refer to a piece of hardware. (They're not literal, physical devices attached to the system.) Instead, these refer to imaginary places. The most common example is /dev/null, which is a "bit bucket," a place you can send data to be discarded. /dev/zero is an endless supply of zeros that can be read by programs. Some systems also have a /dev/random, which produces an unpredictable byte of data. Neither of these is very important right now, though we will talk a little bit more about /dev/null in the next chapter.

Two other kinds of "devices" aren't really devices:[20] *Named pipes*, represented in ls -l by a p, and *FIFOs*, represented by an s, are sometimes present, usually in the /dev directory. Programs on the system use these devices to exchange information. Mostly you should know they're present and leave them to the system administrator.

Filesystems

Because Unix sees all separate disks on the system as part of a single directory tree, and because a system might not always have the same disks attached to it, there's a definite need to be able to attach or detach disks from the directory tree. These processes are known as *mounting* and *unmounting* the disks, respectively. (These terms are a holdover from the days when tapes or large disks would need to be connected to or detached from the drive mechanism by an operator, processes also known as mounting and unmounting. The term carried over from the hardware activities to the associated software processes, much like we talk about "printing" to the screen due to old terminals physically printing everything displayed.)

---

19. Actually, many modems today do compression, which requires blocks of data. For most purposes, you never notice the difference, but old habits die hard, and Unix still thinks of modems as character devices.

20. ...and devices aren't really files either, but who's counting?

A disk can be mounted only in an existing directory on the system. That directory then contains the contents of whatever top-level directory was present on that disk. Generally, only system administrators can mount and unmount disks; some workstations permit users to do so, especially with removable media such as floppies or CD-ROMs. The point where the disk is attached to the system is known as the *mount point*.

So far, I've discussed mounting disks, but what's really being mounted are *partitions* containing filesystems. A partition is a piece of a disk. For convenience, security, or occasionally due to technical limitations of the system, disks are often "broken up" into several pieces known as partitions. The system can address each partition separately, although the device names generally make it clear that these are part of a single physical disk.

A filesystem is a format in which the system expects the data. You can't put a Macintosh floppy disk in a Windows computer and have the system read it[21] because the data on the disk is not laid out in the way the system expects. When you put a PC floppy in a Macintosh, it's treated and identified differently because the different filesystems have different capabilities: There are different restrictions on legal characters in filenames, different maximum lengths of filenames, and so on. Because of its heritage of mixed environments, many Unix systems know how to read several different filesystems.

If you cat /etc/fstab, the file used on most Unix systems to determine the defaults for mounting partitions, you should note that the format is generally the partition to be mounted, where that partition should be mounted, the filesystem type, system defaults, and then sometimes additional system-specific information. (See the man page for fstab(5) for details if you're curious.)

Table 2.1   Some Common Filesystems

ext2fs	The standard Linux filesystem
iso9660	The filesystem used by most CD-ROMs
jfs	AIX's journaling filesystem
xfs	The Extended File System, used on recent SGI systems
efs	An older SGI filesystem
ufs and ffs	Cross-platform filesystems developed on BSD Unix and now available on many different Unix flavors

There also exist filesystems for things that aren't really disks. nfs is the Network File System, which lets you mount arbitrary directories over the network as though they were in fact disks. afs and coda are more advanced network filesystems, with better security and more precise control of the data. The proc filesystem, which is present on some modern Unix flavors, permits you to examine and control aspects of the system by reading and modifying files. These are sometimes readable by regular users but are most often intended for the system administrator.

21. ...without special software, at least.

Processes

On Unix, if you're not working on or with files, you're probably working with processes. A *process*, simply put, is a program running on the system. More precisely, it's an instance of a running program; that is, each time you or someone else using the system runs that program, another process is created.

In many ways, processes are similar to files: Every process is owned by a user, every process has a name, and every process has a number. Processes are owned by the user who ran the program, although suid programs are owned by the setuid file's owner. The name of a process is always the name of the command that the system is executing. Processes also have a size, although this is space in memory, whereas files occupy space on disk.

The system provides the process number. The first process, which controls the execution of all other processes, is init. The process ID (also known as the *PID*) for init is always 1.[22]

Process numbers don't just go up and up forever; they're generally of a fixed length, usually 15 bits. (A 15-bit number is a two-byte number with one of those bits reserved to indicate whether that number is positive or negative.) Some systems have PIDs of 16 bits or more, but there are always a fixed number of possible processes. The reason for this is simply that when a program is written, a fixed amount of space must be allocated for process numbers, and that number must be the same throughout any given system.

Process IDs are doled out sequentially: after process 15321 is created, the next process is always 15322, even if process 15320 is no longer running. After the top process number has been used, the system rolls back to the bottom and then starts handing out process numbers all over again. If a given process is still running, the system skips that one and moves on to the next, not returning again until it has reached the top.

Each process has a parent process, much as each file is within a directory. The consequence of this is that the list of processes on a system can be thought of much like a directory structure. init creates several other processes. Each of these can parent many more processes, each of which can in turn also create any number of processes.

---

22. Usually, computer people start counting with 0. The system administrator's UID is always zero. Sometimes, however, they seem to forget to begin at 0 and begin counting at 1, like everyone else. When people say that Unix is inconsistent, they often are thinking about things like this or about the different arguments taken by commands. To me, though, this is part of what makes Unix more like a human language: It's as though there are different verb endings and different sentence constructions. Unix comes from many sources, like a language, and there was simply some natural variation in those sources.

In Chapter 1, I mentioned in passing that a particular process starts when you log on to a system. This process is the shell, the program that lets you run other programs and that interprets your command line. It's a process like any other, and when your shell dies, you are logged out of the system. There are different shells that operate somewhat differently, as has been mentioned at least once. We discuss shells more fully in Chapter 6.

Looking at Processes

So, what processes are running on your system? Let's take a look at my system and see what's running there:

```
[ jon@frogbog jon ]$ top
  3:04am  up  2:14,  5 users,  load average: 0.11, 0.04, 0.06
68 processes: 66 sleeping, 1 running, 1 zombie, 0 stopped
CPU states:  1.7% user,  2.3% system,  0.0% nice,  95.8% idle
Mem:  191124K av,  86976K used, 104148K free,      0K shrd,   4284K buff
Swap: 204080K av,      0K used, 204080K free                52648K cached
```

PID	USER	PRI	NI	SIZE	RSS	SHARE	STAT	LIB	%CPU	%MEM	TIME	COMMAND
530	root	8	0	10844	10M	2068	S	0	1.3	5.6	0:59	X
2	root	15	0	0	0	0	SW	0	1.1	0.0	1:18	kapmd
1251	jon	11	0	1176	1176	964	R	0	0.9	0.6	0:00	top
900	jon	2	0	3640	3640	1500	S	0	0.3	1.9	0:01	xterm
543	jon	1	0	2472	2472	1644	S	0	0.1	1.2	0:03	wmaker
1	root	0	0	460	460	388	S	0	0.0	0.2	0:03	init
3	root	0	0	0	0	0	SW	0	0.0	0.0	0:00	kswapd
4	root	0	0	0	0	0	SW	0	0.0	0.0	0:00	kflushd
5	root	0	0	0	0	0	SW	0	0.0	0.0	0:00	kupdate
6	root	0	0	0	0	0	SW	0	0.0	0.0	0:00	khubd
7	root	0	0	0	0	0	SW	0	0.0	0.0	0:00	uhci-control
8	root	0	0	0	0	0	SW	0	0.0	0.0	0:00	acpi
225	bin	0	0	404	404	316	S	0	0.0	0.2	0:00	portmap
278	root	0	0	528	528	428	S	0	0.0	0.2	0:00	syslogd
289	root	0	0	928	928	384	S	0	0.0	0.4	0:00	klogd
305	daemon	0	0	484	484	404	S	0	0.0	0.2	0:00	atd
321	root	0	0	600	600	504	S	0	0.0	0.3	0:00	crond
331	root	0	0	556	556	416	S	0	0.0	0.2	0:00	cardmgr

Note that top is an interactive program: It doesn't simply produce output and exit but instead produces output at regular intervals until quit. To quit top, just press **q** at any time. top's output might look different by default on your system, but the program is very configurable and you can adjust it to your liking.

Our habit, as good students, should be to dissect the information presented to us so that we can properly interpret it. Let's start at the top:

```
  3:04am  up  2:14,  5 users,  load average: 0.11, 0.04, 0.06
```

The top line of the screen gives output similar to the uptime command, giving the current time, the amount of time since the computer was started or rebooted, the number of users logged in at the moment, and three *load averages*.

A load average is a simple measure of how much work the computer is doing. Although we generally think of Unix as a multitasking operating system, in reality a given CPU can do only one thing as a time. (Unix does handle multiple CPUs very well, but most systems tend to be single CPU.) Because each CPU can do only one thing at a time, there's a list of programs waiting for CPU time. The higher the number of such processes over a given period of time, the higher the load average. A load average of one, on most systems, indicates the capacity of one processor. On a four-processor system, a load average of four would indicate capacity. In reality, CPU power isn't the limiting factor for most applications, and a load of two to four times the number of processors is reasonable.

The load averages that uptime and top display are for one, five, and fifteen minutes. From these numbers, it's clear that my system's CPU is almost completely idle. The third line of top's display confirms this:

```
CPU states:  1.7% user,  2.3% system,  0.0% nice,  95.8% idle
```

User time is that being used by normal processes on the system. *System time* is that used to write to disks, time spent managing low-level hardware details, and so on. These numbers, together with the idle time, should add up to 100%. The *nice time* can actually be subtracted from this total because it indicates processes that have been given a substantially lower priority by either the user or the system administrator. These processes run only in time not used by other programs.

The next two lines give an overview of the memory usage on the system:

```
Mem:   191124K av,  86976K used, 104148K free,      0K shrd,   4284K buff
Swap: 204080K av,      0K used, 204080K free                  52648K cached
```

Mem: represents memory installed on the system. The machine has 192MB of RAM, of which just under half is used. Most of that RAM, however, is used for buffers and cache, used to speed apparent disk performance. The system also has 200MB of *swap space*, disk partitions used by the system as though they were RAM. None of the swap space is currently used, which indicates that a shortage of memory isn't lowering our performance.

Finally, we approach the list of running processes. Generally, dozens, hundreds, or even thousands of processes run simultaneously on a given machine. top displays only those processes using the greatest percentage of the CPU. (We can use the ps command, which I will soon discuss, to see all processes on the system.) With the process listing header, here's the first several lines of top's output:

```
PID USER      PRI  NI  SIZE  RSS SHARE STAT  LIB %CPU %MEM   TIME COMMAND
530 root        8   0 10844  10M 2068 S       0  1.3  5.6   0:59 X
```

```
   2 root      15  0     0    0     0 SW      0  1.1  0.0   1:18 kapmd
1251 jon       11  0  1176 1176   964 R       0  0.9  0.6   0:00 top
 900 jon        2  0  3640 3640  1500 S       0  0.3  1.9   0:01 xterm
```

The first field is the process ID, the only guarantee that the process you're looking at is the one you think you're looking at. This is followed with the process owner, and then a number representing the priority of the process. A higher number means that more CPU time should be allocated to that process by the *scheduler*, the portion of the system that controls this. The next value, NI, represents the "niceness" of the process; A negative number means that the process is willing to give up CPU time to more important processes.

The STAT field is one of the most important because it gives us the status of the process: Is it actively **R**unning, is it **S**leeping as it waits to be run, has it been s**T**opped by a user, or is it a **Z**ombie?[23]

What's a *zombie*? Programmers, like mad scientists, make mistakes.[24] Sometimes a process exits ("dies"), but its parent process doesn't clean up afterward. These processes remain in the land between the living and the dead until either such clean-up occurs or the parent itself dies, after which the system cleans up. Zombies are unsightly and take up resources but are rarely actually harmful, though they tend to stink up the room…metaphorically, of course.

On my system, the man page for top says that the LIB field doesn't work. If it did, it would indicate the number of library pages used by the application. If you don't know what this means, you probably don't care, even if LIB works just fine on your system.

You probably do care about the %CPU and %MEM fields: They indicate the percentage of the CPU being used by the process as well as the percentage of physical memory. If you want to know what's slowing you down process-wise, these are good indicators. On a system with acceptable performance, it's all right if a process takes up nearly 100% of CPU time because it might only be taking up time that would otherwise be idle. If, by contrast, performance is lousy, see what's hogging memory and the CPU. If you have a multiprocessor system, these values often add up to some multiple of 100% because many systems handle each CPU separately.

TIME shows the total amount of CPU "time" that the process has taken up over the course of its life. This is a rough measure of how much work the CPU has dedicated to handling that process. Long-lived processes often have large numbers in the TIME field even if they're well behaved, because even small increments add up over days, weeks, or even months.

The last field is simply the name of the command being run. This is useful if you haven't memorized what processes are running at what PID. (Yes, that's a joke. Nobody does that, though most admins know that init is always PID 1.)

---

23. Only one process at a time is actually running on a single-user system, and this is by definition *top*, because it couldn't collect the data if it weren't running, so this isn't in itself a particularly useful piece of knowledge.

24. …as do authors. Please email me at jon@lasser.org if you find any.

So how's my system doing? Well, it's almost totally idle, it's got lots of free memory, and no process is currently hogging the CPU. The worst offenders on my system appear to be the X Window System (the Unix GUI), which is taking up a full 10MB of memory and using something less than 2% of the CPU. Something called kapmd is taking up just over 1% of the CPU. This process is handling power management on my laptop, and it's been running since my machine last booted. If you look closely, you'll note that its PID is 2. kapmd is really part of the Linux *kernel*, the part of the OS that controls access to all system resources. It starts up something that looks like a process to handle power management. kapmd has taken up a fair amount of CPU time total, but it would be hard to argue that it's affected my performance.

Next comes top, which is taking up almost nothing, as are xterm (a terminal window, to type commands to the system from X) and wmaker, my window manager. I'll talk about window managers when I discuss X in Part III. Everything else on the system is taking up entirely negligible resources.

A Short Treatise on Unix Genealogy

To understand the ps command, our next subject of investigation, you must know a little bit about Unix genealogy. Any operating system that runs on dozens if not hundreds of different types of computers is liable to obtain a sort of local color in many of those places. Those regional differences are bound to influence the children of those itinerant parents.

The great-granddaddy of all Unix was the Bell Labs version of the software. Back in those days, Bell shared the *source code* with everyone. Source code is what programmers write before it gets turned into *binaries* by a *compiler*.

Let's go over this one slowly. At the most basic level, a computer program is nothing but a long stream of ones and zeros, *machine code*. People don't write machine code (although people used to, when there was no other way to program computers), but instead use other computer languages, which turn source code into machine code, or binaries. Source code is much easier to read than an endless stream of 1s and 0s.

There's an intermediate form known as *assembly language*. Each computer architecture has its own assembly language. Assembly language is usually made up of short mnemonics, three or four letters long, that correspond directly to a single CPU instruction. Some of these mnemonics are followed by the data on which they operate. Most programmers know one sort of assembly language or another, but few use it on a daily basis.

Before Unix, every operating system was written in assembly language. At the time, most programmers could hand-tune assembly language better than the compilers could, and with such relatively simple machines, efficiency was paramount. In the early-mid-1970s, the Bell Labs people rewrote Unix in the C computer language, using assembly language only for small pieces of code that couldn't be otherwise written or that needed an exceptional degree of optimization.

After this was finished, Unix could be "ported" to any other sort of computer with a C compiler available for it. Alternatively, you could write your own C compiler and then build Unix. Because this was easy to do, relatively speaking, lots of people did, and Unix began to take over the world…or something like that.

In the late 1970s, Unix moved to Berkeley and the DEC VAX architecture. Once there, Unix acquired a host of new features. These included advanced networking features, the vi editor, a better printing system, different syntax for some commands, and so on. This new Unix variant was called the Berkeley Software Distribution (BSD). With differentiation came incompatibility, and code had to be written for either BSD or System V Unix, as the Bell Labs (later AT&T) version became known. (SVR4, short for System V Revision 4, is the current version. System V Unix is often referred to as SYSV Unix, or just SYSV.)

In the 1980s, BSD-based Unix flavors were more successful commercially. Today, the situation has turned around. Due to aggressive standardization efforts, SVR4 has become the dominant Unix platform. SunOS, the old BSD-based OS from Sun, has been replaced by Solaris, a SYSV Unix. Irix has moved to a dominantly SYSV architecture. Ultrix, Digital's BSD-like Unix, has been replaced by what Compaq today calls Tru64 Unix, which is SYSV-like. The only holdouts are BSDI, OpenBSD, NetBSD, and FreeBSD, the last three of which are open-source operating systems much like Linux.[25]

Well, sort of. In reality, System V and BSD Unix have moved much closer together at the user level, in terms of both included applications and syntax, and they even interoperate pretty well at the source code level. There are still differences under the hood, but at the user level only two real differences remain: They have different print systems, and ps works differently.

I won't really provide a full discussion of either version of ps. Smart people learn both and occasionally run the wrong command on a given flavor but just shrug their shoulders and type it the other way around. Linux has the smartest ps of all: It can take either BSD or SVR4 options, so you can never make a mistake. Not *that* mistake, anyway. Some SYSV Unix flavors have a /usr/ucb or /usr/bsd directory with various BSDish executables, including ps.

System V ps

To get by with ps, which lists processes in a more typical command-line way than top, you need only know a few things.[26] How do I list my processes on this terminal? How do I get more information about my processes? How do I list all my processes? How do I list all processes on the system?

---

25. Linux has managed to be some of each, but none of either. User commands are slowly moving to a more SVR4 syntax, but Linux itself was a complete rewrite and has code from neither BSD nor AT&T.

26. But you should have already figured that out, with the magic command *whatis ps*, if you didn't already know.

Let's run through this quickly: man ps is your friend, too. For a basic list of all processes on my current terminal, I can simply type **ps**:

```
[ jon@frogbog thinkunix ]$ ps
 PID TTY             TIME CMD
1506 pts/3       00:00:00 bash
1658 pts/3       00:00:00 ps
```

Okay, that's great. I've got my PID for each command, as well as the command name, the TTY, and how much CPU time it has used. ps -f gives a little more information:

```
[ jon@frogbog thinkunix ]$ ps -f
UID        PID   PPID  C STIME TTY          TIME CMD
jon       1506   1504  0 02:04 pts/3    00:00:00 bash
jon       1660   1506  0 02:34 pts/3    00:00:00 ps -f
```

This time I also get the parent process ID, something called C that always seems to have a 0 in it, and the start time of the process. (That's clock time on a standard 24-hour clock.)

I'd be more interested in seeing all processes on the system. I could use ps -e for that, but ps -ef provides more useful information. (Note that options that don't need extra data can be grouped together.)

```
[ jon@frogbog thinkunix ]$ ps -ef
UID        PID   PPID  C STIME TTY          TIME CMD
root         1      0  0 00:06 ?        00:00:03 init
root         2      1  2 00:06 ?        00:04:34 [kapmd]
root         3      1  0 00:06 ?        00:00:00 [kswapd]
root         4      1  0 00:06 ?        00:00:00 [kflushd]
root         5      1  0 00:06 ?        00:00:00 [kupdate]
root         6      1  0 00:06 ?        00:00:00 [khubd]
root         7      1  0 00:06 ?        00:00:00 [acpi]
bin        237      1  0 00:11 ?        00:00:00 portmap
root       290      1  0 00:11 ?        00:00:00 syslogd -m 0
root       301      1  0 00:11 ?        00:00:00 klogd
 .
 .
 .
jon       1504    555  0 02:04 ?        00:00:02 xterm
jon       1506   1504  0 02:04 pts/3    00:00:00 bash
jon       1676   1506  0 02:41 pts/3    00:00:00 ps -ef
```

Note that processes get listed in numerical order and that kernel threads are in brackets.

Perhaps the most important option is -u *username*, used to list a given user's processes. (This can be combined with -f, if you wish, but either way give each option a separate hyphen, as in ps -u jon -f, or place the u last because it requires an argument.)

```
[ jon@frogbog thinkunix ]$ ps -u jon
 PID TTY          TIME CMD
 555 ?        00:00:02 wmaker
 686 ?        00:00:02 xscreensaver
 687 ?        00:00:00 .xsession
 688 ?        00:00:00 xload
 742 ?        00:00:00 xdaliclock
 746 ?        00:00:00 wmbattery
 754 ?        00:00:03 xterm
 756 pts/0    00:00:00 bash
 811 pts/0    00:00:03 vim
1396 ?        00:00:00 xterm
1398 pts/1    00:00:00 bash
1447 pts/1    00:00:00 less
1448 ?        00:00:00 xterm
1450 pts/2    00:00:00 bash
1499 pts/2    00:00:00 less
1504 ?        00:00:02 xterm
1506 pts/3    00:00:00 bash
1678 pts/3    00:00:00 ps
```

Many processes don't have a terminal associated with them. These processes all
happen to run under X directly and are said to be *detached* from a terminal. Now if
I type **kill 742**, my pretty clock goes away, and if I type **kill 555**, my whole window manager goes away and it kills my X session. But I don't want to do that; I'd
rather demonstrate BSD's ps.

BSD ps

BSD's ps distinguishes itself immediately from the SYSV ps by not requiring a
hyphen for its options, shocking and nonstandard though this practice might be.
(What can I say? Those guys at Berkeley did it.) Like SYSV ps, there are three
important options to learn (and several dozen more when you get around to it),
but these are three different options.

A simple ps produces results similar to its SVR4 counterpart:

```
[ jon@frogbog thinkunix ]$ ps
 PID TTY          TIME CMD
1506 pts/3    00:00:00 bash
1689 pts/3    00:00:00 ps
```

No big deal. The first option is to learn is x, which lists all your processes, even
those on other terminals. This is the rough equivalent to a SVR4 -u
your_username:

```
[ jon@frogbog thinkunix ]$ ps x
 PID TTY          TIME CMD
 555 ?        00:00:02 wmaker
```

```
 686 ?              00:00:02 xscreensaver
 687 ?              00:00:00 .xsession
 688 ?              00:00:00 xload
 742 ?              00:00:00 xdaliclock
 746 ?              00:00:00 wmbattery
 754 ?              00:00:03 xterm
 756 pts/0          00:00:00 bash
 811 pts/0          00:00:04 vim
1396 ?              00:00:00 xterm
1398 pts/1          00:00:00 bash
1447 pts/1          00:00:00 less
1448 ?              00:00:00 xterm
1450 pts/2          00:00:00 bash
1499 pts/2          00:00:00 less
1504 ?              00:00:03 xterm
1506 pts/3          00:00:00 bash
1690 pts/3          00:00:00 ps
```

Pretty straightforward. To list all processes on the system if, say, you were the system administrator or simply wanted to see what your fellow users were doing, you would have to use the a option. It's not actually that simple, however, because this would only list processes on your current terminal belonging to all users. This would almost certainly just be your processes. Instead, you must combine the a option with the x option, which lists all user processes on any (or no) terminal:

```
[ jon@frogbog thinkunix ]$ ps ax
 PID TTY        STAT    TIME COMMAND
   1 ?          S       0:03 init
   2 ?          SW      5:08 [kapmd]
   3 ?          SW      0:00 [kswapd]
   4 ?          SW      0:00 [kflushd]
   5 ?          SW      0:00 [kupdate]
   6 ?          SW      0:00 [khubd]
   7 ?          SW      0:00 [acpi]
 237 ?          S       0:00 portmap
 290 ?          S       0:00 syslogd -m 0
 301 ?          S       0:00 klogd
 .
 .
 .
1504 ?          S       0:03 xterm
1506 pts/3      S       0:00 bash
1691 pts/3      R       0:00 ps ax
```

This, unfortunately, isn't entirely useful because it's not at all clear who's doing what. For that, we need the u option as well to indicate the user who owns the process:

```
[ jon@frogbog thinkunix ]$ ps aux
USER       PID %CPU %MEM   VSZ  RSS TTY    STAT START   TIME COMMAND
root         1  0.0  0.2  1104  460 ?      S    00:06   0:03 init
root         2  3.0  0.0     0    0 ?      SW   00:06   5:12 [kapmd]
```

```
root          3  0.0  0.0     0    0 ?      SW   00:06    0:00 [kswapd]
root          4  0.0  0.0     0    0 ?      SW   00:06    0:00 [kflushd]
root          5  0.0  0.0     0    0 ?      SW   00:06    0:00 [kupdate]
root          6  0.0  0.0     0    0 ?      SW   00:06    0:00 [khubd]
root          7  0.0  0.0     0    0 ?      SW   00:06    0:00 [acpi]
bin         237  0.0  0.2  1200  404 ?      S    00:11    0:00 portmap
root        290  0.0  0.2  1156  528 ?      S    00:11    0:00 syslogd -m 0
root        301  0.0  0.4  1568  932 ?      S    00:11    0:00 klogd
.
.
.
jon        1504  0.1  1.4  4756 2692 ?      S    02:04    0:03 xterm
jon        1506  0.0  0.5  1776 1008 pts/3  S    02:04    0:00 bash
jon        1692  0.0  0.5  2664 1016 pts/3  R    02:59    0:00 ps aux
```

This provides a lot more information, including CPU and memory usage, and gives us enough information to kill any of our processes we no longer want. (Only root can kill processes belonging to another user; otherwise, the life of a process would be nasty, brutish, and short.)

On most systems, the precise output of the ps command is highly configurable. However, even most experienced system administrators seem to use one of the default output formats. It's nice to have flexibility, but if you can't use the basic options, all the power in the world won't help. If you're on a system that permits this or if you have access to multiple platforms, I highly recommend getting used to different versions of the ps command.

What's a Thread?

You might have noticed a few paragraphs ago that I slipped in the term *kernel thread* without defining it. I will now correct that oversight: A kernel thread is simply a thread that is really owned by and part of the kernel.

What? That's not helpful? You actually want to know what a thread is? Well, I'll tell you. But first, if you're a programmer, I want you to skip to the next chapter. This explanation glosses over everything even remotely important about threads because users for the most part aren't interested in the things you're interested in. Reading this will only upset you, so don't bother.

Okay, now that I've gotten rid of the pedants, I can let you in on a dirty secret:

As a user, the difference between a process and a thread is irrelevant to you.

No, really. As far as you should be concerned, a thread is just a special kind of process. It acts differently if you're a programmer, but if you're a programmer you should have skipped to the next chapter by now.

Any other questions? No? Well then, onto the next chapter! Let's hope those programmers haven't skipped any farther ahead of us, or we'll never catch up.

Redirection and Pipes

This chapter is the heart of what the Unix mentality is all about. If you took everything else away from Unix but left redirection and pipes, you'd still be doing okay. These are the concepts from which Unix derives its strength and character, and attention paid now will be well rewarded later. I promise. This is a short chapter, but one that contains the ideas which have allowed Unix to flourish for decades while other systems have fallen by the wayside.

The material here is deceptively simple, in that none of these concepts are difficult or take any time to learn. The full power of Unix, however, lies in the informed application of these simple ideas. Practice these concepts until pipes and redirection are a reflex.

Redirection

When I speak of redirection on Unix, I'm speaking of redirecting input and output of individual programs. Redirecting the input and output presupposes that there's a normal place from which data comes and a normal place to which it goes.

The Three Musketeers: STDIN, STDOUT, STDERR

And, in fact, this is the case. We could say that data normally goes from the terminal keyboard through the program and back out to the terminal's display. This does cover the typical case but is technically inaccurate: Data comes from STDIN and goes to STDOUT. *STDIN* is an abbreviation for *standard input*, and *STDOUT* is short for *standard output*.

Both STDIN and STDOUT can be considered as files: streams of bytes. STDIN is a stream being read by the program, and STDOUT is a stream of data being written by the program. Under normal circumstances, these point to the display and keyboard of the user's terminal. If I run cat without any filename on the command line, it reads its file from STDIN (normally the keyboard); cat always writes to STDOUT (normally the screen):

```
[ jon@frogbog thinkunix ]$ cat
This is a test.
This is a test.
I'm typing this in one line at a time.
I'm typing this in one line at a time.
All right I've had enough.
All right I've had enough.
^D
[ jon@frogbog thinkunix ]$
```

As you can see, cat is designed to read text in from STDIN, one line at a time, and send it back to STDOUT. It stops reading its data when it reaches an end-of-file marker (EOF), which on standard Unix systems is represented by Ctrl+D.[1] One more important stream is STDERR, which stands for *standard error*. This is where error messages go, as you'll often find that it's convenient to send errors somewhere different than STDOUT or that it's convenient to send errors the same place as STDOUT, when they'd tend to go elsewhere.

Reading, Writing, Appending

Let's say Elvis wants to take a quick note by catting some text into a file: He's on the phone with Devo about a possible collaboration, and (like us) hasn't yet learned to use a text editor.

```
[ elvis@frogbog elvis]$ cat > devo.txt
Country-Western "Whip It"?

Flowerpot Hats: Jerry's House of Weird Stuff, Pierpont, MI

Get Eddie V.H. to play guitar on new "Jailhouse Rock" album?
^D
[ elvis@frogbog elvis]$
```

A single right-angle bracket (>) redirects STDOUT to a file; it even looks like an arrow pointing into a file. Not surprisingly, to redirect STDIN from a file requires a single left-angle bracket (<). Elvis now wants to see the names in west.txt in alphabetical order because he knows we need a convenient example for redirecting STDIN from a file:

```
[ elvis@frogbog elvis ]$ sort < west.txt
Aristotle
Heraclitus
Plato
Plotinus
Socrates
```

All done, without a troublesome complaint from the system or a good reason why.

Appending to a file is easy, too: It's simply a pair of right-angle brackets without spaces (>>). With appending, Elvis can add to his reading list of Western philosophers:

```
[ elvis@frogbog elvis ]$ cat >> west.txt
Kierkegaard
Pascal
Descartes
Sartre
^D
```

---

1. The more-or-less standard notation for control characters is to put a caret (^) in front of the key to be pressed.

```
[ elvis@frogbog elvis ]$ cat west.txt
Socrates
Plato
Aristotle
Heraclitus
Plotinus
Kierkegaard
Pascal
Descartes
Sartre
```

And the additional names have been added to the list.

Herefiles

Now that I've explained what >, <, and >> do, the obvious question is what <<
does. The answer is that it makes a *herefile*.

"A herefile, huh?" you say. "Never heard of it. What's it do, anyway?" That's a pretty
good question. A herefile lets you input a whole bunch of lines of text to STDIN
until you reach a predefined marker, like so:

```
[ elvis@frogbog elvis ]$ cat > newfile.txt << STOPHERE
> This is a new file. I can put lots of text in it.
>
> I can put text in it all day, if that's what I want to do.
>
> Why would I do this? Because the system will let me.
>
> Of course, the system lets me do all sorts of stupid and worthless things.
>
> Garbage In, Garbage Out, I guess.
> STOPHERE
```

It's immediately apparent that herefiles are more convenient than simply catting
from STDIN. For one thing, they provide a nice-looking prompt at the beginning
of each line, so that we know what to expect from them. For another thing, they
avoid our having to remember that Ctrl+D is the EOF marker on Unix, though
an EOF will still stop input even without the herefile keyword.[2]

Even so, herefiles don't really become important until I talk about *shell scripts* in
Part II. Still, this is the logical place to talk about them in the book. And if I
hadn't, you'd still be wondering precisely what << could *possibly* be used for.

---

2. Nothing works in all shells, but we're not trying to cover all shells: Our reference platform is the
bash shell, though almost everything we do in this book works identically under ksh as well.

In this particular case, csh doesn't provide a prompt when entering text into a herefile, although the
newer tcsh does. We discuss shells in more detail in Chapter 6.

Redirecting STDERR

Now that we've used <, >, <<, and >>, how might we redirect the standard error stream?

Unfortunately, the easy way to redirect STDERR doesn't work in the Bourne Shell, which is what almost everyone uses to write shell scripts. Additionally, the simple and perhaps logical answer would be to extend the existing syntax, using >>>, or to use another symbol, such as], }, or) that bears some visual resemblance to our original symbol. There are actually two ways to do this on Unix: the easy (but not quite so useful) way, and the hard (but more useful) way.

The Easy Way

The easy way to redirect STDERR is to redirect STDERR to STDOUT to a file. You can accomplish this by using >& to redirect to a file. Let's say that we were running a `find` to list all the files on the system, and we wanted to see the error messages inside our output, which we were sending to a file. We could use the command `find / -name '*' -print >& ~/allfiles.txt`. All the output, including `find`'s error messages, would be in that file.

Unfortunately, if we wanted to redirect only the error messages but see `find`'s normal output on the screen, we'd have some difficulty with that. To do that, we must redirect STDERR the hard way.

The Hard Way

The hard way to redirect STDERR relies on a feature present in only some Unix shells: numbered *file handle*s. The Bourne, Korn, and Bash Shells all have this feature. The C Shell and tcsh don't. For more about shells, see Chapter 6. For now, simply type the following command to find out which shell you have:[3]

```
cat /etc/passwd|grep ^ username:|cut -d : -f 7
```

Replace *username* with your own username. That command should print a file and path name. If the program referenced is csh or tcsh, this section doesn't apply to you, unless you change your shell. If it's sh, ksh, or bash, it does.[4] The fact that you can't redirect particular file handles with csh or tcsh leads many Unix experts to pronounce those shells "broken." I take no position on this other than to note that I don't cover those shells. Even if you run those shells and you're not willing to switch, this section is probably still worth reading, just for the theory.

---

3. Assuming your site doesn't use NIS to keep track of accounts. NIS is beyond the scope of this book; however, you can get the NIS account list by typing **ypcat passwd** instead of **cat /etc/passwd**.

4. This seems as good a point as any to point out that Unix shells have two names: their "real names" and the names of the commands that run the shells. The Bourne Shell is also known as sh, the Korn Shell is ksh, the Bourne Again Shell is bash, the C Shell is csh, and tcsh is tcsh.

A file handle is an abstract representation of a file. That is, when a computer program needs to access a file, it doesn't use the name of the file being accessed each time. Instead, the program creates a named file handle. Essentially, the programmer says "Whenever I talk about MY_OPEN_FILE, I'm really talking about /some/really/long/path/to/a/particular/file." This has a whole bunch of advantages for the programmer: first, she doesn't need to type that really long filename each time she wants to read or write from that file. Second, if the file changes its name or directory before the program is finished being written, there's less to change. Third, and more importantly, if the file changes its name or directory while the program is running, or if the program doesn't know the filename beforehand, it can still deal with it.

Most programming languages use names for file handles, but Unix shells use numbers. Names might be convenient, albeit longwinded, but it would be a lot trickier to figure out what part of the command line is a file handle and what part is not. Numbers make this part easy.

All redirection is actually done with numbered file handles (also known as *file descriptors*); most redirection commands simply have a default file descriptor. The generalized format is simply the file descriptor immediately to the left of the redirection command. STDIN is 0, STDOUT is 1, and STDERR is 2. When we run the command cat < ourfile.txt, we're really running cat 0< ourfile.txt. Similarly, when we run ls > whatever, what we're really doing is ls 1> whatever.

Therefore, if we want to direct only STDERR to a file in our previous example with find, we should find / -name '*' -print 2> errors.txt. This prints the normal output of find to the console while sending the errors to errors.txt.

This enables us to get even more complicated and send normal output to one file while getting rid of error messages entirely. find / -name '*' -print > find.txt 2> /dev/null sends the useful output from find to find.txt and sends all the error messages to the bit bucket.

Practice Problems

1. cat /etc/passwd > something.txt. What is contained in something.txt after this command?

2. Using a redirection from a file, display the contents of /etc/group onscreen.

3. Through cat, redirect from /etc/group to something.txt.

4. Using cat, redirect input from /dev/null to a file named null.txt. What are the contents of null.txt after you've done this?

5. Assuming that no directory is named zip in your current directory, change your directory *to* zip, redirecting standard error to null.txt. (If your system gives you an error when you attempt this, feel free to rm null.txt and try again.) What are the contents of null.txt when this is done?

6. `rm something.txt` and, using a herefile, create a file named `something.txt` with the following text:

```
This file is named something.
Presumably, that means something should be in it.
All I see here is a whole bunch of nothing.
How can that possibly be?
```

Pipes

Pipes are what Unix is really all about. I know I said that redirection and pipes were the heart of Unix, but effective use of pipes defines Unix. Although other systems do all right with redirection, only Unix does right by pipes. Although several early releases of Unix were made before pipes were added, pipes made Unix special.

The concept now seems absurdly simple: Rather than redirecting output of a program into a file, we can redirect it into another program. The implications of this concept are staggering, and they delineate what is thought of as the Unix philosophy.

The idea of Unix is like that of a set of good knives. Each has a single purpose. Each does well at its appointed task. Some might be used for another task, but only poorly. The modern GUI-based operating system, with its bloated, monolithic applications, might be thought of as a food processor: It can do all sorts of things, but it's big, complicated, and not as flexible as that drawer full of knives. The food processor certainly does some things better: When I want to make hummus, I run it through the food processor; if I want to carve a turkey, however, I look elsewhere.

There's another lesson here: A food processor permits a person with little experience to do a good job at slicing vegetables. An expert with a good set of knives, however, can probably do the job both faster and better. Some tools, such as knives, reward experience and practice. Some, such as food processors, do not. At least, the learning curve is much more limited with a food processor.

Many people refer to this as the *toolbox philosophy*. In order to effectively connect these individual tools to each other, we need the pipe.

A pipe is represented by the vertical bar (|), and that key is referred to by most Unix people simply as the pipe. The flow of data is from left to right: The program on the left of the pipe sends its output to the program on the right, which sees it as input. A program through which data is piped is known as a *filter*.

Some Common Filters

Now that you have a toolbox, let's fill it with some basic tools! This section is about the hammers, screwdrivers, and wrenches of the Unix toolbox—the ones you use every day. There are drill presses and circular saws, but before you can learn those tools you need to learn the basics.

Pagers

The first filter most users try is `cat` piped into `more`, which is a simple program that stops after each screenful of text and waits for the user to press a key.[5] If you're reading a long text file, `more` is your friend. Just to try it out, type **cat /usr/dict/words | more**. (When you're sick of seeing a long list of alphabetical words, simply press Ctrl+C to break out of `more`.) If your system doesn't have `/usr/dict/words`, try examining `/etc/services` or any other long file on your system.

After you've tried `more`, try `less` instead, if it's installed on your system. If you're not sure whether `less` is installed on your system, just try these commands and see whether they work. If `less` isn't installed, you'll get an error message but nothing will break; you just won't get to see the file you tried to look at. `less` permits you to go backward as well as forward; if your terminal is properly configured, your PageUp and PageDown keys should enable you to scroll a page of text at a time. Because `less` doesn't quit when you reach the end of the file, you'll need to press q to exit. (Unlike most Unix programs, Ctrl+C doesn't exit `less`.) As with `more`, just `cat /etc/syslog.conf | less` to look at a really long file you don't particularly care about.

`more` and `less` are a special subcategory of filter known as *pagers* because they enable users to page through text. Most filters, however, transform the text that passes through them in some way.

Heads or Tails

`head` and `tail` transform text by displaying only part of it. `head` displays the top part of a file, whereas `tail` displays the bottom of the file:

```
[ elvis@frogbog elvis ]$ cat tao.txt|head -2
Lao Tzu
Chuang Tzu
[ elvis@frogbog elvis ]$ cat tao.txt|head -4
```

---

5. You might remember our old friends `more` and `less` from our discussion of documentation in Chapter 1. Not only are `more` and `less` pipes, they can also simply take a filename as an argument and display that file. Many Unix commands are flexible in the same way. Even `cat` can be used as a filter if you don't give it a filename on the command line. You've actually done this already, if you think about it, when you redirected a file into `cat`.

```
Lao Tzu
Chuang Tzu
K'ung Tzu
Meng Tzu
[ elvis@frogbog elvis ]$ cat tao.txt|tail -2
Meng Tzu
Wang Bi
[ elvis@frogbog elvis ]$ cat tao.txt|tail -4
Chuang Tzu
K'ung Tzu
Meng Tzu
Wang Bi
```

By default, head and tail print ten lines apiece. You can specify a measurement other than lines in some versions of these commands, but counting lines is most common.

sort and uniq

Another very popular filter is sort, which simply sorts the file passed to it alphabetically. As with head and tail, there's not a whole lot to say about sort, so I'll just run a few simple demonstrations:

```
[ elvis@frogbog elvis ]$ cat tao.txt|sort
Chuang Tzu
K'ung Tzu
Lao Tzu
Meng Tzu
Wang Bi
[ elvis@frogbog elvis ]$ cat west.txt|sort
Aristotle
Descartes
Heraclitus
Kierkegaard
Pascal
Plato
Plotinus
Sartre
Socrates
[ elvis@frogbog elvis ]$ cat tao.txt west.txt|sort
Aristotle
Chuang Tzu
Descartes
Heraclitus
Kierkegaard
K'ung Tzu
Lao Tzu
```

```
Meng Tzu
Pascal
Plato
Plotinus
Sartre
Socrates
Wang Bi
[ elvis@frogbog elvis ]$ cat west.txt tao.txt|sort
Aristotle
Chuang Tzu
Descartes
Heraclitus
Kierkegaard
K'ung Tzu
Lao Tzu
Meng Tzu
Pascal
Plato
Plotinus
Sartre
Socrates
Wang Bi
```

As you can see, sort takes all the input it receives via STDIN and sends the sorted data to STDOUT. There is a special numerical mode, accessible via the -n option. With this switch, if the text at the beginning of the line is a number, numbers are sorted in numerical order. This seems redundant, but let's have an example:

```
[ jon@frogbog jon ]$ cat some-stuff.txt
99 Dead Baboons
99 Red Balloons
101 Dalmatians
16 Candles
24 Hours
9 Lords a Leaping
[ jon@frogbog jon ]$ cat some-stuff.txt|sort -n
9 Lords a Leaping
16 Candles
24 Hours
99 Dead Baboons
99 Red Balloons
101 Dalmatians
```

But what would happen without the -n switch? Let's try that, too:

```
[ jon@frogbog jon ]$ cat some-stuff.txt|sort
101 Dalmatians
16 Candles
24 Hours
```

```
99 Dead Baboons
99 Red Balloons
9 Lords a Leaping
```

Hardly what we might have in mind when sorting by quantity: Instead of sorting numerically, this list is sorted alphabetically. (Remember, in ASCII numbers come before letters.)

A related tool of somewhat limited use is uniq, which strips out duplicate lines when they follow each other in the file. For example,

```
[ jon@frogbog jon ]$ cat other-stuff.txt
One
Two
One
One
Two
Two
Two
Three
Three
One
[ jon@frogbog jon ]$ cat other-stuff.txt|uniq
One
Two
One
Two
Three
One
```

This is much more useful following a sort:

```
[ jon@frogbog jon ]$ cat other-stuff.txt | sort | uniq
One
Three
Two
```

Not what you were expecting? How's the computer supposed to know that "Two" and "Three" are numbers? You can, however, see that it works.

wc

By far my favorite filter is wc, which simply reports how many characters, words, and lines, are present in a file.

```
[ jon@frogbog jon ]$ cat some-stuff.txt | wc
      6      16      85
[ jon@frogbog jon ]$ cat some-stuff.txt | wc -c
    85
```

```
[ jon@frogbog jon ]$ cat some-stuff.txt | wc -w
     16
[ jon@frogbog jon ]$ cat some-stuff.txt | wc -l
      6
```

wc is particularly useful for counting anything stored one line per record, such as the output of a ps command:

```
[ jon@frogbog jon ]$ ps -ef|wc -l
     63
```

Obviously, the precise number varies depending on your system and its use when you run the command. How many processes are running on this system right now? If you said 63, you're wrong: Remember that ps has a header line at the top of its output, so only 62 processes are running on the system.

Combining Filters into Longer Pipelines

A single filter by itself might be useful, but filters are most useful when combined with each other to produce a particular effect. The language metaphor for Unix is particularly apt here: Single pipes are like simple sentences, whereas longer pipelines are like complex sentences. In this section, we endeavor to diagram some more complex pipelines to gain a better grasp of the language. Users who don't write complex pipelines can get their work done, which is what computing is intended to do, but they're only speaking pidgin Unix. Being able to speak fluent Unix means being able to get your work done more quickly and more elegantly than you might otherwise be able to.

Remember that earlier in the chapter, I asked you to find out what shell you were using by typing

```
cat /etc/passwd|grep ^ username:|cut -d : -f 7
```

Let's dissect that command and see what's going on with it. First, we're looking at /etc/passwd. Use man 5 passwd to find out what's going on with that file.[6] Simply put, /etc/passwd contains a list of all the accounts that can log in to the system. (On systems with NIS, the YP map passwd contains the same information.) The information in this file is in several different fields, each separated by a colon. On my system, two such lines read as follows:

```
jon:x:500:500:Jon:/home/jon:/bin/bash
elvis:x:501:100:Elvis:/home/elvis:/bin/bash
```

---

6. On Solaris systems, you'll have to use man -s 5 passwd, for some silly reason. I don't know why they took a mind to breaking this, but they did.

The first field in /etc/passwd is the username. Second is the password, but on most modern systems the password is stored elsewhere, and x is the only thing that shows up in this field. Third is the UID for this account, fourth is the primary GID. Fifth is the GECOS field, which contains what passes for a human-readable username. On some systems, this can also contain phone numbers, offices, and so on. Sixth is the user's home directory, and finally we have the user's default shell.

If I want to find my shell, as with the command I mentioned earlier, first I have to find my account. For this, we pipe /etc/passwd through grep, which is an advanced search program. The default is to return all lines that match the regular expression provided on the command line.

I'll talk about regular expressions in Chapter 5, but for now we only need to know that you can look for text with regular expressions and that some characters have special meanings. In the previous example, if I wanted to find my account, that part of the pipe would read grep ^jon:.

Why would I want to look for more than my account name? Because more than one account on the system might have *jon* in its name, I want to search for the entire field. We're lucky, because the username is the first field. Regular expressions have a special character to mark the beginning of the line: ^. Marking the end of the field is easy: All we need to do is put a colon at the end of it. Therefore, the regular expression ^jon: finds the word *jon* followed by a colon at the beginning of the line. This should return precisely one account, mine.

Finally, we can pass the output of grep to the cut command. cut lets you specify what part of a line you want to display and can work either with individual characters or fields. We want to work with fields, but by default cut expects that fields are *delimited*, or separated, by tabs. We want to use a colon instead, hence the -d : portion of the command line. We also want to specify that only the seventh field should be shown, and so we add a -f 7 to finish this command line.

Let's try another example to figure out how many different users are currently running processes on your machine. If you have a System V ps, it would look like this:

```
ps -ef|awk '{ print $1 }'|sort|uniq|wc -l|xargs expr -1 +
```

With a BSD ps, it would look like this:

```
ps aux|awk '{ print $1 }'|sort|uniq|wc -l|xargs expr -1 +
```

The part of the pipe that is providing the data is, in either case, a full listing of all processes on the machine. Although the output of this data is different, in both cases we happen to be interested in the first field, which is the username.

The username is passed onto awk. awk is, in fact, a full-fledged programming language, but it lends itself nicely to one-line commands like this. Like cut, awk can print an individual field. However, awk does an excellent job of figuring out where field breaks are if its input comes in reasonably good columns. ps meets this criterion, and because the fields aren't delimited with a single character, cut doesn't do a good job here.

Even though awk is a full-fledged computer language, many Unix users only use the single command I mentioned before. The single quotes around the curly braces are necessary, and to change the column number output, replace the 1 in the earlier example with the column of your choice.

The input stream for sort is now a single column listing the owner of each command. A uniq would not work in this case without a sort because processes might or might not be grouped by username. So we sort and uniq the output, producing a list of all unique usernames who are currently running processes.

We then pass this list to wc -l, which counts the number of lines in its input. Now we have a number, and a problem: The header for ps is counted in that number, unless a user currently running processes has a username the same as the header field! We have to get rid of that extra number. To do this, we just need to subtract one.

The program that can best do this is expr, which permits you to put in a simple math problem on the command line. So we want to expr <STDIN> - 1 to get our answer. Unfortunately, we have another problem: expr takes its input not from STDIN but from its command line. This means we have to turn our input stream into a command-line argument.

Fortunately, there's a program designed to do just that: xargs takes STDIN and appends it (each line separated by a space rather than a line break, if there are multiple lines in the input file) to its own command line. The first parameter on the xargs command line is required, and it tells the program which program gets the new command line. After that, you can put any number of options that get passed to that command before STDIN.

This is our last problem: We want to subtract one from STDIN, which would mean xargs expr <STDIN> -1, but xargs won't let us put text after STDIN. The simple answer is to add STDIN to –1, giving us a final pipe of xargs expr -1 +.

Right now, this sure looks like a lot of work to get a simple answer. In a way, it is. After some practice, however, command lines such as this will feel like second nature to you. If you use Unix enough, you'll even find that it's difficult to get along without the capability to do this because you'll find that it is central to getting the computer to do what you want. You'll begin to wonder (I hope) why it's so difficult to send matching lines of your word document through a filter that changes them in some consistent way. When you start to ask yourself questions like this, you begin to think Unix from the inside out.

Practice Problems

7. How many entries are in your system's /etc/passwd file?

8. Display the last five entries of your system's /etc/passwd file.

9. Sort the last five entries of your system's /etc/passwd file.

10. Sort your /etc/passwd file and display the last five lines, alphabetically speaking.

11. Display only the usernames of these last five entries.

12. Display only the usernames and UIDs of these entries. (Hint: Read the cut man page to find out how to do this.)

13. Redirect this list of usernames and UIDs to a file named last-users-on-system.txt.

14. Write a pipeline that will kill any of your processes whose names begin with cat and a space. (To create a test case, you can run cat &, which creates a process named cat.) Don't try to kill all processes named cat; instead, kill only those that belong to you.

Networking

Marketing doctrine has entrenched the concept of the "killer app," the idea that huge quantities of hardware are purchased so that a particular software application can run well. In the PC platform, marketers cite particular examples such as the spreadsheets Lotus 1-2-3 and Microsoft Excel, and several database and word processing packages that, they felt, "moved" hardware.

If the concept of the killer app is valid, the ultimate killer app—the one that sells computing devices to those who do not already possess them—is networking. Although untold millions of consumer-grade hardware devices to connect to the Internet have been sold, the Internet itself was largely designed and implemented on Unix. Today, the Unix community seems firmly in control of the IETF, the Internet Engineering Task Force, an ad-hoc group of engineers responsible for the ongoing design and development of the network.

Because Unix and the Internet were designed in parallel, Unix gets most of the good stuff first: The World Wide Web was designed on Unix, and the most popular Web browsers started out on Unix before being ported to Windows and Macintosh.[1] Also as a result of its Unix heritage, the Internet is quite flexible, and most of the higher-level protocols are human-readable. This is great because it means that you're going to see how things *really* work.

A Broad Overview of Networking

Of course, to look at that higher-level stuff first we need to understand a little bit about the lower-level design of the Internet. This isn't going to be very in-depth, so professional network engineers and techies who know about the bit-level design of the Internet should skip to the next section.

Name Lookup

We're not going to start at the absolute bottom level of networking, but a little bit closer to home: hostnames. Every time you send a bit of email or look at a Web site, you must tell the system the name of the machine you want. Like usernames and group names, however, computers prefer working with numbers. Every hostname gets converted to a number before a computer can talk with it.

Aside from simply working more efficiently, there are several advantages to using names that get converted to numbers. First, one machine can respond to multiple names so that it can provide different services depending on what it's called. Second, you can change the machine the name refers to while leaving the old system entirely in place; that is, the name can correspond to an abstract idea of a computer rather than a physical computer. This leads into the third advantage,

---

1. Even Microsoft's Internet Explorer started out as a licensed version of Mosaic, the same Web browser from which Netscape was developed.

which is that multiple computers can be referred to by a single name. The host-name www.example.org can point to three or four different machines at once: The system that converts names to numbers can simply "round-robin" the number it responds with when asked for a given machine. This is important when you have too much traffic for a single computer to handle.

The idea that names are converted to numbers by a system is important. In fact, there are several different services by which names can be converted to numbers, but only two are at all important: /etc/hosts and DNS, Domain Name Service.[2]

Back in the old days, there was only /etc/hosts, a file on every Unix box that listed every other computer on the network it knew about. If somebody added a machine to the network, you had to edit your /etc/hosts file or download a whole new one from a master server.

As you might imagine, this became rather unwieldy, and the system had to be replaced. Today, the only line in /etc/hosts on my laptop is

```
127.0.0.1 localhost.localdomain localhost frogbog.localdomain frogbog
```

so that my laptop knows its own names even when not connected to a network. (This is important because you can use a lot of Unix network tools connecting locally.) Generally, the system administrator can configure which of DNS or /etc/hosts overrides the other. Most admins I know let /etc/hosts override DNS so that they can "fix" problems with DNS servers they can't control, but don't assume that this is true on your host.

DNS

So how is this DNS thing more maintainable than /etc/hosts? Its three distin-guishing features are that it's client/server, it's hierarchical, and it's distributed. We'll talk about each of these in turn.

DNS is client/server. This means machines that want to convert a hostname to a number don't generally do it themselves but look to another machine that does the actual work. The machine making the request and receiving the response is the *client*; the machine receiving the request and responding is the *server*. The primary advantage of a client/server architecture is that the clients don't usually require much in the way of maintenance. All that's required is that they can talk to the server.

The user-level tool for DNS lookups is nslookup. Use of nslookup is dreadfully simple:

```
[ jon@frogbog jon ]$ nslookup www.umbc.edu
Server: defender.localdomain
Address: 192.168.0.1

Name: www.umbc.edu
Address: 130.85.253.114
```

---

2. Actually, there's a third name service that is part of NIS, but few sites I've seen use it, even those using NIS. It works much like /etc/hosts shared over a local network.

The output of nslookup is nearly as simple as the command itself. First, it provides the name of the server that has responded to the name lookup and the address of that server. Second, it responds with the name of the host that has been looked up and the address or addresses of that host.

You can also do reverse lookups with nslookup. If you know a machine's number but not its name, you can simply

```
[ jon@frogbog jon ]$ nslookup 204.71.200.74
Server: defender.localdomain
Address: 192.168.0.1

Name: www9.yahoo.com
Address: 204.71.200.74
```

This is useful when looking at logs of, for example, Web connections to a machine. Many Web servers are set up to log the number but not to waste time or resources looking up the name because (as you just saw) that can be done later.

nslookup also has an interactive mode; just type **nslookup** to start it. It will prompt you with a >. Just type the name of the host whose name you want and press Enter. When you're finished, simply press Control-D as an end-of-file marker, or type **exit** and press Enter. (Yes, you can pipe in a list of hostnames to be *resolved*.)

DNS is also hierarchical. The names are nested, like directory names, only with a dot (single period) separating levels rather than a forward slash: www.yahoo.com is the machine named www in the domain named yahoo in the top-level domain com. Similarly, www.umbc.edu is the machine named www in the domain named umbc in the top-level domain edu. You can have more than three levels: many times machines can be listed two or more subdomains deep, such as my-workstation.my-office. my-company.com.

Being hierarchical means that it's easier to find names for what you want to find. It also means that you can have more names available, as each needs to be unique for a given service at a given subdomain level, just as filenames need to be unique within a given subdirectory. Most importantly, a hierarchy of domain names makes it possible to *delegate* the administration of a given domain or subdomain to another party.

The complement to the hierarchical nature of the domain names is the hierarchical nature of the servers. This relies at least partially on the delegation of responsibility for the domain names themselves. A given server is responsible for only a small number of domains and the names of hosts within those domains. Like the domain names themselves, the servers are in a tree, with a root server that decides which server is responsible for the next level down the tree.

For example, when resolving the name www.linux.org.uk, the top-level server decides that a given server is responsible for the .uk top-level domain. Next, the .uk server decides that a particular server (or itself) is responsible for the .org.uk domain. That server, in turn, decides who is responsible for `linux.org.uk`. The `linux.org.uk` name-server, finally, can return the address of the machine `www.linux.org.uk`.

If every system started out by looking at the root nameserver each time, that would put a lot of strain both on the network and on the higher-level name-servers. Instead, nameservers can be used not only to look up names for that domain but for other domains as well. These servers *cache* the results of previous lookups and only look up sites for which current information is not in the cache. Even then, nameservers look up only what is necessary: If `linux.org.uk` is cached, your server will skip straight there when looking up `www.linux.org.uk`, but if only `.org.uk` is cached, it will begin there instead. Only very rarely do servers need to look at the top-level servers. Some servers are "caching-only" servers: They don't serve authoritative data for any particular domain but only handle lookups. These are particularly useful when a large number of machines share a single slow link.

One of the few unfortunate consequences of this distributed service is that some-times, albeit rarely, your server or another server can be wrong. When this happens, you might want to look up the host's address on a different server. (You might also want to let your administrator know that something's not right with DNS. It might not be her responsibility, but if she has time, she can let the appropriate individual know that something's wrong.) `nslookup` supports this very easily: If you're running in noninteractive mode, just add the name or number of your pre-ferred nameserver after the machine you're looking up. If you are going to run `nslookup` in interactive mode, use a hyphen as a placeholder instead of the machine you want to look up so that `nslookup` knows you're not looking up your name-server.[3] For example, to use `dns.elsewhere.net` as my nameserver in interactive mode, I would run `nslookup - dns.elsewhere.net`.

How do you know which server to use? The command `whois` lets you know who is responsible for the domain name.[4] Let's look up the DNS servers for my place of employment, the University of Maryland, Baltimore County (UMBC):

```
[ jon@frogbog jon ]$ whois umbc.edu
[rs.internic.net]

Whois Server Version 1.1

Domain names in the .com, .net, and .org domains can now be registered
with many different competing registrars. Go to http://www.internic.net
for detailed information.
```

---

3. In fact, many Unix commands use a single hyphen to replace a filename to receive data from STDIN or send data to STDOUT when that command normally uses a file. `nslookup`'s usage of a hyphen is fundamentally similar to this usage, in that you're looking up hostnames from STDIN. In this sense, the hyphen is not a placeholder but a filename.

4. In the remainder of this section, I've dealt with the domain name hierarchy as it exists today. This area, due to legal, regulatory, and other pressures, changes rapidly, so the particular example might not be useful for long; the concepts, however, should still hold.

```
Domain Name: UMBC.EDU
Registrar: NETWORK SOLUTIONS, INC.
Whois Server: whois.networksolutions.com
Referral URL: www.networksolutions.com
Name Server: DNS.SLU.EDU
Name Server: UMBC3.UMBC.EDU
Name Server: UMBC4.UMBC.EDU
Name Server: UMBC5.UMBC.EDU


> Last update of whois database: Tue, 4 Jan 00 02:13:44 EST

The Registry database contains ONLY .COM, .NET, .ORG, .EDU domains and
Registrars.
```

Rather than provide all the information about my domain, the server provides the names of the nameservers for umbc.edu and also the name of the whois server that can give me full information on that domain.

This is a fairly recent change to DNS, in that it is no longer, technically speaking, a monopoly. Because different companies can register domain names, full information must come from a particular company's server. If I wanted full information about umbc.edu, I would need to look it up at whois.networksolutions.com. The syntax for this depends on which version of whois you're running.

There are two common versions of the whois command, the original and fwhois. The latter command takes a different syntax, but there's no good way to recognize which version of the command is installed on your machine without trying it out. To look up umbc.edu at whois.networksolutions.com with the traditional whois, you would type **whois -h whois.networksolutions.com umbc.edu**. But if your site has fwhois installed, you would instead run **whois umbc.edu@whois.networksolutions.com** with the server to the right of the at sign, much like an email address. First try the standard format. If fwhois is installed at your site, it will fail with a usage message showing you the correct syntax.

Routing

If you're trying to connect to a specific host and cannot successfully connect, the first thing to check is that the name resolves. The second thing to check is whether the network is functioning properly. To do this, we need to understand how data flows through the network.

Data travels in small parcels called *packet*s. Packets are something like blocks in block devices, like disks, in that they carry a particular quantity of data. Different types of hardware and different protocols deal with different-sized packets of data; some systems can even deal with variable-sized packets.

These packets can't simply go from one machine across the network to another machine: That would require a direct connection between those computers. Instead, packets hop from one machine to another until they reach their destination. In the old days, these machines could be all sorts of individual computers that were connected to each other through multiple network connections. These days they tend to be special-purpose machines known as *routers*. The path from the source machine to the destination is known, not surprisingly, as a *route*. The program that tells you the route your packets are taking is traceroute, and it works something like this:

```
[lasser@gwyn lasser]$ traceroute www.yahoo.com
traceroute: Warning: www.yahoo.com has multiple addresses; us-ing
204.71.202.160
traceroute to www.yahoo.com (204.71.202.160), 30 hops max, 40 byte packets
1 fe1-1-0.gw1.spg.va.rcn.net (207.96.122.1) 0.568 ms 0.345 ms 0.284 ms
2 fe0-1-0.core1.spg.va.rcn.net (207.172.0.137) 0.995 ms fe0-0-
0.core1.spg.va
.rcn.net (207.172.0.9) 0.660 ms fe0-1-0.core1.spg.va.rcn.net (207.172.0.137)
0.734 ms
3 poet1-1-
1.core1.tco.va.rcn.net (207.172.19.86) 17.439 ms 20.806 ms 16.02
6 ms
4 poet4-1-0.core1.blba.md.rcn.net (207.172.9.214) 61.873 ms poet1-0-
0.core1.
blba.md.rcn.net (207.172.19.157) 77.146 ms 55.340 ms
5 poet1-0-
0.core1.phda.pa.rcn.net (207.172.19.105) 48.697 ms 48.680 ms poet
0-0-0.core1.phda.pa.rcn.net (207.172.9.142) 45.165 ms
6 * poet6-0-0.core1.nyda.ny.rcn.net (207.172.19.154) 87.873 ms 43.038 ms
7 poet6-0-
0.core1.nyd.ny.rcn.net (207.172.9.66) 74.597 ms 39.434 ms 36.092
ms
8 s11-1-1.ar2.JFK.gblx.net (209.143.255.9) 42.787 ms 41.895 ms 38.554 ms
9 pos3-1-155M.cr1.JFK.gblx.net (206.132.253.97) 31.601 ms * 55.290 ms
10 pos7-0-
622M.cr2.3NV.gblx.net (206.132.151.22) 175.302 ms 114.516 ms 157.
831 ms
11 * * pos1-0-2488M.hr8.SNV.gblx.net (206.132.254.41) 133.032 ms
12 bas1r-ge3-0-hr8.snv.yahoo.com (208.178.103.62) 192.717 ms 183.725 ms *
13 w1.yahoo.com (204.71.202.160) 150.220 ms 148.721 ms 105.740 ms
```

First, traceroute puts up a warning that there's more than one www.yahoo.com and tells you which one it's using, the numeric address of that machine, the size of the packets, and the number of hops before it gives up. Then, with numbered steps, it reports the machine associated with each of those hops and the time it took three individual traces to get there. Some networks block the packets that traceroute uses, so this might not work from your system.

Note that on hops two, four, and five more than one machine is listed. These hops sometimes passed through one machine, sometimes through another. This generally happens because the traffic is being "load balanced" between multiple routers to keep them operating at a reasonable capacity. Also, on hops six, nine, eleven, and twelve some of those hop times have been replaced with asterisks: Those packets didn't reach their destination. Sometimes, a given hop will be a whole row of asterisks. This means that the network connection is down (which is likely if the packets don't get to another hop following that hop) or that the machine at that hop rejects traceroute packets. This is fairly uncommon and should be clear from the fact that the packets continue beyond that host.

Sometimes we don't need to know every single hop of the way; sometimes we just want to know if a host is up and how long packets are taking to get there. For this, we have ping:

```
[lasser@gwyn lasser]$ ping www.yahoo.com
PING www10.yahoo.com (204.71.200.75): 56 data bytes
64 bytes from www10.yahoo.com (204.71.200.75): seq=0 ttl=242 time=404 ms.
64 bytes from www10.yahoo.com (204.71.200.75): seq=1 ttl=242 time=117 ms.
64 bytes from www10.yahoo.com (204.71.200.75): seq=2 ttl=242 time=161 ms.
64 bytes from www10.yahoo.com (204.71.200.75): seq=3 ttl=242 time=422 ms.
64 bytes from www10.yahoo.com (204.71.200.75): seq=4 ttl=242 time=187 ms.
64 bytes from www10.yahoo.com (204.71.200.75): seq=5 ttl=242 time=159 ms.
^C
--- www10.yahoo.com (204.71.200.75) PING Statistics ---
6 packets transmitted, 6 packets received, 0% packet loss
round-trip (ms) min/avg/max = 117/242/422 (std = 123)
```

ping starts out by telling us where it's pinging and how large a ping packet it's using. Then it lists the responses from the server to those pings. It lets you know which of the pings it was responding to (sometimes pings or responses get sent out of order because a packet was lost and resent; sometimes the response gets lost and a number is skipped entirely), its ttl, or "time to live," and how long it took the packet to come back. Not all versions of ping return all this output by default; some simply report that the destination machine is "alive."

If your ping keeps doing this, break out of it with Control-C, the standard "break" key on Unix. When you want to interrupt a program, hit Control-C. Interrupt is different from end-of-file (Control-D) in that EOF tells the computer, "That's all the data I'm sending you; time to process it," while interrupt tells the computer "Never mind; stop what you're doing, I don't want to do that any more." After we break out of ping, it responds with statistics about how many of our packets were lost and how long they took to get there.

The ttl is, unfortunately, not particularly useful. Different systems set it differently, so it can't fulfill its designated function of helping you find out how far you are from a given host. In an ideal world, all sites would set their ttl to the same value, and intermediate hops would simply subtract one from that value so that you could see how many hops were between you and your beloved without needing to resort to traceroute. Alas, our world is far from perfect, and the ttl is thus almost totally useless, except when you already know how a machine sets this field and that nothing between you and it will ruin it. This isn't often.

Low-Level Protocols

Already we've talked about packets shuttling between hosts along routes, but we haven't said the first word about how those packets are shuffled. We're not going to say much about this because you have to be a programmer or a network engineer to really care, but knowing the names of these things and a rough idea of what they're like might be very helpful.

To talk to one another, or even (in the case of routers) through one another, they must be speaking the same language: They need to know what part of the packet represents the machine number, what part of that machine cares about the packet, and so on. The agreement among computers on how to divide up this data is known as a *protocol*. The analogy is to social protocols, which tell us how we should behave in polite company. A system behaves according to a given networking protocol by sending out compliant packets. Being Unix people, whose network world is limited (by choice) to the Internet, we care only about Internet protocols.[5] The complete suite of Internet protocols is known as TCP/IP, named after two of the standard protocols.

IP

Several different protocols are used for different purposes on the Internet, but protocols can have layers, and the one on which all other Internet networking protocols run—and thus on which they depend—is known simply as IP, which stands for *Internet Protocol*. The version in use just about everywhere is version four, often referred to as IPv4.

The IP protocol doesn't do much. In essence, it has the source and destination sockets for the packet and a note that it is indeed an IP packet. You can send packets via IP, but it doesn't do much. It doesn't keep track of whether the packets arrived at their destination, it doesn't check the order in which packets arrived at their destination, and it doesn't check how many copies of a given packet arrived at the destination.

What good is IP? Plenty good! It's simple, easy for programmers to implement, and a good foundation for more complicated protocols. The three most popular protocols running on top of IP are known as TCP, UDP, and ICMP.

---

5. Actually, many Unix systems talk to other network types as well, including DECnet, IPX (NetWare), and AppleTalk, but these are diminishing in importance as the Internet grows and, for most purposes, we can ignore all the other protocols.

TCP

TCP, which is short for Transmission Control Protocol, does just about everything I said IP doesn't do: It makes sure that one of each packet arrives, in order. It also runs a *checksum* of the packet to ensure that it wasn't accidentally mangled on its way. Because of the Internet design, TCP implements the resending of garbled or missing packets and generally includes a whole bunch of complicated algorithms to try to ensure the best service. Most Internet services are built upon TCP, including the World Wide Web and most email transfer protocols.

ICMP

ICMP, an acronym for Internet Control Message Protocol, is a simple protocol used for messages between machines regarding the performance and functionality of the network. We've already been exposed to the most common uses of ICMP, which are ping and traceroute. These packets are used to monitor and perhaps adjust network performance. For security reasons, many sites block ICMP traffic.

UDP

The User Data Protocol, better known as UDP, is a lot like raw IP: It doesn't check to make sure that the packets arrive, how many arrived, or in what order. What it *does* do that raw IP doesn't is checksum to verify the integrity of the data. Why do we have UDP? Mostly because lots of programmers like reinventing the wheel and think that they can do better than TCP. Soon they discover that the network isn't as reliable as they thought or that the control algorithms are more complicated to get right than they realized. At this point, they either redevelop most of the important properties of TCP within their own protocol, or they simply switch to TCP.

UDP really does have a number of uses, the most popular of which are broadcast protocols to transmit sound or video over the network. Often, the loss of a single packet from this stream is just a little bit of noise but far from crucial, and because speed is important for these applications they can reduce overhead by not worrying too much about this stuff. Mostly, however, UDP is there so that programmers can't complain about not being permitted to reinvent the wheel.

Sockets, Addresses, and Ports

Some of you might have noticed that I slipped the term *socket* into my description of the IP protocol without describing exactly what a socket is. A socket is a representation of one endpoint of an IP connection, arrived at simply by the combination of the numeric address of the machine with the number of the port being accessed on that machine.

You might have noticed that all the numeric addresses you've seen have four numbers separated by periods. Furthermore, if you've looked at a lot of these addresses, you might have noticed that each of those numbers is between 0 and 255—precisely one byte apiece. The form of four-byte addresses with dots between each byte is known as *dotted quad notation*, for more-or-less obvious reasons. That makes an Internet address 32 bits long, which makes a maximum possible number of hosts on the Internet 4,294,967,296.

A fair number of these addresses are reserved for special features or for private networks connected to the Internet whose machines are never directly accessed over the Internet. This reduces the number of available addresses by around 20 million. Even with the huge number of hosts possible on the Internet, it seems that we might be running short (this point is still under debate, and more strategies are in use to reduce the actual number of IP addresses in use). To solve this and other problems, version six of IP (also known as IPv6) is being worked on.[6] IPv6 will have a 64-bit address space so that every computing device ever made can be connected full-time to the network, and every other device ever made can have a networked computer built into it.[7]

The other part of a socket is the port number. Because we're in a multitasking environment, it's possible—almost certain, in fact— that we'll want to have more than one network connection open at a given time. To handle this, the system needs a different ID for each network connection. A system can have up to 65,536 (2^{16}, or 16 bits) different *ports* to which a network connection can attach.

Some of these ports have special meanings: Port 25 is always used to receive email from other computers on the network, for example. All ports with numbers less than 1,024 (2^{10}) are reserved for special purposes. After an initial connection is made, however, the system does a little sleight of hand and moves that connection to a different port, so that the well-known port (which can have only one connection at a time, to keep from getting confused) can stay open for other connections.

Practice Problems

1. Find out the name of your system by running the command `hostname`. (If this command does not return the full Internet name of the machine, ask your local system administrator for the full name of the system.) Look up your system's IP address with `nslookup`.

---

6. If you're wondering what happened to version five, it was used for experimental purposes.

7. If you want to figure out roughly how many hosts are available on the IPv6 Internet, simply take 2 to the 64th power. 2^N is always equal to the maximum possible value of an N-bit number because each bit has two possible states, 0 or 1. Each of those states can be different independent of all other bits, so to find the maximum number of combinations you simply multiply 2 over and over out to the number of bits. If you did any work with probabilities in middle-school math, this will probably make sense if you spend a minute to draw it out on paper.

2. Look up information about your domain with whois. If whois refers you to another server, follow up.

3. Look up the IP address of a Web site you frequent. Look up information about its domain.

4. Use ping to verify that this Web site is up, and if so use traceroute to find how many hops are between you and that Web site. (Your site might have disabled the capability to ping or traceroute to other sites on the Internet. If these commands fail but you can still access the site through normal means, ask your system administrator if these functions have been disabled.)

Talking with Other Machines

The point of a network is not to learn all this mumbo-jumbo about protocols and sockets and name service but to talk with other machines. Talking with other machines falls into two general categories: sharing data and resources over the network and actually using a computer via the network. On Unix, these two concepts are closer than you might imagine, due to the preponderance of cleartext higher-level protocols.

Telnet

The basic tool for both using other machines remotely and accessing the resources available on them is telnet, which simply connects you to a particular port on the host you specify. The default is to log on to a machine remotely by connecting to an appropriate port.

```
[ jon@frogbog jon ]$ telnet razorback
Trying 192.168.0.10...
Connected to razorback.localdomain.
Escape character is '^]'.

Red Hat Linux release 6.1 (Cartman)
Kernel 2.2.12-20 on an i686
login: jon
Password:
Last login: Wed Jan 5 01:11:54 from frogbog.localdomain

Campus sidewalks never exist as the straightest line between two points.
- M. M. Johnston

    No mail.


    [ jon@razorback jon ]$
```

There! I'm now accessing razorback, one of the machines on my home network, remotely. Note that I did enter my password at the password prompt, but the system's too smart to show it. Note also that the hostname in my prompt is now set to razorback, and all programs that I run between now and the time I log off of razorback are done on that machine. Everything works pretty much as it does when you're logged in to the local machine except that starting X programs is a little more complicated, but we'll ignore X for the time being.

It should go without saying that you should attempt to log on to systems on which you have a legitimate account and should never attempt to access systems for which you do not have appropriate permission. Logging on to systems without permission is the network equivalent of breaking-and-entering and can land you in hot water with the law. Furthermore, it's in bad taste to share accounts among multiple individuals because this makes the system administrator's job much more difficult with regard to tracking down intrusions and unauthorized access. (Many systems do have specific accounts that are intended to be shared among users, but typical user accounts should not be shared.)

Direct Lines: Talking to Services

To talk directly to a service that communicates in plaintext (or one that doesn't if you *really* know what you're doing), simply telnet to the appropriate port by appending a space and the port number to your telnet command. What ports run what services? For a large list, look in /etc/services. Many of those don't actually run via plaintext messages, but a large number of them do. As an added bonus, you can use the /etc/services protocol name instead of a port number, if you can't remember what the correct port number is.

SMTP

Besides telnet itself and DNS, for which good tools are available, the most important text-based protocol is *SMTP, Simple Mail Transfer Protocol.* This is how email is sent between machines on the network. This is different from *receiving* your mail, which is done with either the POP3 or IMAP4 protocols; instead, SMTP is what is used when you send email in response to a message you've read or when you send out an entirely new message. Let's look at an SMTP session and see how it works:

```
[ jon@frogbog jon ]$ telnet razorback 25
Trying 192.168.0.10...
Connected to razorback.localdomain.
Escape character is '^]'.
220 razorback.localdomain ESMTP Sendmail 8.9.3/8.9.3; Wed, 5 Jan 2000
09:32:34 -0500
```

After I've connected, the mail server displays a header showing the host name, the time, the date, and the version of the mail server. More important, however, is the three-digit number before the message. When an automated program talks to a mail server, it doesn't read the message, just the three-digit status code.

```
HELO frogbog.localdomain
250 razorback.localdomain Hello IDENT:jon@frogbog.localdomain [192.168.
0.33], pleased to meet you
```

First, we identify ourselves to the mail server with a `HELO frogbog.localdomain`. Because my home network is not connected to the Internet, I use `.localdomain` as my top-level domain. Most SMTP commands are a few letters long. Although SMTP commands are not case sensitive, capitalizing them certainly makes it more obvious what's a command and what's an argument. Some servers support a `HELP` command, which lists all valid commands; other SMTP servers don't support this command, which is unfortunate when you've manually connected to the SMTP server.

The `HELO` command is used to authenticate the host sending email for the server logs and as an anti-spam measure. An ever-dwindling number of servers don't require this command. The mail system checks to see whether the machine you claim to be (in this case `frogbog.localdomain`) can possibly be correct. It might also try to figure out what user you are on that system. (In this case, the response notes that I'm `jon@frogbog.localdomain`.) In some cases, the system might not care who you claim to be, as when for example you're sending mail within a system. The mail *daemon* (a Unix term referring to a constantly running system process) responds with some information and, more importantly, a 250 status code. 250 essentially means, "All okay, go ahead."

```
mail from: jon@frogbog
250 jon@frogbog... Sender ok
rcpt to: jon@razorback
250 jon@razorback... Recipient ok
```

Next, we tell the system who we are to send mail—jon@frogbog, again—and the system verifies that this is a reasonable combination, again as an anti-spam measure. Some systems make sure that the domain name or even the host name is legitimate, and some systems have further restrictions on this. The system responds with a 250 again, and we let it know whom we're sending mail to. It checks that this is a valid user and responds in the affirmative with a 250.

```
data
354 Enter mail, end with "." on a line by itself
From: Jon <jon@frogbog>
To: Myself <jon@razorback>
Subject: Demonstration of email

I'm just typing this message in entirely by myself, just over telnet. If
you're curious, the name for the service on port 25 is 'smtp' (no
```

```
quotes), and other than that, this message is entirely content-free.
.
250 JAA05993 Message accepted for delivery
```

Next we give the DATA command, and we can input our message. It's very important that the from: and to: we've already set don't need to match the headers in
the message itself. Most users only see the headers that are part of the message, the
ones I manually typed in the previous case (From: jon To: myself, and so on). If
the data given directly to the mail daemon is saved at all, it ends up in a received:
header hidden by most mail clients. We enter a dot on an empty line to end the
message, and the system responds back with a 250 telling us we're okay.

```
mail from: jon@frogbog
250 jon@frogbog... Sender ok
rcpt to: elvis@razorback
550 elvis@razorback... User unknown
quit
221 razorback.localdomain closing connection
Connection closed by foreign host.
[ jon@frogbog jon ]$
```

Just for kicks, I tried to send a message to Elvis, who doesn't have an account on
razorback, and the system responded back with a 550 error, letting me know that
Elvis was *not* in the building. Finally, we QUIT. The system responds with a 221,
gives us a "quitting" message, and kicks us out.

The Story of Email

What happens after we finish our email and the SMTP daemon (usually a program
called sendmail but sometimes a different application) accepts our message for
delivery? Well, that all depends. On Unix, email is broken down into several conceptual pieces. Let's talk about each of them in turn.

The life of an email message begins with the sending user's *MUA*, or *Mail User
Agent*. This is whatever program or set of programs the sender uses to compose and
send mail. Some common MUAs include pine, elm, Netscape Communicator, and
mutt, my personal favorite. In our previous example, our MUA is telnet direct to
the destination server.

Depending on the MUA and its configuration, sometimes the message will be
passed off to a local program on the sender's system, sometimes even a local copy
of sendmail. That program, in turn, sends the message to the MTA, or Mail Transfer
Agent, on the destination system. In the preceding case, that's the sendmail process
we've connected with on our destination system.

Sometimes, however, we don't want to send the mail ourselves. If the destination
server were down, we'd have to try repeatedly to reach it. This would require a
program on our system (again, usually sendmail) to go through the mail queue on

a regular basis and try to send these messages again. Rather than handle this ourselves, we might send these messages to a different SMTP server our organization has set up for just this purpose. That server is known as a *relay host*.

Technically, messages can pass through multiple relay hosts on their way to the destination system. This was very useful in the old days, before most sites had full-time Internet connections: Alice's system could dial Bob's system once a day and download its email. Perhaps Carol, who's on Dave's system, knows that Alice and Bob trade email on a regular basis, and she wants to get a message to Bob. Dave, however, only talks to Alice, so Carol could route her mail through Alice to Bob. This used to happen a lot, when connections were expensive and slow. It doesn't happen much anymore, so you rarely get mail that has been relayed through more than one host. In fact, many people have turned off relaying, because spammers have taken to multiple relays as a means of covering their tracks. *Open relays*, those that permit anyone to forward a message through that server, are now frowned upon in the Internet community.

Just about the only circumstance when you'll see a message passed through more than two or three SMTP servers is if you forward your mail from place to place or if you're on a mailing list. A mailing list works pretty much like a relay where one incoming name means a whole bunch of outgoing names. You might also see this if your site has a main email gateway through which all your mail comes before being distributed to a multitude of smaller mail servers.

After being passed through the MTA, it arrives on the destination system and is given to the *MDA (Mail Delivery Agent)* for delivery. The MDA is often `sendmail`, but is sometimes `procmail` or even just plain old `mail`. Whatever program this is, it might follow a couple of extra rules before depositing mail in your inbox. All of these MDAs permit you to set up a `.forward` file in your home directory, into which you can put an email address to which all your mail should be forwarded. In addition, if `procmail` is present on your system but `sendmail` is your standard MDA, you can write a `.forward` file that will pass your mail off to `procmail` to be delivered, or indeed to any Unix program in general.[8]

Finally, the message (which is generally stored in a *mail spool* on the system with the username of the recipient as the filename and the messages in the folder separated by a specially formatted `From:` line) is read by the user via the destination MUA or downloaded to a home PC via the POP3 or IMAP4 protocols, at which point the message might be deleted from the mail spool.

---

8. In general, the format of a `.forward` file is simple: a list of email addresses, one per line, to which mail should be forwarded. To pass each message off to a program, the first character of the line should be a pipe, and the rest of the line should be the pipeline to which the message should be passed. See the `forward (5)` man page on your system, if it's present.

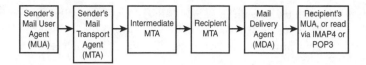

Figure 4.1

An email's path through the system.

Reading Mail Using POP3

Most people don't have their computers set up to be on the Internet all the time (although that's changing rapidly even as this book is being written). Also, most people don't have their PCs set up to receive mail, because Windows and Mac OS aren't reliable enough to do that invisibly in the background and because it's not worth setting up unless you are always connected to the Internet. Many organizations don't like all those machines exposed on the network for security reasons anyway. For all these reasons, many sites have centralized mail servers from which everyone can pull their mail.

SMTP "pushes" mail to machines: It assumes that, as a rule, machines are available to receive mail over the network, and it takes the initiative to send that mail out. Mail servers, however, suspect that their clients are probably not always ready to receive mail, and instead wait for those clients to connect and ask for, or "pull," their mail from the server. IMAP4 and POP3 are pull-oriented protocols designed for reading mail. These protocols can't be used to send mail, which is why mail clients that use IMAP or POP ask you not only for your IMAP or POP server but also for your SMTP server, so that they can send outgoing mail.

Although PC and Macintosh users most frequently use these mail-reading protocols, their clean design and use of plaintext makes clear that these were developed by the Unix and Internet community. More importantly, it also means that it's possible for us to read mail directly from our mail server when we're not at our own computer without having to run and configure a mail client on the machine we're on. Let's walk through a manual connection to a POP server a piece at a time:

```
[ jon@frogbog jon ]$ telnet razorback 110
Trying 192.168.1.10...
Connected to razorback.localdomain.
Escape character is '^]'.
+OK POP3 razorback.localdomain v7.59 server ready
USER jon
+OK User name accepted, password please
PASS MyPasswordHere
+OK Mailbox open, 2 messages
```

Port 110 is the standard POP3 connection port. When we connect to our server, it responds with a banner message indicating the protocol, host, and server version. *POP* stands for *Post Office Protocol*, and the number three represents the version of that protocol supported. Communication protocols, such as software, evolve as need dictates. Also like software, these versions are numbered, so that you know what you're getting and can have an idea as to what's supported.

All POP status messages, including the banner when connected to a server, have one of two status indicators, as opposed to the many numbered status codes supported by SMTP. These codes are +OK for successfully executed commands and -ERR for unsuccessful commands. This makes it possible to write incredibly simple client software that nevertheless supports error checking. Anything on the rest of the line is, as far as the protocol is concerned, simply a comment intended for human consumption; these comments are fairly informative, to help us debug problems when we manually connect to our server.

Our first mission, when we connect, is to authenticate ourselves so that the server knows whose mailbox to look at. Unlike SMTP, it matters that we are who we claim to be, and so we're asked for a password. Because this is a simple, direct network connection, the password is displayed onscreen as you type it, so take a good look and make sure nobody's watching before you do this. The syntax of the USER and PASS commands is fairly simple and self-evident. Commands are not case sensitive, like in SMTP, and I've capitalized them as in our previous examples to make clear what is a command and what's an argument.

```
LIST
+OK Mailbox scan listing follows
1 518
2 707
.
```

LIST shows us the messages in our mailbox and their size, in case we're over a slow link and don't want to read the larger messages. There are two messages in my mailbox right now, numbered one and two, with lengths of 518 and 707 bytes, respectively. Whenever a POP server responds with more than a single-line response, its response is terminated by a period by itself on a line. (If you'll remember, this is also how we told the SMTP server that we were finished typing in our message.) Otherwise, we'd have no way to tell the difference between a slow server or congested network and a completed command.

Let's read our first message:

```
RETR 1
+OK 518 octets
Return-Path: <elvis@frogbog.localdomain>
Received: from frogbog.localdomain
        by razorback.localdomain (8.9.3/8.9.3) with SMTP id OAA05093
        for jon@razorback.localdomain; Sat, 15 Jan 2000 14:00:36 -0500
Date: Sat, 15 Jan 2000 14:00:36 -0500
```

```
Message-Id: <200001151900.OAA05093@razorback.localdomain>
From: The King <elvis@frogbog.localdomain>
To: Jon <jon@razorback.localdomain>
Subject: you
Status: O
```

I've noticed you've not been reading your mail lately; is everything okay?
.

RETR is short for *retrieve*. Note again that the message is terminated with a single period so that we know the server's finished. There are more mail headers here than you're probably used to seeing: Many mail clients hide the lines they assume you're not interested in. We're going to talk about some of them here, however, because they're often useful when debugging mail problems. (You didn't think that we're teaching you how to talk directly to services just because it's fun, did you?)

The Return-Path header's purpose is simple: If the message doesn't get through, who gets the bounce message? This is generally set by the sender's MTA, although many mailing lists change it so that the list administrator gets bounce messages, not the sender of the message to the mailing list. In this case, Elvis sent it, and he would have received the error message if it hadn't gotten through.

The Received header is one of the most important: It's a log of every system the message has gone through on its way to its destination. Each intermediate MTA adds a single Received header on a per-message basis, newer headers above older headers. These are sometimes interspersed with Delivered-To headers indicating that the receiving mail system did something with that message. Think of these headers like the provenance of a piece of art or a forensic chain of evidence: The goal is to have a complete list of intermediate possession of the message. (We'll talk more about this in a minute.) In this case, the message went from one system (frogbog) to the target system (razorback). This is a multiline header; continuation lines are distinguished by indentation. This header also indicates the time of receipt.

The last relevant header is the Message-Id. This is theoretically unique on a per-message basis. That is, if you received the same message from multiple sources, such as different mailing lists, each of those messages would possess the same Message-Id, and you could thus filter out additional copies, but no other message should have the same number. This is, unfortunately, not always the case in practice, and thus most people don't discard messages with duplicate IDs.

Deleting the message, now that we're through with it, is simple and straightforward:

DELE 1
```
+OK Message deleted
```

Whether this message is immediately deleted or whether deletion is reserved for the termination of your connection somewhat depends on what server is being used. Never delete the message until you're certain you no longer want it.

```
RETR 2
+OK 707 octets
Return-Path: <peasants-errors@localdomain>
Received: from mailbox.localdomain
        by razorback.localdomain (8.9.3/8.9.3) with SMTP id 0AA05102
        for jon@razorback.localdomain; Sat, 15 Jan 2000 14:06:37 -0500
Received: from frogbog.localdomain
        by mailbox.localdomain (8.9.3/8.9.3) with SMTP id 0F905155
        for peasants@localdomain; Sat, 15 Jan 2000 14:05:17 -0500
Date: Sat, 15 Jan 2000 14:05:17 -0500
Message-Id: <200001151905.0F905155@mailbox.localdomain>
From: The King <elvis@frogbog.localdomain>
To: My Loyal Subjects <peasants@localdomain>
Subject: Appropriate behavior
Status: O

You SHALL bow before me.

Do I make myself clear?
.
```

This message has a more interesting set of received headers. It was not sent to me personally, but to a mailing list, peasants@localdomain. The bottom Received header shows that this list is handled by the machine mailbox.localdomain and sent to list members from there. The header above this shows that it was sent to my address on razorback immediately afterward: Assuming that the clocks on these machines are synchronized, one minute and 20 seconds elapsed between the time the message was received on mailbox and when it was received on razorback. This delay might be affected by whether all the machines are on the network simultaneously, the number of people on the mailing list, and other factors.

It's clear that every host that the message passed through is accounted for: Each header lists the host that the mail came from and the machine that received it. Even if a machine didn't add its own header, its name would still appear in the header above where that would be. Any omitted header or multiple passes through the same machine for the same target would be evidence of a mail configuration problem on that machine.

Sometimes, spammers or other evildoers might attempt to hide the origin of their mail by adding fake Received headers at the top of their mail, which would appear below the actual headers. You can often recognize this by the presence of other inappropriate or irrelevant headers stuck between Received headers. The Delivered-To header is a special case because it is another piece of evidence in the forensic chain, but the intrusion of other headers is often evidence that the sender forged some of the headers.

The legitimate `Received` headers are your only good evidence as to the source of the message: It's trivial to provide any `From` header that you want in the message. I could change Netscape or Mutt to claim that all my mail is from `president@whitehouse.gov`, but the `Received` headers would show the actual machine from which the mail was sent. Whenever you receive a piece of mail from an unusual address or unlikely individual, examine these headers to get a good idea of who might have actually sent that mail.

Finally, let's delete this second message and quit:

```
DELE 2
+OK Message deleted
QUIT
+OK Sayonara
Connection closed by foreign host.
[ jon@frogbog jon ]$
```

HTTP

Lest you think that all plaintext protocols revolve around email, let's briefly discuss one last protocol we can use on a daily basis: *HTTP*, the *Hypertext Transfer Protocol*.[9] HTTP is the protocol underlying the World Wide Web, the language in which Web browsers talk to Web servers. It's a large and fairly involved protocol, but we're going to discuss only a small (albeit useful) piece of it. We're not going to discuss every possible header or error, either; this is mostly so that you can get the flavor of a somewhat different sort of protocol.

The simplest sort of HTTP request (and, generally speaking, the only sort we're going to discuss) is one where you simply ask for a particular Web page on the server:

```
[ jon@frogbog jon ]$ telnet localhost 80
Trying 127.0.0.1...
Connected to localhost.localdomain.
Escape character is '^]'.
GET /~jon/
<!DOCTYPE HTML PUBLIC "-//W3C//DTD HTML 4.0 Frameset//EN">
<html>
<head>
<title>Jon Lasser's Home Page</title>
</head>
. . .
</html>
Connection closed by foreign host.
```

9. There *are* many other plaintext protocols, such as *NNTP*, the *Network News Transfer Protocol*, but after you have the basics down, you can learn any of them. I've picked important protocols, those you use every day, because relevance counts.

In this request, we simply ask for a Web page, my homepage. This would be expressed by the URL http://localhost/~jon were we to enter it directly into our Web browser. We enter our GET request and hit Enter, and the Web daemon responds with the raw text of that Web page, closing the connection when it's finished.

This is the original form of the Web connection. The HTTP protocol has evolved, however, and eventually HTTP 1.0 was created. To send an HTTP 1.0 request, simply append the text HTTP/1.0 to your GET request, with a space between the pieces:

```
[ jon@frogbog jon ]$ telnet localhost 80
Trying 127.0.0.1...
Connected to localhost.localdomain.
Escape character is '^]'.
GET /~jon/ HTTP/1.0

HTTP/1.1 200 OK
Date: Sun, 16 Jan 2000 02:13:08 GMT
Server: Apache/1.3.9 (Unix) (Red Hat/Linux)
Last-Modified: Mon, 20 Dec 1999 23:52:53 GMT
ETag: "c710-741-385ec155"
Accept-Ranges: bytes
Content-Length: 1857
Connection: close
Content-Type: text/html

<html>
.
.
.
</html>
Connection closed by foreign host.
```

When we simply add the version number of the protocol to our request, the server knows that we can understand the headers it sends back to us. It also knows that we can send headers to the server as well, so it waits for headers after we enter our GET command. Because we are not adding any additional headers, we can just hit Enter, after which it will respond with its own headers followed by the HTML.

Some of these headers are obviously useful, such as the Last-Modified header, which lets us know when the Web page was last edited. The Content-Type header is used by the target Web browser (if there is one) to determine what external program to use, if any, to display this sort of content. Some of the headers are less useful. When it's done with the headers, the server adds a blank line, displays the requested Web page, and closes the network connection.

Eventually, Web developers realized that there were a couple of problems with the Web. Two of the most pressing problems were that too many Web servers required multiple IP addresses, and Web servers were rather lagged in their responses.

The first problem was a result of the fact that if you wanted to run multiple Web sites on a single computer, each one would require its own IP address. This is because, although many names can be aliases for a single IP number, the server can't tell what name was requested. The solution, initially, was to give the Web server a different IP address for each site it would serve: Based on this number, the server could return different sets of pages.

Some network engineers claimed that one reason Web servers were so slow is that the system's overhead each time you create or end a network connection was adding up. With some Web servers servicing hundreds of connections per second, this had in fact become a real problem. HTTP 1.1 was designed to solve these and other problems that had been discovered when employing HTTP in the real world.

Let's look at a simple HTTP 1.1 connection. As you'll see, it's not too different from an HTTP 1.0 connection:

```
[ jon@frogbog jon ]$ telnet localhost 80
Trying 127.0.0.1...
Connected to localhost.localdomain.
Escape character is '^]'.
GET /~jon/framed/contento.html HTTP/1.1
Host: frogbog.localdomain

HTTP/1.1 200 OK
Date: Sun, 16 Jan 2000 02:26:25 GMT
Server: Apache/1.3.9 (Unix) (Red Hat/Linux)
Last-Modified: Mon, 20 Dec 1999 23:52:53 GMT
ETag: "9a06d-59f-385ec155"
Accept-Ranges: bytes
Content-Length: 1439
Content-Type: text/html

<html>
. . .
</html>
GET / HTTP/1.1
Host: frogbog.localdomain
Connection: close
HTTP/1.1 200 OK
Date: Sun, 16 Jan 2000 02:29:35 GMT
.
.
.
</html>
Connection closed by foreign host.
```

In an HTTP 1.1 connection, the `Host:` header is mandatory so that the Web server can be certain of which set of pages you desire. If you don't have a `Connection: close` header, the server will leave the connection open until it receives a request on that connection *with* this header, until you manually break the connection, or until the request "times out."

These headers are important for programs, but less so for people. As a result, when I just want the Web page I tend to tell the server I'm an HTTP 1.0 kind of guy. It's just less work for me that way.

Practice Problems

5. Send yourself email with `telnet`. (If you don't receive email on the machine to which you log in, you might need to know the incoming SMTP server for your domain. Ask your helpdesk or system administrator.) Examine the `Received` headers and see which machines your mail passed through.

6. If a POP3 mail server is available, read some of your email using `telnet` via the POP3 protocol. Look at the `Received` headers on several messages, and trace the path from their initial sender through to the recipient.

7. Pick a familiar Web site and, using `telnet`, retrieve the main page of the site without specifying an HTTP version. Repeat this process, first specifying Version 1.0, and then again specifying Version 1.1 of the HTTP protocol.

8. Using HTTP 1.1, retrieve multiple pages from a single site without closing your connection.

Using Machines Remotely

We've already discussed how to use telnet to log in to another machine remotely, although at this point we've mostly used it to use email and to browse the Web.[10] Logging on to another machine is fundamentally different from using another system's services: When you do the latter, you rely on your local machine only for its display, for input, and for network services. All actual computation and storage occur on the remote system. When you use a remote system to provide services, processing or storage of data generally occurs on your local system. (Except, of course, when the service the remote system is providing is storage.)

---

10. Most people don't do that, but we're not most people: We're Unix people. Most people just use `telnet` to log on to other systems and use them remotely.

Healthy Paranoia

Unfortunately, all is not sweetness and light when dealing with `telnet`: Although it doesn't show up when you type it in, your password is going across the network in the clear. Anyone who can see the network traffic can read your password. Normal users on a Unix box can't look at the network traffic, but PC or Mac users can if you're all on a shared network. (If you don't know, ask your local network guru if your network is switched or shared. If you're connecting over the Internet, that's almost always a shared connection.)

"But wait," you say, "I typed my password in the clear when I used POP3 to read email. Why was that okay?" Well, it's not okay, really. I hope you looked over both shoulders and still shivered before typing that password in. Although I've checked my mail that way, I try to avoid it. For much the same reason, I try to avoid using POP3 to check my mail from public and semi-public access stations, and avoid `telnet` like the plague.

Most Unix guides, in their section on networking, talk about the rsh (Remote Shell) suite of utilities: `rsh`, `rlogin`, `rcp`, and `rexec`. These tools let you act on a remote system as though you were acting on a local machine. They also transmit passwords in cleartext across the network or, worse, sometimes even permit you to escape authentication altogether. Smart administrators disable these tools wherever possible, especially on Internet-connected systems.

Some jaded types are probably wondering why I'm discussing security because they see security as a problem for the system administrator. In a strict sense, that might be true, but that presumes users lack any investment in the content or security of their systems, a presumption I believe to be false. Furthermore, informed users (readers, this means you) tend to behave more responsibly than users who are unaware of the security implications of their behavior.

In any case, you should use a strong password. A strong password contains uppercase and lowercase letters as well as at least one digit and one symbol. Most Unix systems restrict passwords to eight characters. What I always do is take a phrase, take the first letter of each word, and stick in a number and a symbol. For example, "This is not a good password (because it has been published)" yields "TiN!agp(" which should be hard for anyone to guess. Under no circumstance should your password be your name, nickname, significant other's name, pet's name, your phone number, your social security number, the words *secret* or *password*, any bit of common profanity, any dictionary word, your favorite sports team, and so on. The object is to create a password that is hard for somebody to guess (even somebody who knows you!), but is nevertheless easy to remember.

Security Solutions

Now that I've stirred up some doubt and concern, you're probably expecting a solution. In fact, there's no universal solution to this problem, and various sites have solved different parts of the problem in different ways. These include implementing *VPN* (*Virtual Private Network*) solutions, to create secure *tunnels* between sites over public networks; implementations of POP3 and IMAP4 over SSL, the encryption standard that Web sites use to protect e-commerce and sensitive information; and various one-time password devices, to prevent passwords *sniffed* over the network from being reused against your system. Ask your system administrator what your site uses.

The most popular Unix-specific tool is `ssh`, Secure Shell, a replacement for the rsh family of programs. SSH encrypts not only your passwords but all network traffic over its connection. As a result, nobody can see anything you do between those two machines on your network. SSH clients exist for both Windows and Macintosh as well. On the Windows side, a nice shareware client is Secure CRT; for Macintosh, NiftyTelnet + SSH is a very good freeware client.

Digression: SSH and the Law

As of the time of this writing (January 2000), SSH is encumbered with various legal issues that have prevented it from becoming a universal solution. These are patent problems, U.S. export law, and the license for the ssh program itself.

The first problem is that one of the encryption technologies used by ssh is patented in the United States, a patent for which licensing fees are required when used in commercial or other applications. This is the simplest problem to solve, requiring only a modicum of patience: The RSA patent expires September 20, 2000.

U.S. export regulations regarding encryption are presently in flux, are poorly understood by lawyers due to a lack of applicable case law (several cases are presently working their way through the courts, but the regulations are changing even as the cases progress), and are often wielded by the government in surprising and perhaps unfair ways. Days prior to this writing saw new regulations that look to make it possible to export cryptographic software from the United States with only modest interference, but the practical details are not presently clear.

The SSH program itself has two versions: The older version, 1.2, is in wide use, while the newer 2.0 version is not yet popular. One reason for this is that the license for the earlier version restricts use for commercial gain, but is fairly nonspecific as to what that means. The newer license is more particular, making it difficult to use SSH 2 in commercial environments without the payment of hefty licensing fees. Nevertheless, many institutions are unable to implement either version of SSH due to these licensing issues.

Work is in progress to address the licensing issues: One project is producing a tool, lsh, which interoperates with version 2 of SSH. Another tool, OpenSSH, bases its work on an earlier version of SSH with a still-different license and is compatible with SSH version 1.2.

One thing is certain: Computer security, and cryptography in particular, is a fast-changing area and no book can hope to keep up. As such, the best advice I can offer is to ask your system administrator, who knows what your site implements (and who might be familiar with the current status of various tools), and to ask a lawyer when appropriate.

The syntax for ssh, the program that replaces rsh, rlogin, and rexec, is fairly straightforward. If I'm at razorback's console and Elvis, who is looking over my shoulder, wants to log on to frogbog, I might let him:

```
[ jon@razorback jon ]$ ssh elvis@frogbog
elvis@frogbog's password:

Last login: Sat Jan 15 13:55:14 2000 from localhost
No mail.
[ elvis@frogbog elvis ]$
```

Some older versions of ssh don't accept the user@host notation and require ssh -1 username host.domain instead.

Sometimes, though, you just want to execute a command on a remote machine and log out. ssh lets you do that, too:

```
[ jon@razorback jon ]$ ssh jon@frogbog hostname
jon@frogbog's password:
frogbog.localdomain
[ jon@razorback jon ]$ ssh -1 elvis frogbog whoami
elvis@frogbog's password:
elvis
[ jon@razorback jon ]$
```

You can also pipe data through ssh as though it were just another program. My laptop, frogbog, doesn't have printing configured; razorback, my desktop, does. From my laptop, I can print through the lpr program on razorback:

```
[ jon@frogbog jon ]$ cat snorkel.ps | ssh -1 jon razorback lpr
```

And, lo and behold, the file prints. (lpr is part of the BSD set of print tools; lp is its rough equivalent on SYSV boxes. Both send jobs to the print queue.)

One other neat trick ssh lets you do is automatic forwarding of your X connection. Any X Window program you run while logged in to your remote system appears on your local display. If you're familiar with X, this is both more and less of a trick than it seems at first. If you're not familiar with X, we'll talk about it in Chapters 10 and 11.

scp, SSH's replacement for rcp, has a syntax similar to good old-fashioned cp. In fact, you could use scp as a replacement for cp if you wished, though you wouldn't exactly get any benefit from this. Much more useful is the capability to securely copy files between computers:

```
[ jon@frogbog tmp ]$ ls .
[ jon@frogbog tmp ]$ scp jon@razorback:some_file.txt .
jon@razorback's password:
some_file.txt | 0 KB | 0.7 kB/s | ETA: 00:00:00 | 100%
```

```
[ jon@frogbog tmp ]$ ls
some_file.txt
[ jon@frogbog tmp ]$
```

As with cp, you can use the -r flag to copy entire subdirectories.

This is far from everything there is to know about Unix networking. The subject is quite broad, and it's possible to spend several large books discussing it. I hope this is enough to give you a flavor for how Unix does things over networks, and that it provides enough for you to learn about other Unix networking technologies.

Practice Problems

9. If you have access to more than one host, find out whether ssh is installed on both systems. If so, log on to one system from the other using ssh.

10. Having done this, run the command uptime on the first system via ssh while logged on to the second system.

11. Using ssh and the cat command, cat a file on one system and sort it on another machine.

12. Use scp to copy a file from one system to another.

HARD LINKS • SOFT LINKS • REDIRECTION AND PI
REDIRECTING STDERR • NAME LOOKUP • ROUTII
READING MAIL VIA POP3 • VI AND REGULAR EXF
FILENAME GLOBBING VERSUS REGEXPS • INTERA
COMMAND-LINE EDITING • HISTORY SUBSTITUTIC
CONTROL • VARIABLES AND QUOTING • CONDI
EXECUTION • WHILE AND UNTIL LOOPS • ALIASE
FUNCTIONS • THE X WINDOW CLIENT/SERVER M
WIDGETS AND TOOLKITS • CONFIGURING X • PE
AND OWNERSHIP • USERS AND GROUPS • HARI
SOFT LINKS • REDIRECTION AND PIPES • REDIREC
STDERR NAME LOOKUP • ROUTING READING MA
• VI AND REGULAR EXPRESSIONS FILENAME GLC
VERSUS REGEXPS • INTERACTIVE COMMAND-LIN
HISTORY SUBSTITUTION • JOB CONTROL • VARIA
QUOTING CONDITIONAL EXECUTION • WHILE A

vi, Dotfiles, and Regular Expressions

Somehow, we've managed to get all the way up to Chapter 5 without teaching you a text editor. (No, this wasn't easy, believe me!) The most widely available full-screen text editor on Unix is vi. Many, many versions of vi are available. There's the original, the improved nvi (which stands for "new vi"), elvis, vim, and many others. The version of vi I'm using in this chapter is vim version 5.4 in its vi compatibility mode. This turns off some very useful features, such as multiple undo and redo, but makes it behave more like other versions of vi. vim is the version of vi installed by Red Hat Linux, and compatibility mode is its default behavior.

The other popular editor in the Unix world is Emacs, which is an abbreviation of "editor macros." There are two popular versions of Emacs, GNU Emacs and XEmacs, but (as with the multiple versions of vi) users of one can move with fairly little pain between the two. Emacs is much larger than vi and is almost entirely customizable in LISP, an unusual but particularly powerful computer language. In fact, Emacs is so customizable that you can make it act like vi, if you want. Many Emacs users don't simply use it as an editor but also use it to read email and Usenet News, as a scheduler, and even to browse the Web. Partisans of vi note that their computers already have operating systems and that all they want is a fast and efficient text editor. Editor preference is a religious war in the Unix world, eliciting eloquent and passionate arguments for and against both vi and Emacs.

Without taking a formal position in the editor war, this book chooses to cover vi but not Emacs.[1] Reasons for this include the fact that Emacs has effective online tutorials available, as well as dozens of books, and that a single chapter on Emacs can't convey any of the good reasons to use it. A single chapter on vi, while also insufficient, can convey much more of its flavor and flexibility. Furthermore, any system with Emacs installed almost certainly has vi as well, and there are still systems without Emacs that do have vi. Finally, if you administer Unix systems, or if you intend to administer Unix systems in the future, it's much easier to get vi working on a mostly crashed system than it is to access emacs. Many "rescue disks" have vi, but emacs won't fit on a floppy.

In addition to vi proper, this chapter also covers two important and related concepts that have wide applicability elsewhere in Unix. Dotfiles are the most common way to customize Unix applications and utility behavior. Regular expressions are an advanced sort of search-and-replace mechanism that is nearly standard across Unix applications and far more powerful and expressive (that is to say, far more cryptic to outsiders and difficult to learn, albeit well worth the effort) than anything available on Windows or Macintosh. Understanding these ideas is critical to effective use of Unix.

---

1. Personally, I use vi, and this entire book was written in vi. Although Emacs has many nice features, the most immediately useful of these for writers and programmers are present in vim. Nevertheless, Emacs is clearly more flexible.

Surviving `vi`

`vi` is a microcosm of the Unix world. Don't expect to learn all of it at once; perhaps you shouldn't expect to learn all of it at all. First learn just what you need to get by, and learn more as you need to do more. This chapter is written as though it were to be read straight through, all the material learned at once. That's an artifact of what it means to be a book, not what it means to learn `vi`. Even now, I use only a small subset of `vi`'s features. I know only what I need, and my `vi` knowledge grows slowly but surely as time goes on. To try and learn all of `vi` at once will only make you frustrated. Also, editors are only ever learned in terms of finger habits. You'll do well to read this chapter sitting at a terminal, trying things as you go.

Most text editors and word processors you've probably used operate pretty much the same way throughout: that is, a given key combination probably works the same more-or-less everywhere and you can always enter additional text. These editors are modeless. `vi` is a *modal* editor.[2] This means that it has different interfaces based on context.

There are three commonly used modes in `vi`: *input mode,* wherein you can modify or enter text; *command mode*, wherein you can operate on blocks of text or the entire document; and `ex` *mode*, a special subset of command mode in which you can do other sorts of editing operations. Practically speaking, however, you can treat `ex` mode as part of command mode. Also, there are different input modes (append, replace, and insert), but these can be treated more-or-less identically too.

That `vi` is a modal editor is partly historical. The original Unix text editor was `ed`, which was enhanced and integrated into the more advanced `ex`. Both of these were line-oriented text editors: They operated on a single line of text at a time. Eventually, Bill Joy and others at Berkeley wrote `vi`, a "visual interface" for the `ex` editor.

Although difficult at first, the division between writing and editing text implied by `vi`'s different modes becomes second nature with only moderate use. One way to think about it is to treat `vi` as though it was always in command mode and to treat entering text as a single long command.

In Through the Out Door

The first thing you need to know about any program is how to get started. You, readers, are not Dummies, and can guess that you enter `vi` by simply typing **vi** and hitting Enter. You've probably already guessed that to edit a particular file, you can simply type **vi my-file.txt**, so we don't need to discuss how to start `vi` and can start with the much trickier issue of *quitting* `vi`.[3]

---

2. As is Emacs, though in quite a different fashion.

3. It might be worth noting that most of the `vi` clones and enhanced versions also can be started by simply typing **vi**. To figure out what version of `vi` is started by that command, you can simply **ls -l `which vi`** and see whether it's a symbolic link to some other editor. On my system this points to `vim` but it might point elsewhere on your system. It might also be that `vi` is a hard link to the same editor as `ex`, `ed`, or `nvi`. When all else fails, check your documentation.

Not surprisingly, there's more than one way to quit vi. It all depends on what you want to do, but every way to leave vi requires that you be in command mode. If you've just started vi and have a nice blank screen, you're already in command mode. If you're not sure, hit Esc to leave insert mode, if you're in it. If you're not, hitting Esc doesn't hurt anything. Heck, when I want to be *really* sure I'm in command mode, I'll just hit it four or five times in a row. If you've started typing a vi command but lost track or made a mistake, Esc also cancels a partially entered command and lets you begin again.

The simplest way to leave vi is just to type **zz**. This will save any changes you've made and exit. Another popular way to accomplish the same thing is to enter **:wq** (the colon means that this is an ex command, which in this case is write and quit). If for some reason you need to force the system to write the file, just type **:wq!** instead. (You might want to do this if you haven't changed the file but want the system to think you have.) Most people use either this last command or zz as their preferred method of quitting vi. It doesn't really matter which of these you use; I'd pick one and stick with it, at least for a while.

In vi (and most other editors) you're not actually editing the file, you're editing something called a *buffer*, which is a bunch of text in memory usually (but not always) associated with a file. The file doesn't actually change until the buffer is written to disk. What if you don't want to save the changes to the file because you've completely wrecked the buffer or just changed your mind? Simply quit with **:q!** In general, ex commands that end with an exclamation mark, or bang, force the command in some way or deal with filters. (We'll talk about that case later.)

You might want to try entering and leaving vi several times, just to become comfortable with it. Try all these different methods and find what works for you.

Basic Movement Keys

Before we really learn to write in vi, we need to learn to move around. When vi was new, every computer keyboard was entirely different. You couldn't even guarantee that a particular terminal had arrow keys. Although most modern vi implementations support the arrow keys, even that is not universal. All vi flavors support an unusual but consistent set of movement keys: h, j, k, and l. As with all vi commands, these keystrokes are case sensitive and are to be entered in command mode.

Although these might appear to be the most ridiculous keystroke commands you've ever heard, there's some internal logic. Of these four keys, h is the leftmost, and hence moves the cursor left; similarly, l is the rightmost, and thus moves the cursor right. Slightly less logical is the choice of j to move downward; I fancy that this is because Control-J, ASCII code 10 (decimal), is the control character that moves the cursor down a line. That leaves k, which moves upward.

There are two basic ways to learn these key commands. The first, somewhat less enjoyable, is to enter vi and move around a large document. The more enjoyable way is to play games. Rogue and Nethack, two popular dungeon exploration games for Unix, use the vi movement keys to move your adventurer through the dungeon. Nethack in particular is a good way to waste several hours, as for example when writing a book, and you can comfort yourself with the knowledge that you're improving your Unix skill set.

Sometimes you want to move through text faster than a single line at a time. Control-F moves down a full screen of text, and Control-B moves back an equal distance. You can think of these as *Forward* and *Backward*. When you've found the screen with the text you're most interested in, you can press H (perhaps the Head of the screen, or simply a variant on the standard h command) to move to the top line on the screen, M (presumably short for Middle) to move to the middle line on the screen, and L (representing Last) to move to the bottom line on the screen.

Moving to the beginning or end of a line is equally simple and equally unintuitive: $ moves to the end of the current line, and 0 moves to the beginning of the current line. ^ moves to the first nonwhitespace character on the line, which is perhaps important if you're a programmer type.

You may also move through the text in logical rather than physical units: w moves forward one word, b moves back one word, and e moves to the end of the word. W, B, and E do the same thing as their lowercase variants, but without regard to punctuation. The keys) and (move forward and back one sentence, respectively; you might imagine them as blunt arrowheads pointing right and left. Fancier arrowheads, } and { move forward and back one paragraph.

Remember, you don't actually need to know all these commands to move effectively through your document. Personally, I use the four directional keys, back and forward one page keys, and beginning and end of line keys. Sometimes I use the others, but only rarely. As I write this book, I find that I'm using more and more of them, but you certainly shouldn't pressure yourself to learn all of them right away. (I say that now, but the practice problems later in the chapter will assume knowledge of most of these keys. Feel free to use a cheat-sheet when answering these questions.)

Adding and Inserting Text

The simplest way to add text into a buffer is to type a (for append), which moves to the space following the cursor, if there is one, and puts you straight into insert mode. Type away and (as always) hit Esc to exit. This raises the obvious question as to how to edit the first character in a line if there's already text there. Simply type i, short for insert, which enters insert mode right under the cursor. If you only had i, you'd never be able to add text after the last character in the line; conversely, if you only had a, you wouldn't be able to insert text before the first letter on the line.

As with the movement keys, there are some shortcuts for dealing with text: A appends to the end of the current line no matter where the cursor is when you hit it, and I inserts text at the beginning of the current line no matter where you are when you type it. To insert an entire blank line below your cursor position and enter insert mode, type o, and to enter insert mode on a blank line above your cursor position, use O.

Deleting and Editing Text

Adding text to a document is only part of the picture: To get work done, you also need to remove and alter text. (And believe me, I *know* about removing and altering text!) Generally speaking, while in insert mode (including append) you can backspace (or delete, depending on your keyboard configuration) over text on the current line of the display that you have typed in since entering insert mode. This is the one sort of editing you can do without switching into command mode.

Two other useful keystroke editing commands available in insert mode are Control-W and Control-U. Control-W deletes the last word you typed, and Control-U deletes the entire current line.[4] These only function as far back as where you entered insert mode or the beginning of the line, whichever is nearer. That is, if halfway into a line you enter insert mode and type Control-U, it won't delete the first part of that line.

After switching into command mode, several other deletion commands become available. x deletes the single character under the cursor, and dd deletes the current line. Either of these can be pasted back into place with either p or P. When pasting complete lines, p places the text on the line below the cursor, and P places it on the line above the cursor. When pasting individual characters, it works much the same way: p pastes the text after the character, and P places it before the cursor.

Even with these few commands (there are quite a number of others, some of which we'll discuss shortly), you can do all the basic editing you need to do in a document, albeit not as efficiently as you might want. There are several neat tricks you can do with just these keystrokes; my favorite is swapping two characters when I've accidentally typed them in the wrong order. From command mode, place the cursor over the first of the swapped characters and type xp. This will reverse the order of those two letters.

---

4. Actually, Control-U is really your terminal's "kill" key and might be different on different systems. Generally you can reconfigure the kill key with a command like stty kill *keykill* where *keykill* is replaced by your favorite control key. To input a control key literally, as in the above, so that it is not interpreted by your system, preface it with a Control-V. To switch your "kill" key, you would type stty kill ^V^B. In fact, the Control-V keystroke is used to escape literal control characters by many Unix programs, including vi. If for example you needed to insert a literal escape into the text of your document, while in insert mode you would simply type Control-V followed by Esc and just keep typing away, because Control-V does not take you out of insert mode and keeps the escape from doing so.

It's important to understand that vi's conception of a line of text is different from a line of text displayed on your screen. For vi, a line of text doesn't end in the last row of your display but at the next carriage return character. A single line, therefore, can "wrap" over multiple screen lines and still be treated as one line by the editor. This is appropriate for both configuration files and for programmers, but less appropriate for writing large quantities of text. We'll talk about how to make vi behave reasonably regarding line breaks in text documents later in this chapter.

What if you've accidentally deleted the wrong line, or you meant to delete only the sentence but not the paragraph? What if you didn't mean to join those lines, or that's not where you meant to paste that? vi's undo command is u, although :u works as well. Standard implementations will undo your undo (that is, redo your edit) by running the undo command a second time. Some fancy implementations, such as vim, allow you to undo multiple commands and have implemented a :redo command to reverse your undo commands.

Saving and Loading Files

We've already discussed how to save a file when you leave vi, but the user who waits to leave the editor to save the file is in for a nasty surprise when the power goes out, when the network goes down, when the modem disconnects, or when the system crashes. (Yes, it does happen, even with Unix. It happens much less frequently, of course, than on traditional desktop operating systems, but even Unix isn't perfect.) Fortunately, it's easy to save your file's current status. From command mode, simply type :w and hit Enter, and the file will be saved.

What if you've been working for hours on a file, only to realize that you don't have write permission for that file? Save the file under a different name: :w *new_filename*.txt to do this. If you type :w and then Enter, most vi implementations will try to resave the file under its original name.

To escape this problem, we might want to edit the new file rather than the old file. To do this without leaving vi, you can type **:e** *edit_me*.**txt** and the system will load whatever file you've specified. If you've altered the file and want to lose your changes since the last time you've saved, you might need to force the system with :e! *open_me*.txt instead. You can use :e to edit any other file on the system, not just a variant on your current file.

One more useful file command is :r *readme*.txt, which inserts the specified file into the current document right underneath the current cursor. To insert the /etc/group at your current position, you could simply type **:r** **/etc/group**.

Suggested Exercises

1. Enter vi. Leave vi. Repeat, using a different command to quit.
2. Enter vi, specifying a file that exists on the command line. Make changes to the file and then quit, discarding your changes. (Make sure this isn't an important file, just in case!)

3. Enter vi, specifying a file that does not exist on the command line. In this new document, type at least four paragraphs.

4. In your multiparagraph document, use the h, j, k, and l commands to navigate. Move to the top of your document using these keys, and then move to the bottom. Move your cursor to a word in the middle of a line in the middle of your document.

5. Delete this word. Delete the line of text this word was on, and paste it above the current line.

6. Save this file to disk. Append the /etc/passwd file to the document and then, without saving your document, edit a different document on disk instead.

Thriving in vi

By now, you should be fairly comfortable with vi. That doesn't mean knowing and using every single command, but it does mean knowing enough to wander around and edit files. Few people use all the features, and fewer still remember them all. I keep a vi reference card close at hand and refer to it frequently. This section covers some parts of vi that aren't crucial if you occasionally use vi to edit some configuration files but which are great if you spend any significant amount of time working in vi.

If you're not yet comfortable in vi, return to this section when you're ready. You won't get much benefit from the rest of this chapter until then anyway.

More Editing Commands

Besides simple line-oriented editing, vi allows you to work with logical units in your document. Instead of just deleting single lines or characters, you can combine a single d with one of the movement commands we discussed earlier: d{ will delete from your cursor position back to the beginning of the paragraph, d) will delete from your cursor position forward to the end of the sentence, de will delete from the cursor to the end of the current word, dw will delete to the beginning of the next word, and so on.

The delete command works much like "cut" does in modern GUI systems, and the paste command works similarly too. The GUI's "copy" command in vi becomes yank. yy copies the current line so that it can be pasted back into the text. You can combine a single y with movement commands in the same way as the d command can be combined with movement keys. For example, y) copies the text between the cursor and the end of the sentence, and yw copies to the beginning of the next word.

A different sort of text editing is accomplished with the change command: c followed by a movement command lets you replace the text up to the point marked by the movement command. If you continue to type past that point it will insert the text rather than replace the old text. c$ lets you replace the text from your current position to the end of the line, c| lets you replace text from the cursor back to the beginning of the line, and so on. My favorite is cw, which lets me replace a given word with my choice of words.

The change command works a little bit differently in different versions of vi. My favorite behavior is vim's behavior when not in compatible mode: vim simply deletes the text between your cursor and its destination and lets you type away. In compatible mode, it behaves like a traditional vi implementation, temporarily replacing the last character in the block of text you want to replace with a dollar sign and removing extra text when you're finished. Other vi replacements might display still different behavior; try it out yourself or check your manual for details.

There are a few more editing commands that you might find useful. The single letter r replaces one character under the cursor with whatever letter you type following that r; R replaces characters from your current position until you hit Esc, each time replacing the character under the cursor with the one you type on your keyboard. The join command, represented by a J, attaches the line of text below the cursor to the line of text on which the cursor sits, replacing any whitespace at the end of one line or the beginning of the next with a single space. This is useful for combining short lines into longer ones as well as manually reformatting small paragraphs.

Blocks of Text

Lots of times, we might want to work with arbitrary blocks of text rather than simple words, sentences, or paragraphs. vi lets us work with these arbitrary blocks of text. To do so, we can mark points in the document and move to these places. Movement to these marked points in the document, when combined with yanks and deletions, permit us to work with these arbitrary pieces of our edit buffers.

Instead of a single mark point, vi lets us use any single letter as a mark in the document. To specify a point as mark "a," type ma; to specify a point as mark "q," type mq. Move to a previously assigned mark with a back-quote and the mark name: `v moves to point "v," and `t moves to point "t."

To delete from the current cursor position to "a," type d`a: The movement to the mark works identically to other logical units of text, albeit with an extra character. You may also type y`c to copy text from the cursor to position "c," or c`x to change the text up to mark "x." You may reassign marks at will; just assign them as you would unassigned marks.

Configuring `vi`

The more we can customize our software to work like us, the more powerful and flexible that software is. Language-like software, that with a full set of ideas which can be put together in a deeply expressive fashion, is certainly the most powerful. Even in these software packages, however, there's a need to change simple behaviors in a simple fashion.

`vi` has several variables that can be used to configure the program. These variables are set with the `:set` command. Those variables that require strings or numbers are set with a command that looks like set *variable=value*, where *variable* is the setting you would like to change, and *value* is what this variable should contain. For example, `:set` wrapmargin=8 sets an eight-character margin at the end of each line. On an 80-character-wide display, the default on many systems, this produces 72-column output. (You can unset this by typing **:set wrapmargin=0** if you no longer want to have a margin.)

Some settings can only be either on or off. Programmers call these *Boolean* values, after George Boole, who invented the binary (true/false, 0/1, yes/no) logic at the heart of modern computing. To set line numbering on, you can simply **:set number** and to turn it off, you can **:set nonumber**. This prefixing a Boolean variable name with "no" to turn off that variable works for all such values in `vi`. The showmode variable determines whether an indicator at the bottom of your screen indicates when you are in insert mode.

Useful variables differ among `vi` flavors. Check your documentation for other useful settings.

`vi` also allows other sorts of customizations; one especially useful sort is *abbreviation*. If you're familiar with the autocorrect feature found in current word processing software, you're already familiar with abbreviations. An abbreviation is just a way to type a short phrase and have the computer replace it with a long phrase. They are fairly simple and straightforward to use: `:abbr` *shortform longform* replaces *shortform* with *longform* whenever you type the former into the text. For example, `:abbr` jtl Jonathan Thomas Lasser means that when I'm in input mode and I type **jtl**, `vi` replaces that with Jonathan Thomas Lasser. To remove this abbreviation, simply type **:unabbr jtl**.

You can also use abbreviations to correct common spelling errors: `:abbr` teh the will fix that common typo without requiring human intervention. You can extend this with as many of these minor corrections as you like.

Saving Your Configuration: `.exrc`

This raises the question of how to maintain a particular configuration. It would obviously be quite inconvenient to retype all our abbreviations and reset all our variables every time we edit a file. vi gives us a configuration file in which we can save our settings. This file is .exrc. Why .exrc? Remember that vi was originally built on top of the line-oriented ex editor, which explains the first half of the name. Many configuration filenames on Unix either begin or end with rc, which is short for "run control"; that is, they control what the programs do when they run. (These files are collectively referred to as *rc files*, although they don't share a common configuration format.) Configuration files stored in user home directories are usually dotfiles to avoid cluttering up directory listings.

The format of vi's .exrc is simple: It's just a series of ex commands, one per line. (Remember, ex commands are the ones with colons in front of them.) Because vi expects only ex commands in the configuration file, omit the colon that leads off each command.

My .exrc is as follows:

```
" Number lines
set number

" Show what mode we're in on the modeline
set showmode

" Wrap after 72 characters.
set wrapmargin=8

" The F10 key should always save and quit, but stop if there are
" problems
map <F10> ZZ
map! <F10> ^[ZZ

" K will delete to the end of the document. However, xxxK will delete to
" line xxx of the document. Neat! (This breaks on some specific
" versions of vi, but works on most.) Thanks to David Lesher for this
" one.
map K dG

" ^X always reformats the current paragraph. If editing text, it starts
" writing text again right below the last line of that paragraph.
map ^X {!}fmt -uw 72^M}
map! ^X ^[{!}fmt -uw 72^M}A

" ^A reformats the entire document, when in command mode.
map ^A 1G!Gfmt -uw 72^M

" Some common spelling corrections
abbr teh the
abbr thier their
abbr THe The
```

```
" My initials (when not capitalized) should print my name
abbr jl Jon Lasser
abbr jtl Jonathan Thomas Lasser
```

Let's go over this configuration point-by-point. First, comment lines begin with double quotes. Because ex commands are not necessarily transparent, I comment just about everything. Up at the top of the file, I set some defaults, which we've already discussed, and at the bottom I set some abbreviations. This leaves the various map commands in the middle. Conveniently enough, these key mappings demonstrate most of the other vi features we'd like to look at. (Funny how that works out, isn't it? Let me tell you, being an author is great!)

Key Mapping

Key mappings are like macros in word processors or spreadsheets or like abbreviations for commands: A single keystroke can represent one or more commands. vi supports two types of key mapping: one for command mode and one for insert mode. The :map command is for command mode, and the :map! command is for insert mode. The syntax for mapping is similar to the syntax for abbreviation with the caveat that, generally speaking, all mappings are limited to a single keystroke. They represent a sequence of more-or-less arbitrary length of keystrokes that you would type. These could be either text or commands.

Let's take a look at the first two mappings in my .exrc:

```
map <F10> ZZ
map! <F10> ^[ZZ
```

First, and perhaps most interesting, you can map the function keys available on most keyboards by just putting the name of that function key between angle brackets. If it hasn't been mapped yet, a function key will insert its name when pressed. The first of these two mappings, then, lets you hit the F10 key when in command mode to save your buffer and exit. The second of these mappings is for insert mode, and there's a funny control character before the ZZ.

If we had a key mapping for insert mode that was just some text, the default behavior would be to simply insert those characters into a document. To enter a command, we first need to enter command mode. We do this by pressing the Esc key, so we need to insert an escape into our :map! command. We do this the same way we insert any other control character into a buffer: Control-V Esc, which produces the Control-[that appears in the document. (In fact, you can type that key combination instead of Esc if you want to.)

Repeating Functions

Most vi commands can be repeated simply by prefixing the number of repetitions desired. To move up 30 lines, I can simply type **30k**, or to insert 30 hyphens, I can type **30i-** and finish off insert mode with an Esc. For some commands, the repetition prefix works differently: **6G** doesn't go to the end of the document six times, but instead goes to the sixth line of the document. **7|** moves the cursor to the seventh column in the current row rather than moving to the first column of that row. Simple enough, and quite useful all by itself. Sometimes, however, it can be more:

```
map K dG
```

If you simply type a **K**, **vi** removes your current line and every other right up to the end of your document. *That* part works right with every flavor of **vi**. On most modern versions, however, if you type a number before K, **vi** deletes from your current line until the line number you specified. That is, if I'm on line 13 and I type **35K**, most versions of **vi** delete lines 13 through 35, inclusive. Some older, crankier versions still just delete to the end of the document.

Why does it do that? **vi**'s behavior is undefined with regard to repetition and multiple key actions—to which part the repeat applies is unspecified. Should the number apply to the delete command or the go command? If it applies to the delete command, **vi** deletes from the cursor to the end of the document *N* times; this is what some versions of **vi** do. If you apply the number to the go command, however, the delete applies between the initial cursor position and its eventual resting place, a much more useful result. Try it out, and see how your version of **vi** behaves.

vi also possesses a simple "repeat" function. To repeat the last change made to the edit buffer, simply type a single period. If you just deleted to the end of the word with **dw** and you move the cursor to a new location, you can hit **.**, and text is deleted from the current cursor position to the end of *that* word. If instead you insert a single "a" into the document, each time you press the **.** another "a" will be inserted.

Filtering Text

Up until now, **vi** has been described as just another program. A strange, complex, powerful program with lots of historical cruft, to be sure, but not particularly special as a Unix program.[5] With the addition of filtering, however, **vi** becomes the quintessential Unix program.

As with most other **vi** features, there's the trivial way to filter text and there's the complex but powerful way to filter text. To insert the output of a Unix command right into your editing buffer, you can type **:r !run_me**, where *run_me* is the command you want to run. For example, you can insert the current date and time in your document by typing **:r !date**. You may of course append any options and arguments to that command, as in **:r !uname -a**.

---

5. Unless you insist that the essence of Unix is the cryptic, a notion I hope this book helps refute.

To send the current document to a program as input, simply type `:w !this-way`. To send the current document to lpr, the BSD and Linux print program, I can type `:w !lpr`, or I could create a key mapping to do precisely the same thing. This operation sends the data but leaves your document unchanged.

Still more powerful are the filtering commands that allow you to alter the buffer via a filter; all of a sudden, you can use good old-fashioned Unix pipelines to process text any which way. Let's look at a thoroughly contrived example and see how this works; after that, we can finish our look at my `.exrc`, try some practice problems, and move on to regular expressions.

Okay, time for Contrived Example Number One: I am putting together a shopping list for the grocery store, sorted by the aisle that had those items. I've been putting one item per line in the file to make it easy to remove or delete items. This is a good thing because all of a sudden I realize I've been imagining the grocery store backward, and the last aisle in the list is actually the first aisle in the store! This being Unix, I think to myself "If only I could pass this list through tac!" Of course, I could save and quit, pass the list through tac and return to vi, but that would ruin my train of thought.[6] Instead, I simply type `:1,$!tac` and get on with my life (such as it is).

Wow! What was *that?* vi can run ex commands on groups of lines. For ex commands, the default is simply to act on the current line. We can, however, specify line numbers prior to the command names. The general format for this is `:Xcommand`, with no space between the line number (X) and the command. You can also specify a range of lines by replacing X with two line numbers separated by a comma. There are several special replacements for line numbers that we'll talk about in a minute.

The command to filter text is simply a bang. (We saw this earlier in the section with `:w !command` and `:r !command`.) One of the features that distinguishes Unix is a certain "slippage" of concepts, where similar ideas are expressed with an identical symbol. This is analogous to English words with multiple definitions. (Often those definitions cluster around a general concept, although this is not always the case.) Therefore, if I want to run line 18 of my grocery list through rev, another truly trivial filter, I can type `:18!rev`, and it will be done.

You probably noticed in the earlier example that I had one line number, a comma, and then a dollar sign in place of a second line number. In this context, $ means the last line in the document. In general, $ means "the end" with the object defined by context: When moving around in vi, $ means the end of the current line; when replacing text, $ represents the end of the text being replaced; and in ex mode, $ represents the last line of the document.

Another common placeholder on Unix is a single period. One dot means "this": The directory . is *this* directory; the vi command . tells you to do *this* last command again; and in ex mode, . represents *this* line of the file. Therefore, if I typed `:.,5w tempfile.ttt`, vi would write all lines from the current line to line five

---

6. No, we haven't discussed tac because it's entirely trivial and not especially useful except for contrived examples like this one. man tac if you're curious, or just read on.

inclusive to a file named `tempfile.ttt`. You can combine the dot with addition and subtraction: `1,.-4` acts on text from the first line of the buffer through to four lines above the current line. The expression `.,.+1` acts on the current and next lines.

All this seems well and good, albeit not especially useful. Now, however, we can examine the last three unexamined lines of my `.exrc` and move on to the next topic.

```
map ^A 1G!Gfmt -uw 72^M
```

What does Control-A do? It goes to the first line of the document (`1G`) and filters through to the last line of the document (`!G`) with the command `fmt -uw 72`, remembering to provide the carriage return. (Enter is ASCII code 13, which is also Control-M.) The command `fmt -uw 72` is the GNU version of `fmt`, which reformats each paragraph. `-u` fixes the spacing at one space between words, two between sentences; `-w 72` assumes 72 characters for the width of my document. Given that I've set a `wrapmargin` of eight, this is perfect for a standard 80-column window. Not coincidentally, turning line numbering on takes up the first eight columns in the document. Therefore, typing Control-A reformats my entire document to be the proper width and to look nice.

This is especially important because `vi` doesn't do full-fledged word wrapping. Although turning on a `wrapmargin` causes lines to wrap, subsequent editing (deletes, joins, changes, and the like) do not cause lines to wrap backward. That is, if you shorten a line by 15 characters, the first 15 characters of the line below that will not come back and wrap properly. Also, some text-processing software and some email software don't put carriage returns within a paragraph, assuming that the software on the other end will do appropriate line wrapping. This macro fixes that in a single keystroke.

So what about the final pair of macros in my `.exrc`?

```
map ^X {!}fmt -uw 72^M}
map! ^X ^[{!}fmt -uw 72^M}A
```

These are virtually the same mapping, only the second mapping is for insert mode. Let's look at the first of these and treat the modifications to this in the second as just that, a minor appendage. By now, you've learned everything in these, so we'll just dissect them piece by piece. You might want to try and figure them out on your own before reading on, to judge your knowledge.

Control-X, when in command mode, goes back to the beginning of the paragraph (`{`) and filters through to the end of the paragraph (`!}`), via the same `fmt` command we just talked about, to reformat the paragraph. When it does this, `vi` generally places the cursor at the beginning of the paragraph, where it was before the format command, so we advance to the end of the nicely reformatted paragraph and can thus continue editing. The insert-mode variation has an Escape at the beginning of this so as to enter command mode, and eventually it returns into insert mode at the end of the paragraph (A) .

Topics We've Skipped

We've covered a large part of vi, but this isn't the whole story. We haven't covered opening multiple documents, named cut buffers, tricks with indentation, and more. We also haven't covered search and replace operations, although we will after a brief detour. Suffice it to say, if you spend a large portion of your time editing text, it might be worthwhile to dig even deeper into vi, or perhaps even to explore Emacs. Many computer users spend a majority of their time working with text, and up-front effort learning to work efficiently in an editor will be repaid hand-somely. (Contrast this with the design philosophy behind most typical word pro-cessing applications, which these days seek to minimize the learning curve at the expense of both power and efficiency.)

Practice Problems

1. In vi, turn on line numbering.
2. Set a 12-character right margin for your document.
3. Map the F7 function key, if it is present on your keyboard, to quit vi without saving your document. (If F7 is not present, pick a different key to use for this mapping.)
4. Make a second mapping that will do the same thing while in insert mode.
5. Map F8 to reformat your entire document through sort.
6. Map F9 to reformat your entire document through sort and then uniq.

Regular Expressions

In this chapter's introduction, I noted that regular expressions (often shortened to *regexps* by users) are an advanced search-and-replace feature that is nearly standard across Unix applications. Most search-and-replace functions look for the exact string of text you specify, but what happens when you want to find one of several variations on that text? Regular expressions can contain *metacharacters*, which can stand for one or more characters in your string. In this sense, it's like filename globbing but significantly more powerful. You could think of regexps as a sort of small computer language used only for describing strings of text, if that helps you think about it. (If it doesn't, just think of them as normal strings of text with a number of special characters that mean different things.)

Unfortunately, regular expressions are only *nearly* standard across Unix: Different programs were written differently and thus support different regular expression functionality. All these are close to compatible but never quite perfectly so. In this section, I use the GNU versions of grep and sed, and I'm still using vim as my ver-sion of vi. If the regular expressions don't work in your versions of these programs, check your documentation and see how your flavor handles regular expressions.

Some Unix programs don't even support regular expressions in their search-and-replace features. After you learn to use regexps, however, you'll begin to find yourself avoiding these programs in favor of ones that support them. As with vi and most other Unix applications, don't expect to learn all regular expressions at once. Learn what you need, and return to the subject occasionally to learn more.

Lots of little pieces make up regular expressions. First we'll look at these pieces, often using grep for our examples. After this, we'll discuss using sed to search and replace on the command line, and then we'll return to vi and talk about how search and replace works in the text editor we all know and love. (If you don't know and love vi, work on that part some more.)

Lots of Little Pieces

We took a look at grep in Chapter 3; you should remember that you can pipe text into grep and search for text in that input stream. We even looked at a single metacharacter: ^. grep also lets us pass any number of filenames after that regular expression; you can search for my username in the /etc/passwd file by typing **grep ^jon: /etc/passwd**. This searches for jon: at the beginning of a line in the file /etc/passwd.

As in vi, ^ has to do with the beginning of a line. Given what you've learned about vi, what metacharacter should mark the end of a line of text? If you said $, you've been paying attention; to look for the word *nevermore* at the end of a line, we can type **grep nevermore$ raven.txt**.

Filename Globbing Versus Regexps

What if the word *nevermore* is capitalized? In shell globbing we would look for [Nn]evermore, and in regular expressions we can look for the same thing. That said, regular expressions are not just an extension of filename globbing; some metacharacters with special meanings for shell globbing mean different things in regexps.

In filename globbing, * means any character, group of characters, or no characters at all. In regular expressions, * means any number, including none, of *the metacharacter that precedes the asterisk*. (Strictly speaking, characters with no special meaning are metacharacters that represent themselves. Wrap your head around that one for a minute. All single letters and digits are that sort of metacharacter.) In filename globbing, t* means the letter *t* followed by any number of other characters—it matches *t*, *ta*, *tcp*, *tipper*, and so on. In a regular expression, t* matches (that's nothing at all, if you couldn't see it), *t*, *tt, ttt, tttt, ttttt*, and so on. As a regular expression, it *wouldn't* match *ta, tap, tapper*, or anything with any character other than *t* anywhere in the expression.

A single question mark (?) is used to match any single character with filename globbing; in regular expressions, a single dot (.) is used. lo. matches *lob, log, lop*, and so on, but it won't match lo because the dot requires a character to match.

We can use these two characters to emulate the file globbing's *: .* matches any number (the star) of any character (the dot). Although it's an extra character as compared to the filename globbing version, the capability to combine metacharacters makes regular expressions incredibly powerful.

What, then, of the lonely ?, whose job has been usurped by the dot? In some programs that use regular expressions, ? matches the preceding metacharacter one time or not at all. .? would match any single character or a null string—that's geek speak for "no characters at all." To match one or no instances of the letter *z*, you could use z?, and to match lowercase or capital Zs, once or not at all, you could use [Zz]?. Not all regular expression engines support this meaning for the ? so, as always, check your program's documentation.

Matching Word Boundaries

To use grep to match anything containing the letters *va*, we could cat thisfile | grep 'va.*'. (We'll talk more about those quote marks in the next chapter, but for now assume that you want to put them around any regular expression you input on the command line. They're not part of the regular expression itself.) This would match *va*, *vamoose*, *vagrant*, *varnish*, even *va183sdfaljsf12esd sdgofiu sakfdljsf 1924 fsafd,!* (whatever that means); but because the expression doesn't specify that those letters need to be at the beginning of a line, it will also match *nova*, *covalent*, *sf sdjfasg sfjliuvvax dsflkjqtosfj*, or any other line of text with those letters. To match only lines that begin with *va* we could cat thatfile | grep '^va.*', which would match the first five entries above.

If I wanted to match any *word* that begins with *va*, the simplest way to do it is to simply match a pattern either at the beginning of a line or with a space before it: cat yetanotherfile | grep '[^]va'. In doing this, however, you might find it doesn't always work as you might expect: Had I reversed the order of the bracketed metacharacters and typed '[^]va' instead, the pattern would only match occurrences of *va* at the beginning of a line (as we would expect) or in the middle of a word (which we wouldn't expect). Hmmm... this is funny... what's going on?

We've run across an interesting feature of regular expressions. If a caret is the first character in a bracketed list, that matches any character *not* on the list! Therefore, [^] matches anything other than a space. Why do words that begin with *va* show up when they're at the beginning of a line? Because they don't start with a space; they start with a new line marker. (Actually, the new line marker marks the end of the previous line, so these words don't really start with anything other than *va*.)

If you want to match the end of a word, whether there's an easy way to do it depends on how your program handles regexps. Some programs support the expression [[:>:]] to refer to the end of a word, some use \>, and some use \b.[7] In the last case, to find all lines with the letters *tion* at the end of a word I could search for tion\b and in the first case I would search for tion[[:>:]]. Most versions of grep don't support these extensions, but many systems include an egrep, which stands for "Extended grep," that can handle more complex regular expressions.

---

7. To search for the beginning of a word, you would use [[:<:]], \<, or \b. That last expression actually refers to a word boundary, not to either the beginning or end of a word specifically.

What if I actually wanted to search for \b rather than a word boundary or [abc] instead of one of the letters *a*, *b*, or *c*? I would have to escape the characters with special meanings with a backslash. In the above cases, I would search for \\b or \[abc\]. If you were typing these on a command line, you would need to escape the backslashes themselves from the shell, and would need to search for \\\\b and \\[abc\\]. What a mess! Another way to solve this problem is to protect the string for which I am searching in single quotes: Rather than cat my-file.txt | grep \\\\b, I can cat my-file.txt | grep '\b'. I'll talk more about single quotes in Chapter 7 when we discuss quoting.

Matching This or That

Sometimes we want to match one of a number of things. You might want to search for either this or that, to find URLs that begin with http or ftp, or to look for the name of any one of your cats. To search for these things, we need to group our individual words with parentheses and separate them with a pipe. To find this or that, I could search for (this|that). If I wanted to search for anything beginning with http or ftp followed by a colon and two slashes, we would search for (http|ftp)://, and to search for my cats, I could search for (Mallet|Dashigara|Spike) .

Practice Problems

7. grep standard input for an exclamation mark at the end of a line.
8. grep standard input for the letter *n*, any other character, and the letter *t*.
9. grep standard input for *a* word beginning with the letter *n*, any other letter, and then ending the word with the letter *t*.
10. grep standard input for the word *kitten* or the word *puppy*.
11. grep standard input for the word *the* at the beginning of the line, with the letter *t* either lowercase or uppercase, and with any number of tabs or spaces before the word.

Search and Replace in sed

As with awk, sed is a very powerful program that is often used in minimal ways. Specifically, although sed is a fairly complex programming language most users simply use it to search and replace text on the command line. Like most good Unix programs, sed takes input from STDIN and sends output to STDOUT. You can either specify a file with your sed commands or provide them on the command line.

To change every occurrence of *dog* to *cat*, we could do something like the following:

```
cat animals.txt | sed -e 's/dog/cat/g' > animals.txt.new
```

sed runs through its input line-by-line, does the search and replace, and sends each line to its output. The term to search for is a regular expression, and the replacement term is a normal string of text with a couple of special regular-expression symbols permitted. It wouldn't make sense to replace one regular expression with another, in broad terms, because the computer would not know what to replace. If you replaced [Dd]ogs? with [Dd]oggies, it might be obvious to you as a person that a capital letter in the search pattern should remain capitalized in the replacement pattern, but what if you were replacing [aeiou]ths with [cb]uts? Because of the difficulty of solving this problem in the more general cases, Unix makes the decision not to try to solve the problem.[8]

By default, sed uses the forward slash to separate the search pattern, the replacement pattern, and whatever options you append to that command. However, you can use any other character for that separator as long as you use it consistently within that command. For example, s#[hlm]ouse#noun# or sX[sm]endXverbX are both valid, but s#[tr]ube/thingy/ is not.

So what's that option g at the end of our original search example, cat animals.txt | sed -e 's/dog/cat/g' > animals.txt.new? That g stands for "global," indicating that the search and replace matches not only the first occurrence on a given line but every occurrence on that line. The other frequently used option is i, which does non–case sensitive matching; that is, s/dog/cat/gi replaces every occurrence of *dog*, *DOG*, *Dog*, *dOG*, and so forth on the given line with *cat*. For the reasons discussed above, cat is always lowercase. I know of no general solution to the problem of replacing one string with another one while preserving case.

Arbitrary Numbers and Hold Buffers

Sometimes it might be necessary to keep part of a pattern while replacing other parts of it. Imagine I had a long list of phone numbers all in slightly different formats: Phone numbers might be listed as (410) 555-1212, (410)5551212, 4105551212, 410 555 1212, or 410-555-1212. To make this file more readable, I want to rewrite all these phone numbers as that last form.[9] I can cat this file through sed with

```
sed 's/(*\([0-9]\{3\}\)\)[) \-]*\([0-9]\{3\}\)\)[ \-]*\([0-9]\{4\}\)/\1-\2-\3/g'
```

and sed will regularize all the phone numbers in this file in the form 410-555-1212, regardless of whether those phone numbers stand alone on a line or are mixed in

---

8. Unix tends to err on the side of predictability. Rather than a complex and difficult algorithm that correctly predicts what you want 90 percent of the time but does something strange and unpredictable the rest of the time, Unix will use a simple and straightforward algorithm that is predictable 100 percent of the time. Complete predictability is a crucial attribute of powerful tools.

9. Being a U.S. resident, and thus believing that the world revolves around my country, I shall pretend that only ten-digit U.S. phone numbers exist.

with other text. If you look at the preceding search pattern, you'll see three things you haven't seen before. The first two are more immediately obvious: backslash-escaped curly braces and similarly escaped parentheses.

The curly braces permit you to match a pattern more than once but no more than a certain number of times; they work similarly to a range of lines in an ex command. \{4\} matches exactly four of the previous metacharacter or bracketed expression. [0-9]\{4\} matches a string of precisely four digits, the logical equivalent of [0-9][0-9][0-9][0-9] but rather shorter.

Sometimes it's useful to give a range of numbers for possible matches. Let's say I was looking at the /usr/dict/words on my system looking for words of two to four letters that begin with e. I could run cat /usr/dict/words | grep '^e[a-z]\{1,3\}$'. If I were looking for words that are *at least* three letters but with no maximum, I could instead write cat /usr/dict/words | grep '^e[a-z]\{2,\}$' to do that. According to the documentation, if I wanted to match all words beginning with e that are four characters or less, I could match for ^e[a-z]\{,3\}$, but my version of grep complains if I try that. Instead, I use ^e[a-z]\{0,3\}$.

Why must I specify the beginning-of-line and end-of-line characters in the preceding expression? If I don't provide the caret, grep returns any word with an *e* and the appropriate number of letters following that *e*. If I don't provide the buck, grep returns any word beginning with an *e* with *at least* the given number of letters following it. However, because the word can match any substring of the line, specifying a minimum number of letters is useless.

Note that the replacement pattern in our phone number rewriting example is \1-\2-\3: The numbers escaped with backslashes represent *hold buffers*, parts of the earlier regular expression that are being reused in our replacement pattern. The hold buffers are delimited by the escaped parentheses, and the numbers in the replacement pattern indicate which hold buffer should be replayed. The numbers are determined simply by order of appearance: The first expression in escaped parentheses becomes \1 and the sixth becomes \6.

Let's say your boss gave you a list of instructions that looked like this:

```
Item 1: Ignore item 2.
Item 2: Ignore item 1.
Item 3: Ignore item 3.
Item 4: Ignore all previous items.
Item 5: Ignore all previous items.
```

and you wanted to reformat the list to look like this:

```
1. Ignore item 2.
2. Ignore item 1.
3. Ignore item 3.
4. Ignore all previous items.
5. Ignore all previous items.
```

You would want to retain the number in a single hold buffer. Your best bet would be to match up to the colon with `Item \([0-9]+\):` and to replay the parenthesized expression with `\1`. . (That's a tab at the end of the replacement expression, if you can't see it.) That would match any arbitrary number of items and make it all look nice in your reformatted version.

If I had written a document where I referred to my older two cats as Dashigara and Mallet and I wanted to reverse the order of their names in every instance, I could run this document through

```
sed 's/\(Dashigara\) and \(Mallet\)/\2 and \1/g'
```

which would save me a tiny bit of typing. This is much more useful in search strings with complex regular expressions within the parentheses, but the preceding example should be enough to demonstrate the feature.

The third thing to notice in the phone number example is the bit that reads `[ \-]`. The hyphen must be escaped so that the hyphen is matched rather than considered an open-ended range that contains every character with an ASCII value equal to or greater than that of space. If we wanted to match the literal pattern `\(`, we would have to escape the backslash and look for `\\(`.

Practice Problems

12. Using `sed`, replace every occurrence of the word *Yes* with the word *No* on standard input, ignoring the capitalization of the input.

13. Using `sed`, switch the words *Yes* and *No*, leaving intact any text between those two words. Assume that the word *Yes* occurs on the line before the word *No*.

14. Using `sed`, replace the second occurrence of the word *No* on each line with the word *Yes* in a case-sensitive fashion.

15. Using `sed`, replace three forward slashes with two forward slashes.

16. Using `sed`, replace any three consecutive digits with a single instance of the word *know*.

Search and Replace in `vi`

In `vi`, we can run `sed`-style search-and-replace commands in `ex` mode. A simple `:s/search-term/replacement-term/g` will work.

You didn't think it was really that simple, did you? Remember that `ex` commands work on single lines or numbered ranges of lines. If you want to replace text on a line other than the current line, you will have to specify line numbers, as in `:5,10s/findme/myreplacement/g`. To search and replace across the whole document, then, you would `:1,$s/this/that/g`.

There is an easier way. Sort of. There is a global command that will execute any ex command on every line of the document that matches a given regular expression. You can combine this with a standard search-and-replace command: `:g/My Old Line/s//My New Line/g`. This saves few if any characters over the line-range version of the command but has a pleasing symmetry. Note that you need not repeat the search pattern twice: A blank search pattern matches the last pattern searched.

If you're not actually replacing any characters but only searching for a regular expression, there is a pair of vi commands you need to know: / does a search from your current location forward in the document, and ? does a search from your cursor backward in the document. Both honor the "last searched" usage of the null string.

Practice Problems

17. On the current line of your vi document, replace the first occurrence of the word *whale* with the word *monster*.

18. On the current line of your vi document, replace all occurrences of the word *whale* with the word *Jonah*.

19. Replace all occurrences of the word *whale* with the word *krill* in your entire vi document.

20. Replace all occurrences of the word *start* at the end of any line with the word *finish*. Do this in a non–case sensitive manner.

REDIRECTING STDERR • NAME LOOKUP • ROUTIN
READING MAIL VIA POP3 • VI AND REGULAR EXF
FILENAME GLOBBING VERSUS REGEXPS • INTERA
COMMAND-LINE EDITING • HISTORY SUBSTITUTIC
CONTROL • VARIABLES AND QUOTING • CONDI
EXECUTION • WHILE AND UNTIL LOOPS • ALIASE
FUNCTIONS • THE X WINDOW CLIENT/SERVER M
WIDGETS AND TOOLKITS • CONFIGURING X • PE
AND OWNERSHIP • USERS AND GROUPS • HARI
SOFT LINKS • REDIRECTION AND PIPES • REDIREC
STDERR NAME LOOKUP • ROUTING READING M/
• VI AND REGULAR EXPRESSIONS FILENAME GLC
VERSUS REGEXPS • INTERACTIVE COMMAND-LIN
HISTORY SUBSTITUTION • JOB CONTROL • VARIA
QUOTING CONDITIONAL EXECUTION • WHILE A

Shell Concepts

HARD LINKS • SOFT LINKS • REDIRECTION AND
REDIRECTING STDERR • NAME LOOKUP • ROUTIN
READING MAIL VIA POP3 • VI AND REGULAR EXF
FILENAME GLOBBING VERSUS REGEXPS • INTERA
COMMAND-LINE EDITING • HISTORY SUBSTITUTIC
CONTROL • VARIABLES AND QUOTING • CONDI
EXECUTION • WHILE AND UNTIL LOOPS • ALIASE
FUNCTIONS • THE X WINDOW CLIENT/SERVER M
WIDGETS AND TOOLKITS • CONFIGURING X • PE
AND OWNERSHIP • USERS AND GROUPS • HARI
SOFT LINKS • REDIRECTION AND PIPES • REDIRE(
STDERR NAME LOOKUP • ROUTING READING MA
• VI AND REGULAR EXPRESSIONS FILENAME GLC
VERSUS REGEXPS • INTERACTIVE COMMAND-LIN
HISTORY SUBSTITUTION • JOB CONTROL • VARIA
QUOTING CONDITIONAL EXECUTION • WHILE A

Muddling Through Shells

Once or twice already we've run across the concept of the *shell*, the Unix program
that interacts with the user. This doesn't just include allowing the user to run programs but also allows redirection of output and piping output from one program
through to another. The logout command is actually built into your shell, as are cd
and umask. The shell is also responsible for several features that we haven't yet discussed. In this chapter we will discuss command-line editing and job control. In
the next three chapters we will discuss other important shell concepts, including
quoting, using variables, loops, conditional execution, and more.

There is, strictly speaking, no requirement that a shell function in accordance with
the standard Unix way of doing things. If one wanted to create a new shell that
worked identically to MS-DOS that would be eminently possible. In fact, there's
no requirement that a shell even *have* a command line—you could potentially
write a shell with a menu-based interface. In the Unix world, however, most shells
fall into one of two historical "families" and work along those lines.

Shell Wars

A long time ago (if for you 1978 is long past), in a laboratory far, far away (unless
you happen to be near Murray Hill, New Jersey, home of the fabled Bell Labs,
which was the birthplace of Unix), the Bourne Shell was written. This shell,
named after its author, Stephen Bourne, was a replacement for the original Unix
shell, known simply as "shell." At about the same time, a heroic band of rebels (if
the stories are to be believed) centered around Berkeley, California, created another
shell, the C Shell. (The vast majority of that work is credited to Bill Joy.)

Each of these shells offered significant improvements over the previous shell: The
Bourne Shell (/bin/sh) allowed for advanced scripting and the use of the shell to
write relatively complex programs, and the C Shell (/bin/csh) had advanced functionality used for command-line editing and the control of multiple simultaneous
processes (*job control*). It combined these features with a programming syntax reminiscent of C, the programming language in which most of Unix is written.

Several things happened that conspired to keep all users from standardizing on a
single shell. While the Bourne Shell didn't have advanced command-line editing
features or fancy job control, the C Shell's redirection features were somewhat less
powerful than those of the Bourne Shell, and its programming features were a little
buggy. As a result of this, the default at many sites was to use the C Shell for interactive use but to write shell scripts in the Bourne Shell.

Later, both of these shells were found to be inadequate in one way or another, and
many other shells were written to compensate. The three most popular replacement
shells are (in no particular order) the Korn Shell (/bin/ksh or /usr/bin/ksh, depending
on your system), the Bourne Again Shell (/bin/bash, /usr/bin/bash, or

/usr/local/bin/bash, depending on your system), and tcsh (/bin/tcsh, /usr/bin/ tcsh, or /usr/local/bin/tcsh, depending on your system). Because of the more recent vintage of these shells, it is entirely possible that one or more of them will not be present on your system. Rare is the Linux system that doesn't have the Bourne Again Shell (also known as bash), while most other systems these days possess the Korn Shell (also known as ksh). Both of these shells are enhancements of the original Bourne Shell and are almost entirely compatible, in that almost everything that runs on the Bourne Shell works in ksh and bash as well. (The reverse is not necessarily true: Features in ksh and bash aren't necessarily present in the Bourne Shell.) Many Linux systems don't have the original C Shell (csh) but contain tcsh in its place. As always, check your system and its documentation for details.

What features do bash, ksh, and tcsh offer that aren't found in the standard sh and csh? Advanced job control and command-line editing features found their way into bash and ksh, while tcsh improved upon csh's existing command-line editing features and worked the bugs out of the programming features. Still, for historical reasons, many sites remain with csh or tcsh for interactive use, while just about all sites still write shell scripts in good old-fashioned sh. Which shell should you use? Personally, I see no particular reason to learn csh or tcsh, especially given that ksh and bash are virtually identical and that one or the other is available on virtually every system. Most of what you learn for shell script programming in these shells is useful in the Bourne Shell, and the command-line editing is quite similar to that of csh and tcsh. From my perspective, it makes no sense to learn one shell for interactive use and another for programming, especially because there is such little functional difference these days. Shell choice, like editor choice, is a religious argument in Unix circles, and ultimately you should probably use whatever is supported at your site.

In Chapter 3, we looked at one way to determine your default shell, to wit:

```
cat /etc/passwd|grep ^ username:|cut -d : -f 7
```

One way to determine your current shell family is to look at the prompt displayed. If your system displays a $ as the last character of your prompt, you're using a Bourne Shell derivative. If the last character of your prompt is a %, you're probably using csh or tcsh. If the last character of your prompt is #, you're probably logged on as root, which is a Bad Thing, and you should exit to a user account before determining your current shell.

If you would like to try another shell temporarily, simply type the command name of the shell you would like to test. (On most systems you can find a list of valid shells in /etc/shells.) When finished with that shell, press Control-D or type **exit** to return to your previous shell. To permanently change your shell, you can use chsh, ypchsh, chfn, or ypchfn, depending on your system and its configuration.

This section of the book deals primarily with the Bourne Shell and its derivatives, bash and ksh. Due to the historical tangle of shells and their subsequent borrowing of features from one another, their features overlap but not always in predictable ways. For programming features, we deal only with the Bourne Shell derivatives: sh itself, ksh, and bash. That's because they're all compatible. When it comes to fixing mistakes, however, the picture is somewhat more complex. ksh, bash, and tcsh support interactive command-line editing, unlike sh and csh. At the same time, csh, tcsh, and bash support csh-style history substitution commands.

Fixing Mistakes

We make three kinds of mistakes when working on computers: typing errors, logical errors, and errors in judgement. Errors in judgement are beyond the scope of this discussion, but the effects of the other two might be ameliorated with command-line editing and history commands. Command-line editing allows us to interactively correct mistakes on previously typed commands, and history functions allow us to rerun or alter commands we have already run. If these sound similar, they are, but because different shells support different mechanisms, it behooves us to learn both groups of features. We'll cover interactive command-line editing first because it's simpler to use. If you're just getting started, you might want to learn this right away and return to history substitution only when you're comfortable and ready to learn more.

Interactive Command-Line Editing

Interactive command-line editing is supported by all the more recent shells: tcsh, ksh, and bash all support similar sets of commands for editing previously typed commands.[1]

The most popular of these commands are the arrow keys. You can use the up arrow to scroll through all the previous commands you've typed, and when you've found the command you'd like to execute, simply hit Enter. If you find that you've passed the command for which you are searching, hit the down arrow until you've found it.

If you're using the Korn Shell or the Bourne Again Shell and this doesn't work, type the command **set -o emacs** and see whether it works then. If you're using tcsh, type **bindkey -e** to reset it. Note that all these commands implement emacs-style editing. Most of the keys you'll use are similar to their vi counterparts, but we'll take a look at how to switch to vi-style editing in a few moments.

---

1. The subtext, of course, is that none of them support precisely the same set of commands as any of the others. Unix is a language, and there are many dialects. Although these dialects are a modest impediment to those armchair anthropologists who would like to learn everything in a single sitting, they make for a richer set of cultural interactions. Without these subtle differences, what would Unix wizards argue about?

What if you made a mistake on the previous line? Hit the up arrow, and then use the arrow keys, Control-W, or Control-U, and just fix the line you're on as if you were in a simple text editor. tcsh behaves somewhat differently from the other two shells in this regard. If you run tcsh and would like to see a full list of keystroke commands, you can run `bindkey` with no options to see how things are set up. In ksh you can run `bind` to the same effect. The default key bindings for bash are listed in the man page in a section titled "READLINE," which also contains extensive (although obtuse) information about configuring these keystrokes.

If you're a thorough vi addict, to the point where you find that you're hitting Escape and trying to use h, j, k, and l to edit your command lines, you might want to switch to vi mode. In the two shells I said we would discuss in this chapter, type the command **set -o vi** to switch to vi mode. In the modern shell that I said we would not discuss, type **bindkey -v**.

The vi style of command-line editing has three major differences from vi itself: First, there's no ex or ed mode, only vi mode; second, you can see only one line at a time, that being the current line; and third, you begin in insert mode rather than command mode. This means that if you want to run through your previous commands, you need to hit Escape. After that, you may use h, j, k, and l to navigate as you would use the arrow keys. To insert additional text somewhere in the line, you'll need to type **a**, **i**, or the capital letter variations of those commands. When in command mode, you can use all the standard vi single or double character commands, such as **dw** to delete a word.

Although vi mode is amusing and sensible, in practice many users find it quicker to use the arrow keys and related key combinations in emacs mode. tcsh still permits you to use the arrow keys in vi mode, but ksh and bash do not. Ultimately, your shell is your own work environment, and you should personalize it to suit your work style.

History Substitution

The csh, tcsh, and bash shells all support csh-style history substitution. These history commands allow some powerful features not easily accessible through simple command-line editing.

The simplest history command is !!, which simply repeats the last command you typed. (This is equivalent to hitting the up arrow and Enter in command-line editing mode.)

```
[ jon@frogbog jon ]$ echo "Test"
Test
[ jon@frogbog jon ]$ !!
echo "Test"
Test
```

```
[ jon@frogbog jon ]$ !! some more
echo "Test" some more
Test some more
[ jon@frogbog jon ]$
```

As you can see, !! can have further pieces of a command line appended to it. This is especially useful for building pipelines one step at a time to make sure you're getting the right data to your pipe:

```
[ jon@frogbog thinkunix ]$ ps
PID TTY TIME CMD
3947 pts/3 00:00:01 bash
5182 pts/3 00:00:00 ps
[ jon@frogbog thinkunix ]$ !! | awk '{ print $1 }'
ps | awk '{ print $1 }'
PID
3947
5183
5184
[ jon@frogbog thinkunix ]$ !!|grep -v PID
ps | awk '{ print $1 }'|grep -v PID
3947
5185
5186
5187
[ jon@frogbog thinkunix ]$ !!|sirt
bash: sirt: command not found
[ jon@frogbog thinkunix ]$ ^sirt^sort^ -n
ps | awk '{ print $1 }'|grep -v PID|sort -n
3947
5188
5189
5190
5191
[ jon@frogbog thinkunix ]$
```

Not only can we add steps to our command line one-by-one, but we can also use the caret to edit the text of that command line. The format for caret replacement of text is simple: One caret leads off the term to be replaced, one caret separates the replacement from this term, and a final caret ends the replacement term. This final caret is optional if you do not want to add text to the end of the command line.

The history command gives us a list of commands we've already executed. Depending on how your shell is configured, the number of commands displayed varies. (We'll discuss this configuration in Chapter 7.) The first command you typed into your shell is number one, the second is number two, and so on. A bang followed immediately by a number executes that command number in your history: !33 executes the thirty-third command in your history:

```
[ jon@frogbog thinkunix ]$ history|tail
1159 whoami
1160 vi some-file.txt
1161 w
1162 uptime
1163 cd thinkunix/
1164 ls -l
1165 ls -l *.sgml
1166 vi wholebook.sgml
1167 cat introduction.sgml |head
1168 history|tail
[ jon@frogbog thinkunix ]$ !1162
uptime
  5:52pm  up 14:18,  5 users,  load average: 0.11, 0.08, 0.07
[ jon@frogbog thinkunix ]$ !1164 *.dsl
ls -l *.dsl
-rw-r-r-  1 jon       jon           3281 Dec  3 15:26 thinkunix.dsl
```

As with the other history commands, you can append to your command line simply by typing more at its end. You can also refer to history commands relatively: !-X executes the command executed X commands earlier. !! is therefore equivalent to !-1 because it executes the command typed before the current one.

```
[ jon@frogbog thinkunix ]$ !-2
uptime
  5:53pm  up 14:19,  5 users,  load average: 0.10, 0.08, 0.07
[ jon@frogbog thinkunix ]$
```

One last pair of useful history commands are !string and !?string?. You can run the most recent command that begins with a specific string by typing !string. Thus, to execute the last command that began with ls, I would type !ls. If instead I wanted to execute the last command *containing* the string sgml, I could type !?sgml?:

```
[ jon@frogbog thinkunix ]$ !up
uptime
  5:56pm  up 14:22,  5 users,  load average: 0.09, 0.07, 0.06
[ jon@frogbog thinkunix ]$ !?sgml?
vi wholebook.sgml
```

These commands are relatively underutilized by users, which might be as effective an argument for command-line editing as any I've heard; nevertheless, Unix gives you a choice of working styles.

Practice Problems

These practice problems are for bash, csh, and tcsh, the shells that support csh-style history commands.

1. How many commands are in your shell's history?
2. echo the last command you executed.

3. echo the command you executed four commands ago.

4. echo the last command you executed with the word *cat* in it.

5. Rerun the last command you executed with the word *cat* replaced by the word *dog*.

Job Control

Because Unix is a multitasking operating system, there's a very good chance that you might be doing more than one thing at a time. (In another era, this would be thought of as "hyperactive," or perhaps "lacking focus," but today we can call it "Making effective use of technology." How times change!) Given that we're doing more than one thing at a time, there's a pretty good chance that we might want to have some influence over what we're doing and when we are doing it. In a system developed today, this would probably be done through some cute little graphical control panel, but because Unix's multitasking heritage goes back nearly 30 years, there are several command-line tools for controlling our jobs.

What's a Job?

"Wait," you say, "I was just getting used to processes! What are these job things you're talking about?"

Good question. Back in the old days, before users had so much as a teletype with which to talk to their computers, if you wanted the computer to do work, you would need to submit a large pile of punch cards onto which you had punched out your instructions. You would hand your large pile of punch cards to the wizards in charge of the machine, and much later you would receive back your pile of cards and some output (hopefully the output you were hoping for, but more likely an error message because you punched one of your cards wrong) from the computer. That pile of cards was your *job*.

In Unix terms, a job is a process or series of processes you're running. That is, it's based on what was entered on a single command line rather than on a per-process basis. You can have more than one job at a time, and thus need tools to suspend jobs, run them in the background, switch foreground jobs to the background, and switch them back to the foreground again.

Suspending jobs is usually easy: most programs permit you to type your suspend key, which on just about every system defaults to Control-Z.[2] Some programs by default will disable the suspend key. Notable in this regard are many mail readers and editors. Often there will be an option to prevent the program from disabling suspend. Being a Unix user who prefers that the system gives me enough rope to hang myself, I tend to reenable suspend in my applications, but opinions on this matter differ considerably.

---

2. As with your erase and kill keys, this can be reconfigured with stty: stty susp Control-V *newkey*.

A Brief Demonstration

Let's start and stop some useless jobs and see how it all works out:

```
[ jon@frogbog thinkunix ]$ cat
Control-Z
[1]+ Stopped                cat
[ jon@frogbog thinkunix ]$ pr
Control-Z
[2]+ Stopped                pr
[ jon@frogbog thinkunix ]$ jobs
[1]- Stopped                cat
[2]+ Stopped                pr
[ jon@frogbog thinkunix ]$ fg
pr
Control-Z
[2]+ Stopped                pr
```

After starting cat, which sits waiting for input from STDIN, we suspend it and start pr, which also sits waiting for input when we suspend it with Control-Z. We run the shell built-in command jobs, which shows us that we have two jobs stopped. The most recent job is marked with a plus sign, the job before that is marked with a minus sign, and other jobs are unmarked. We continue the most recent job in the foreground—that is, as the process with which we are currently interacting—by typing **fg**, and then we suspend it again so that we can play a little bit more with job control.

```
[ jon@frogbog thinkunix ]$ bg %1
[1]- cat &
[ jon@frogbog thinkunix ]$ Enter
[1]+ Stopped (tty input)    cat
```

We can act on a job other than the last job by specifying it with a percent sign and the job number. Here, we send the first job into the background so that it can continue to run while we interact with other programs. When returned to the prompt, we hit Enter and see that, despite our admonition, cat stopped itself again, because (so the system reports) it's waiting for input from the terminal.

```
[ jon@frogbog thinkunix ]$ fg cat
Control-C
```

Because there's nothing we really want to do with cat anyway, we hit Control-C to kill it. Let's kill pr too:

```
[ jon@frogbog thinkunix ]$ kill %2
Enter
[2]+ Stopped                pr
[ jon@frogbog thinkunix ]$ Enter
[2]+ Terminated             pr
 [ jon@frogbog thinkunix ]$
```

We can also pass the job ID to other programs in the same way that we can use it with fg and bg, just specifying the job number prefixed with a percent sign. Note that a job's number remains constant, even if jobs with lower numbers have terminated. Unlike process IDs, job numbers will be reused beginning with the lowest available. It's also worth noting that we had to hit Enter twice after our kill command in order for the process to terminate. (We could have typed other commands in between, rather than simply hitting Enter repeatedly, but this is the clearest demonstration of the fact.)

This is not for deep technical reasons, but simply because the shell doesn't clutter up your display with informational messages after the prompt is displayed. The first time we hit Enter, the shell sees that the job has been stopped, lets us know, and displays the prompt. The second time, the shell sees that the job has actually terminated and displays the message before returning us to the prompt. The reason that more of these messages don't happen at once is that the system must signal jobs to stop before actually ending them, and processes that quit often spend a few brief moments cleaning up after themselves.

One interesting consequence of this behavior is that it's possible to kill a job, start a new one, and have the new job have a higher job number than the old, dead job. This isn't of any real consequence, but it might be confusing if you haven't previously experienced it.

Foreground, Background

Up to this point we've been playing fast-and-loose with defining foreground and background processes. Put simply, a *foreground process* is the process currently accepting input from the terminal. A *background process* is any process that is currently running but is not accepting input from the terminal. A suspended (or stopped) process is one that is not running and thus is not accepting input from the terminal but which has not yet terminated and thus might be restarted either in the foreground or in the background.

Starting a process in the foreground, suspending it, and restarting it in the background is a lot of work. Unix provides a simple way to put a process in the background from the beginning: Simply append an ampersand to the command line, and it will begin in the background. The shell should report a job number, so you can still control the process easily.

Although a background process will not accept input from the tty, it might send output to STDOUT or STDERR, which might display to the terminal even if another program is currently running. If you're not prepared for it, this can be mighty confusing; many full-screen applications will redraw the screen if you type Control-L. This is useful when a background process unexpectedly sends output to the screen.

One smart way to solve this problem is to not send the output of processes you intend to run in the background to the terminal at all:

```
[ jon@frogbog jon ]$ really-verbose-program &> program-output.txt &
[1] 21217
[ jon@frogbog jon ]$
```

We've redirected STDERR and STDOUT to a single file (program-output.txt) and run the command in the background. The system reports the job number and process ID and lets us go on our way. As long as really-verbose-program doesn't stop to wait for user input, we won't see any messages from it on the screen. If it does stop and we thus need to foreground it, we won't see any prompt on the screen; we'll need to look in program-output.txt to see what the system wants to know.

Eventually the job might terminate. When this happens, we will get a message onscreen as we did when it stopped. We can hit Control-L to redraw our screen, continue what we were doing, and examine the output file at our leisure.

What happens if you start a background job and you log out of the system? In the old days, your shell would helpfully kill the processes for you, preventing your really long-running scientific program from completing its work while you went away and watched TV for a few hours. To solve this, the command nohup was written. You can run nohup with your command appended to it, and it will intercept the HUP (hang-up) signal to stop it from killing your program. nohup will send all your program's output to the file nohup.out. By default, nohup will start in the foreground, so you still need to background the process manually or append an ampersand to the command line.

Most modern shells will not send the HUP signal to kill backgrounded processes when the shell exits, instead leaving them to run uninterrupted. If, however, you try to exit a shell with some jobs not running but stopped, the shell will complain:

```
[ jon@frogbog jon ]$ logout
There are stopped jobs.
[ jon@frogbog jon ]$ jobs
[1]+ Stopped                    cat
[ jon@frogbog jon ]$ logout
Connection closed by foreign host.
```

After complaining once, the shell will still let you exit. Unlike jobs running in the background, stopped jobs will be terminated on exit. There is no standard way to reconnect a tty to a process's STDIN after the terminal connected to that process has disconnected. Because there's no way to feed new input into that stopped process, chances are there will be no way for that program to do what it intended, and it might as well be killed.

There are, by the way, several nonstandard solutions to disconnect and reconnect processes to different terminals. The two most popular are screen and dislocate. The screen program allows you to have multiple virtual terminals in a single real terminal or xterm and allows you to reconnect to those virtual terminals from a different real terminal at a later time. dislocate is a simple script for the expect programming language that is included with that package. screen is much more powerful, and many power users have grown quite attached to it, but you might not run background processes or move between physical machines enough to care.

What, No Bat Signal?

Several paragraphs back, I referred to the HUP signal. Unix can send various signals to processes to inform them of specific conditions. Because we're most likely to want to send the QUIT signal to programs, the kill program lets us send signals to individual processes.

You can get a list of signals your platform supports by typing **kill -l** at the prompt:

```
[jon@frogbog thinkunix]$ kill -l
 1) SIGHUP       2) SIGINT       3) SIGQUIT      4) SIGILL
 5) SIGTRAP      6) SIGIOT       7) SIGBUS       8) SIGFPE
 9) SIGKILL     10) SIGUSR1     11) SIGSEGV     12) SIGUSR2
13) SIGPIPE     14) SIGALRM     15) SIGTERM     17) SIGCHLD
18) SIGCONT     19) SIGSTOP     20) SIGTSTP     21) SIGTTIN
22) SIGTTOU     23) SIGURG      24) SIGXCPU     25) SIGXFSZ
26) SIGVTALRM   27) SIGPROF     28) SIGWINCH    29) SIGIO
30) SIGPWR
```

The first thing to note is that each signal has a name (that begins with SIG and a number). You can use either the signal name (minus SIG) or the number with the kill command: kill -9 %1 is equivalent to kill -KILL %1, and kill -STOP 31337 does the same thing as kill -19 31337.

Signals should be more or less constant between platforms, although there can be some variation. As a user not interested in programming the system, you're probably interested in only a few of these signals. If you don't specify a signal when you run kill, the default is signal 15, SIGTERM. This signal politely asks a process to quit. The process is encouraged to clean up after itself before exiting, removing temporary files, and so on. If a program ignores TERM, the next course of action is to *demand* that the program quit, immediately: KILL, signal 9, is used for this purpose. It's much harder for a process to avoid being terminated with this signal.

If for some reason we can't suspend a process with Control-Z, we can send SIGSTOP to stop it, and we can send SIGCONT to let that job continue.[3] Another interesting signal available to us is SIGWINCH, which is sent to the system when a terminal changes its geometry—when you resize an xterm, for example, and the number of rows or columns change. Smart programs watch for this signal and can resize their display areas appropriately. Sometimes not-quite-so-smart programs try to do this but must be sent another SIGWINCH signal to do it right, or that signal must be followed up by a manual redraw command, usually Control-L, as we discussed earlier.

One final signal of importance is SIGHUP, the signal we discussed earlier, which lets a program know that it has been disconnected from a tty and should exit. Some programs that are intended to be run when disconnected from a terminal use this signal to tell them to reread their configuration files. Many of these programs are *daemons*, the system-level programs that run in the background, spinning away. (The programs that connect you to a mail server or Web server when you telnet to the appropriate port are one kind of daemon, and are particularly likely to respond to a SIGHUP asking them to reread configuration files.)

One last note about signals before we move on to some practice problems: Unless you're root, you can send signals only to processes you own. This is an obvious security measure so that as another user on the system I can't stop your program that is important but getting in my way. Of course, root *can* send signals to your processes, which is useful if you have processes that are misbehaving and you're not logged in or you're not paying attention.

Practice Problems

6. Start rev with no options, and then suspend the process. Next, start tac with no options and suspend that. Finally, display all running jobs.

7. Restart rev as a background job.

8. Using kill, stop rev without ending the process.

9. Terminate both rev and tac.

10. Start cat in the background. Then bring this job to the foreground and terminate it with Control-C.

---

3. The version of bash that we're using as our reference shell, Red Hat's build of bash 1.14.7, has a bug in that it does not acknowledge jobs restarted with SIGCONT as actually running. You can check it out with top, however, and see that these processes are running even though they're listed as stopped. The newer version of bash included with Red Hat 6.1, bash 2.03, functions correctly in this regard. (This newer version of bash is referred to by Red Hat as bash2 and is located in /bin/bash2.)

7

Variables
and Quoting

The fundamental fact of computer operation is the *manipulation of symbols*. In fact, besides working with literal numbers, symbolic manipulation is all that computers are capable of doing. Word processors do nothing but rearrange numbers (which represent letters) and other numbers (representing font size, style, and paragraph margins) that are connected to each other. As the writer, of course, you are also manipulating symbols—words, ideas, and representations of places and people— albeit at a higher level than that at which the computer works. When the computer program attempts to work with those higher level symbols, that's where it makes the most mistakes. Spell checkers, notoriously, accept any correctly spelled word rather than just the correct word, and grammar checkers are even worse because the level at which they must function is so much higher than spell checkers.

Up to this point, I've mostly discussed relatively low-level concepts: files, processes, packets, and lots and lots of data. Now, however, we're stepping up into the realm of higher-level symbolic manipulation. If you enjoyed discussing shell history manipulation and regular expressions, that's great, because that's where we're headed. Writing regexps can be thought of as a specialized form of computer pro- gramming, and the remainder of Part II in *Think Unix* can be thought of as an introduction to *shell scripts*, computer programs written in the syntax of whatever Unix shell you're using.

Don't let the thought of programming a computer scare you away, even if you've never done it before. In fact, you already have if you did the regular expression practice problems or wrote any complicated vi key mappings. Although some of the things I do in the next couple of chapters might be rather over-the-top, each one of them can be broken down into smaller pieces and digested.

This chapter is about two of those smaller pieces: *variables* and *quoting*, for those who didn't glance at the chapter title before pressing onward. Variables are symbols that represent other symbols, and quoting is simply a way to tell the shell what you mean literally and what you mean symbolically.

Variables

If you think you're new to variables, you're not. All the way back in Chapter 1 I wrote "you can display a man page by typing man *ManPageIWantToRead*." In that case, you didn't actually type the word *ManPageIWantToRead*, you replaced that word with the name of the man page you actually wanted to read. You replaced one symbol with another. In computing, a symbol that stands for something other than itself is called a *variable*. It's like the *X* in algebra that stands for an unknown quantity.

In practical terms, a user will set a variable to a given value and then recall that later. You may use arbitrary variables in your shell for whatever purpose you desire, but there are also special variables that the system uses for particular purposes. I will use some of these special variables to discuss variables more generally before returning to arbitrary variables.

csh and tcsh have completely different commands for dealing with variables than do sh, bash, and ksh. As always, I use bash as the model for how these commands work. If you use csh or tcsh, read your documentation to see how to use variables and to find what variables will work in your shell. Users of ksh and sh should find that all these commands and variables work just fine but might want to check the documentation to see how those shells differ.

Paths and Manpaths

By now you know that most Unix commands (those not built into the shell, to be precise) are files on disk, like any other, and you know that every file must be referenced by either an absolute or relative path if the system is going to find it. Have you ever wondered why you need not type /bin/cat every time you want to run cat, or why the system doesn't try to run ~/docs/about/my/cat instead?

The reason is that, when looking for files, the system looks in several particular directories for commands to execute. The precise list of places to search varies by the flavor of Unix because one major difference between flavors is the precise location of directories that contain executable files. The executable search path, which can be configured within the shell, is a list of places where the shell should look for commands that can be executed.

The path is simply a list of directories separated by colons. Each entry is an absolute path to a particular directory. A very simple path might be /usr/local/bin:/usr/bin:/usr/X11R6/bin:/usr/sbin:/bin:/sbin. With that path, the system would first look for commands in /usr/local/bin, then /usr/bin, /usr/X11R6/bin, /usr/sbin, /bin, and then finally /sbin, stopping the first time it finds a command with the given name in one of those directories. If the command is not present in any of those directories, the shell will return a file not found command along the lines of bash: *someweirdcommand*: command not found.

The name of the variable representing the executable search path is simply PATH. To see what your path is set to, type **echo $PATH** at your prompt:

```
[ jon@frogbog jon ]$ echo $PATH
/usr/local/bin:/usr/bin:/bin:/usr/games:/usr/X11R6/bin:
/usr/local/games:/usr/sbin:/sbin:/home/jon/bin:
[ jon@frogbog jon ]$
```

Note that I've added several other directories to my path, such as /home/jon/bin, where I can place programs I've added to the system and programs I've written without needing any special permission to do so. I've also rearranged the order of some of the directories in the system to move more likely locations earlier in the path. Given the excellent performance of contemporary computers, this is probably not necessary, but old habits die hard.

Variables need not be named entirely with capital letters, although it is traditional to do so for important or persistent variables. As in the preceding example, when I want the shell to replace a variable with its contents, I prepend the variable name with a dollar sign. At execution, the variable's name is replaced with its contents. For example, imagine that I have a variable named WHATEVER that is set to /etc/passwd and I type the command *cat $WHATEVER*. The shell would substitute the contents of $WHATEVER for the prefixed variable name, and thus would interpret that command as cat /etc/passwd. If, however, I had entered the command cat WHATEVER, the shell would *not* substitute the variable's contents for its name, and the command would be interpreted by the computer as cat WHATEVER, which wouldn't do much unless I happened to have a file named WHATEVER in the current directory.

This brings us to the question of how to set a variable. Generally, you can simply type VARIABLE=value at the prompt; for example:

```
[ jon@frogbog jon ]$ PATH=/usr/local/bin:/usr/bin:/bin
[ jon@frogbog jon ]$ echo $PATH
/usr/local/bin:/usr/bin:/bin
[ jon@frogbog jon ]$ PATH=$PATH:/sbin
[ jon@frogbog jon ]$ echo $PATH
/usr/local/bin:/usr/bin:/bin:/sbin
[ jon@frogbog jon ]$ unset PATH
[ jon@frogbog jon ]$ echo $PATH

  [ jon@frogbog jon ]$ exit
```

A variable can be used in combination with plain text and other variables. In the third command above, I add /sbin to the path I set in the first command. And in the fifth command, I get rid of my path: unset clears a variable, removing any value it has. I can use the set command to set a Boolean variable, one that either is set or not set but has no contents. (You saw a variation on that command when I used set -o vi to set vi mode for command-line editing: set -o is used to set shell options.)

For the same reasons as those why Unix needs a PATH variable, it needs a MANPATH variable as well. The purpose of the MANPATH is to list those places where man pages may be stored on the system. Man pages are stored in subdirectories named man1, man2, man3, and so on in a top-level directory generally named /usr/share/man or /usr/man, along with parallel directories such as /usr/local/man. My MANPATH is as follows:

```
[ jon@frogbog jon ]$ echo $MANPATH
/home/jon/man:/usr/man:/usr/local/man:/usr/X11R6/man
[ jon@frogbog jon ]$
```

As with my PATH, I have added a directory underneath my home directory where I can place man pages I have added to the system.

Shell Configuration Variables

In addition to PATH and MANPATH, the shell has other variables that provide configuration information. Chief among those variables that users should not alter (although in many cases the shell will let you do so) is HOME, which holds as its value the name of your home directory. Whenever you want to refer to your home directory, you can always use $HOME instead. This has the same effect as using ~ to refer to your home directory, except that you can't use HOME to refer to another user's home directory. In fact, the original Bourne Shell does not permit you to use the tilde, so all Bourne Shell scripts must use $HOME to refer to the home directory of the user running the script.

Another important variable which should not be written to is PWD, which contains the full pathname of the directory you are currently in. It produces the same output, as does the pwd command:

```
[ jon@frogbog jon ]$ which pwd
/bin/pwd
[ jon@frogbog jon ]$ pwd
/home/jon
[ jon@frogbog jon ]$ echo $HOME
/home/jon
[ jon@frogbog jon ]$ echo $PWD
/home/jon
[ jon@frogbog jon ]$ cd tmp
[ jon@frogbog tmp ]$ echo $HOME
/home/jon
[ jon@frogbog tmp ]$ echo $PWD
/home/jon/tmp
[ jon@frogbog tmp ]$ cd
[ jon@frogbog jon ]$ echo $PWD
/home/jon
```

Although you *can* change the values of PWD and HOME in your shell, I don't suggest doing so on a regular basis. You might want to try it once or twice to see how it works, but it isn't a good way to run your life—or your computer.

Some variables are meant to be changed to alter the behavior of your shell. Some trivial configuration options include MAILCHECK and HISTSIZE, and a more complicated (sometimes) pair of variables, PS1 and PS2.

MAILCHECK is a number that represents how many seconds the shell should wait between checking to see whether you have received mail. If I set MAILCHECK=600, the shell will check for new mail in my mailbox every 600 seconds, which those of us who don't always count in seconds might refer to as 10 minutes. If you want the shell to look in a different place for your mail files, the MAILPATH variable is a colon-separated list of files in which the shell should look for new mail.

HISTSIZE controls how many commands are stored in your command history. If you set HISTSIZE=10, only 10 commands will be stored in your history before rotating out. That means that, with either variety of command-line editing, you can only look at a small handful of commands. If instead you type HISTSIZE=5000, that provides a fairly substantial list of previously run commands for you to work with. It also means that you might well spend more time looking for just the right command. *C'est la vie.*

The PS1 variable sets the prompt on your command line. You can do simple and silly things with this:

```
[ jon@frogbog jon ]$ PS1='What now?'
What now?PS1='What now? '
What now? PS1='Hailing Frequencies Open: '
Hailing Frequencies Open:
```

Note that I needed to put a space after the question mark in the first prompt to insert a space between the prompt and where I could input my command line. Note also that there's little practical point in doing this because my default prompt was much more informative.

The PS2 prompt is like the PS1 prompt, but it is used when the shell needs more information, as for example when you use a herefile:

```
Hailing Frequencies Open: PS2='Need More Input: '
Hailing Frequencies Open: echo << EOF
Need More Input: Test One
Need More Input: Test Two
Need More Input: Test Three
Need More Input: EOF

  Hailing Frequencies Open:
```

That is marginally more useful because the prompt makes the shell's current need clear.

How does the default PS1 prompt work? All the way back in Chapter 1 I briefly discussed how the echo command uses special sequences of characters to produce special results, such as \n to produce a newline. The bash shell uses similar metacharacters to put strings into your prompt. (Although ksh doesn't do this, it is possible to alter your prompt to contain useful information using ksh. I'll talk about this in the second part of this chapter.) All the metacharacters that bash uses for prompts are documented in the bash man page; let's play with some of them:

```
Hailing Frequencies Open: PS1='\d\n\t\n\w\n\u: '
Sun Feb 20
17:13:10
~
```

```
jon: cd /tmp
Sun Feb 20
17:14:10
/tmp
jon: cd /usr/local/etc
Sun Feb 20
17:15:02
/usr/local/etc
jon:
```

Gosh, that's a lot of information—and a lot of screen real estate, too. Perhaps I just need the current working directory and the history number of the current command, so that I can do more effective command-line editing:

```
Sun Feb 20
17:15:02
/usr/local/etc
jon: PS1='[\!] \w\$ '
[1033] /usr/local/etc$
```

Maybe I don't need the whole name of the current directory: bash lets us use \w to refer to the whole name of the current working directory and \W to refer to the *basename* of this directory. (basename is a Unix command that displays part of a file's name. Type **man basename** for more information.) Let's use \W to switch our prompt back to the default, but without those annoying spaces just inside the brackets:

```
[1033] /usr/local/etc$ PS1='[\u@\h \W]\$ '
[jon@frogbog etc]$
```

The \$ command sequence is replaced with a $ under most circumstances but a # when your effective UID is 0: that is, when you're running as root. This is a simple indicator to help remind you not to run any stupid and dangerous commands. Depending on the way you work it might or might not help at all. All these special characters work as well in the PS2 prompt, although most people tend not to use them in that situation.

Terminal Settings

Several shell variables affect your terminal settings: They alter how the system interacts with your display terminal, whether you're running a Linux console, an ancient VT220 terminal, or an xterm window. Some of these variables are LINES, COLUMNS, DISPLAY, and TERM. These variables should be present in every shell, although of course they're set with different commands in C Shell derivatives than in the Bourne Shell family of shells I discuss in this chapter.

LINES and COLUMNS should almost always be set by your system and only rarely need help from the user to work correctly. COLUMNS is a number indicating the width of your display, in characters, and LINES is, not surprisingly, the number of lines that your terminal displays. Theoretically, all programs that want to draw all over your screen (full-screen programs such as most mail readers, editors, games, and the like) should look at these values to determine where onscreen to draw.

Unfortunately, some programs make bad assumptions, such as assuming that all screens are 80 characters wide or 25 lines high. These programs are, generally speaking, beyond hope. Expect that they will mess up your screen pretty badly, and there's not much to be done about it besides rewriting the program if you've been blessed with access to the source code. Some other programs miss the SIGWINCH that tells them you've resized your windows, in which case you might need to exit to the shell and restart the programs. In some cases, these programs might even have blocked the SIGWINCH from getting to your shell, and you might have to send that signal to your shell to force it to figure out the size of your terminal. On the other hand, some programs do an excellent job of paying attention to SIGWINCH and resizing, and those of you who are easily amused can have hours of fun resizing editor windows and email programs.

The DISPLAY variable is used by the X Window System to determine where programs run on this terminal should be drawn. X is a distributed multiuser system that is eminently capable of handling multiple displays per user. The DISPLAY is made up of a hostname followed by a colon and then a display number, which is two integers separated by a decimal point. We'll discuss the meaning of DISPLAY in Chapter 11, but for now it's best simply to know that it's here and that it can be used to display a program running on one machine on a machine somewhere else, although this is quite slow if you don't have a very fast network. One of the nice features of ssh is that it does a good job of setting this automatically.

The most important of all terminal control variables is TERM. This variable tells Unix what sort of display you're using and what it's capable of doing. Way back in the distant past, before computers were small and cheap, most people accessed Unix by way of a terminal. A terminal is, for those of you too young to remember, a monitor and keyboard with a serial cable sticking off the back that connects to the actual computer. (The terminal might also be connected to a modem, which could be used to connect to the actual computer over a telephone line. On the other end of that telephone line, a modem would be directly hooked up to the serial port. It amounts to the same thing in the end.) Most old Unix boxes (and even many new ones) could support literally dozens of keyboards and monitors connected via serial cables to the system unit.

This was very good and very bad. It was good because it allowed effective use of limited resources; it was bad because dozens of companies made and sold terminals, and each one of them supported a different set of features. Some might be printers and keyboards while others might have a CRT screen. Some might have an *addressable display*, where the cursor could be moved about at will, while others might not. Some might support color, while others might be black and white; and so on.

Around the time that vi was written, this had clearly become an important problem. The solution to this was the TERM variable and a file called /etc/termcap that contained information about the capabilities of various terminals. The user would set a TERM variable when logging on to a machine so that screen-addressable programs would work properly.

Eventually, the terminal industry settled down, and several terminal types became de facto standards that other manufacturers would emulate. Several DEC models became popular targets for emulation, chief among these the vt100 and vt102 terminals, although the vt220 was also quite popular. The vt102 was just an update of the vt100. The most notable difference was a fix for some display bugs. (I'll come back to this in a minute.)

Not too surprisingly, none of the terminals that emulated the vt100 or vt102 did so perfectly. As a result of this, many different terminal emulations are still listed in the /etc/termcap file and in the /etc/terminfo directory. The /etc/terminfo setup was another attempt to solve the same problems as /etc/termcap and is the infrastructure upon which the curses and ncurses full-screen programming interfaces rely. (Traditionally, /etc/termcap was the BSD Unix solution to these problems and /etc/terminfo was the System V solution.)

In fact, many programs that claim to emulate a vt100 terminal actually emulate the vt102 due to the absence of a bug regarding the display of attributes such as bold or underline. If your display is correct except for the underlining or bolding of text, try switching your TERM from vt100 to vt102 or vice versa.

Arbitrary Variables

Of course, no shell limits you to the built-in variables with special functions. Instead, you can create any number of arbitrary variables that you desire, as long as their names do not conflict with special-purpose variable names. (In bash you can type **help variables** to see a complete list of reserved variable names. Check the documentation for other shells as necessary.)

Why would you create a variable? Some variables are used by other programs on your system to provide configuration information. One interesting pair of variables is EDITOR and VISUAL. In the Korn Shell, these variables control whether you edit your command line with Emacs or vi style command-line editing keys, as we saw in the previous chapter. In other shells, however, these variables are accessible by running programs to determine what editor to use when an editor is required. VISUAL usually overrides EDITOR, though this is not always the case. Similarly, PAGER defines the default pager (more, less, cat, or whatever else you desire) for displaying long informational screens. Depending on the software you run, other variables might be useful for configuration.

If you write shell scripts, you might also want to use arbitrary variables to store information used at runtime. For example, if I generate a random filename for a temporary file, I can save this value in TEMPFILENAME so that I can delete it when I'm done with my script, or I can set a number of variables for particular projects to save me some typing:

```
[jon@frogbog jon]$ BOOKDIR=$HOME/docs/unixbook/thinkunix
[jon@frogbog jon]$ echo $BOOKDIR
/home/jon/docs/unixbook/thinkunix
[jon@frogbog jon]$ cd $BOOKDIR
[jon@frogbog thinkunix]$ pwd
/home/jon/docs/unixbook/thinkunix
[jon@frogbog thinkunix]$ cd
[jon@frogbog jon]$ rm $BOOKDIR/tempfile
[jon@frogbog jon]$
```

As you can see, you may use variable names as parts of strings, commands, or other variables: The system replaces variable names with their values in the command line before it is interpreted.

Environment Variables

Shell variables are, for the most part, available only to the current shell. If you want programs running within the shell to have access to a variable (when you use a variable to provide configuration information to a program, for example), you need to *export* that variable to your *environment*.

Huh? What's that? Your environment is a collection of information about your current configuration, consisting primarily of specific shell variables that are made available to running programs. Some variables (TERM and PATH, for example) are automatically exported to your environment by your shell. Others are not. Many newsreaders use the NNTPSERVER variable to know what NNTP server to use for reading Usenet news. This variable must be exported manually:

```
[jon@frogbog jon]$ NNTPSERVER=news.example.org
[jon@frogbog jon]$ export NNTPSERVER
```

If you know you will need to export a variable, you can set and export it all at the same time:

```
[jon@frogbog jon]$ export WWW_HOME='http://www.tux.org/~lasser/'
```

The WWW_HOME variable is used by the lynx Web browser to determine the starting home page.

Shell Startup Scripts

Just as vi has a configuration file named .exrc that stores its configuration defaults and runs whenever you start vi, each shell has one or more startup scripts that are executed whenever a shell is started. Which startup file is executed depends on whether the current shell is a *login shell*.

A login shell is almost what it sounds like: When you log in to a system via a text terminal, ssh, telnet, or the console, you get a login shell. In general, login shells read from different configuration files and are listed when someone runs the who command to see who is logged on to the system. xterm windows can run your shell either as a login shell or a non-login shell. (We'll talk more about that in Part III.)

If you run bash as a login shell, it first looks at the system's generic startup script in /etc/profile. After running that, it looks for one of the following three files, in order: ~/.bash_profile, ~/.bash_login, or ~/.profile. After it finds one of those files, it doesn't look for any of the others but just runs that.

When not run as a login shell, bash runs the commands located in ~/.bashrc. To make sure that my environment is almost always the same, I create a .bash_profile with several useful commands, the first of which is source $HOME/.bashrc, to set my environment variables and run my complete configuration. (The source reads in the specified file and executes the commands in the current shell. It's built into the shell, so check your shell's man page for details on usage.) My general rule is anything that should be run only when logging into a box should be in the .bash_profile, and anything that should be set in any xterm should be set in .bashrc. In practice, that means most of my configuration is done in my .bashrc, but that might be different in your environment.

When invoked as a login shell, ksh first looks for /etc/profile, just like bash. It then will look for a ~/.profile file. Because some configuration options should be different in bash, I need to have a .bash_profile so that bash doesn't try to read the Korn Shell .profile file in my home directory. If, unlike me, you don't switch between shells like a maniac, this might be unnecessary in your configuration.

If your system sets the ENV environment variable, ksh will also read that file for startup information. Many systems set this to ~/.kshrc, but that might or might not be true on your system. You can, of course, set ENV to an appropriate value in your .profile to make your systems behave appropriately.

The C Shell uses ~/.cshrc and ~/.login. The latter of these is equivalent to a ~/.profile file in the Bourne Shell derivatives. Unlike the Bourne Shell derivatives, however, the ~/.cshrc file is processed before the ~/.login file. If you use tcsh, it will use a ~/.tcshrc file in preference to a ~/.cshrc file, if both are present. (You might source the latter from the former, if you so desire, as tcsh is entirely backward-compatible.)

Each shell also has a shutdown script, which is run when the user logs out of the shell: bash uses the file ~/.bash_logout, and csh, tcsh, and ksh all use the file ~/.logout. Because these shells might use different syntax, I strongly recommend *not* putting anything other than a simple command in this file. Personally, I avoid .logout files altogether because they can create subtle incompatibilities and aren't really all that useful in the first place. One common use is to insert a clear command in the .logout file, to make the terminal look nice for the next user or to hide confidential data after logging out.

Practice Problems

1. Create a variable named EXTRAPATH and set its value equal to your current path.

2. If you do not already have a directory named bin within your home directory, make that directory. If it is not already in your PATH, add it to the end of your path. (If you do have a directory of that name already, pick a different name and try that.)

3. Create a new variable named THIRDARM that contains the contents of your new, modified PATH. Export this new variable to your environment.

4. Reset your path to the contents of EXTRAPATH.

5. Unset the variable EXTRAPATH and the variable THIRDARM. Re-export this empty THIRDARM to your environment.

   If you are not using bash as your shell, skip the next two problems.

6. Set your prompt to two blank lines followed by a closing parenthesis and a space.

7. Set your prompt to the base name of the current working directory followed by a space, a square bracket, the history number of the current command, another square bracket, a dollar sign, and a space.

Quoting

Several times now I've used single quotes to keep the shell from interpreting certain strings, and once or twice I've used the backslash to "escape" certain shell characters. In fact, these are only two of the four types of quoting that Unix offers: Backslashes escape individual characters; backticks execute code and are interpreted as the output of that code; single quotes keep the shell from interpreting anything within those quotes; and double quotes preserve some of the text within the quotes while substituting other portions of that text.

The different sorts of quoting are one of the most powerful features of the Unix shells, and one of the most confusing. Quoting works almost identically between shells, but as always check your documentation to be certain. Because the different quote marks are so similar, it is sometimes difficult to be sure which sort to use in a given situation. This section will try to clarify this important subject.

Backslash (\)

Although it's not technically a sort of quote, the backslash (\) is used to escape, or "quote" individual characters. There are two different ways it is used, and in some sense they are opposite to each other, but on a deeper level there is a unity of purpose for the lowly backslash. Consider the backslash as a sort of toggle. It makes special characters literal and literal characters special.

The first use of the backslash is to turn a regular character into a metacharacter. We saw this both with the echo command and with bash's interpretation of the PS1 and PS2 command strings. For the prompt strings, \n represents a line break ("newline") character; \u represents your username; \w the name of the current working directory; and so on; while \\ represents an actual backslash. For the echo command, \n is still a newline; \t is a tab; \a rings your terminal bell, if it has one; and \\ still represents an actual backslash.

The second use of the backslash is to treat the following character literally: to disable its special purpose. Many punctuation marks have a special meaning to the shell, including single quotes, back quotes, double quotes, exclamation marks, question marks, carets, ampersands, pipes, asterisks, parentheses, semicolons, brackets, greater-than signs, less-than signs, and tildes. Any of these characters can be treated literally rather than have a special meaning simply by prepending a backslash to that character.

One use of this is when you have a file with a funny name and want to work with it. Imagine you have a file whose name is an asterisk, and you want to remove it. rm * would delete every file in the current directory; unless you use rm -i, it won't even ask before doing so. To remove a file named *, you need to escape it; rm * will remove that file. Similarly, if you have a file named !, you may cat it by typing *cat* \!. As when it gives another character a special meaning, \\ represents a literal backslash.

Because in most circumstances it tells the shell to treat the next character literally, you can use a backslash to tell the shell that the next line is part of the same command:

```
[jon@frogbog jon]$ echo one\
> two\
> three \
> four
onetwothree four
[jon@frogbog jon]$
```

Consider for a moment what just occurred: The shell was told that the line break was to be treated literally, so why didn't one, two, three, and four appear on separate lines? The shell essentially ignores whitespace. In practice, this means that newlines are discarded and more than one space between words is compressed into a single space:

```
[jon@frogbog jon]$ echo one two
one two
[jon@frogbog jon]$
```

Why are spaces only compressed while newlines are dispensed with entirely? From the shell's perspective, spaces are discarded: In the second example, one and two are separate arguments to the echo command, and each argument to the echo command is returned, with a single space between arguments.

Single Quotes (')

If you want each space to be included in your echo command, they all must be part of a single argument. Single quotes delimit a string that the shell will take literally, treating it as a single unit, or *token*:

```
[jon@frogbog jon]$ echo 'one two'
one two
[jon@frogbog jon]$
```

Everything between single quotes is taken literally. This includes backslashes, newlines, variable names, double quotes, backticks, and on and on:

```
[jon@frogbog jon]$ echo 'three
>
> four
> five `@#$%^\"[]'
three
four
five `@#$%^\"[]
[jon@frogbog jon]$
```

In fact, the only character that you can't put between single quotes is another single quote: If you did, how would the system know that you intended it as a display quote? (Sometimes, an exclamation mark will also cause a problem, depending on shell configuration related to history commands.)

If you have a file with more than one funny character in its name, single quotes are a great way to deal with that:

```
[jon@frogbog jon]$ cat 'a funny file name (with lots of characters, but no
single quotes in the whole darn thing)'
Nothing to see here, move along!
[jon@frogbog jon]$ mv 'a funny file name (with lots of characters, but no
single quotes in the whole darn thing)' a-shorter-name.txt
[jon@frogbog jon]$
```

Of course, so far we've used single quotes to protect find, grep, sed, and awk commands from being interpreted by the shell. All the way back in Chapter 3, we first used single quotes to protect a command when we ran find / -name '*' -print >& ~/allfiles.txt. In that case, the single quotes keep the shell from converting the asterisk they surround from being interpreted by the shell. Without those quotes, the shell would replace that asterisk with a list of every file in the current directory.

Yes, you heard right: It is the shell and not the application that interprets filename globbing. Although this is confusing at first, the reason is simple: If you wanted, you could write a shell that implemented filename globbing in a different fashion. In fact, you could write a shell that used regular expressions, or even a completely different scheme, instead of filename globbing. As a result, however, you do need to protect anything the shell could confuse with filename globbing or any other "reserved" symbol. That includes bangs and carets, which could be confused with history substitution commands; dollar signs, which might indicate the presence of a variable; backslashes; parentheses; and anything else that has a special meaning within the shell.

Another use for single quotes that I've already demonstrated was in the last chapter, when we used single quotes to keep the shell from interpreting the prompt string. I set the PS1 variable to What Now? with the command PS1='What Now? '. In this case, the single quotes both keep both words of this prompt as a single unit in the eyes of the shell and make certain that the question mark is not interpreted. When I set PS1 to [\u@\h \W]\$ using the command PS1='[\u@\h \W]\$ ', the single quotes prevent the shell from interpreting the brackets or the backslash-escaped characters as well as keeping the spaces intact.

Back Quotes (`)

One complaint about setting the prompt to that last value is that it only works in bash, not sh or ksh. To duplicate the effect of this command in those shells, we must be able to include the output of one Unix command in another command. Because this is a new concept, let's detour a moment and look at a couple of simple examples before coming back to altering the prompt sting.

Back quotes interpolate the output of one command in another. The command within those quotes is replaced by its output within the whole thing being run. This sounds confusing, so let's look at a couple of examples:

```
[jon@frogbog jon]$ expr 1 + 3
4
[jon@frogbog jon]$ echo The `expr 1 + 3` horsemen
The 4 horsemen
```

In this case, the `expr 1 + 3` in the second command is replaced with the output of the command expr 1 + 3, which I've cunningly demonstrated returns the number 4. The shell, therefore, interprets the command echo The `expr 1 + 3` horsemen as echo The 4 horsemen.

```
[jon@frogbog jon]$ whoami
jon
[jon@frogbog jon]$ echo `whoami`
jon
```

In this example, the command whoami is replaced with the output of the command whoami, which evaluates to jon. Of course, echo jon will produce the same output as the command whoami does, although it gets there in a different way.

```
[jon@frogbog jon]$ cat /etc/shells
/bin/bash
/bin/sh
/bin/tcsh
/bin/csh
/bin/ash
/bin/bsh
/bin/bash2
/bin/ksh
/bin/zsh
[jon@frogbog jon]$ ls -l `cat /etc/shells`
-rwxr-xr-x 1 root root 63196 Sep 12 00:09 /bin/ash*
-rwxr-xr-x 1 root root 373176 Apr 6 1999 /bin/bash*
-rwxr-xr-x 1 root root 456244 Sep 24 17:41 /bin/bash2*
lrwxrwxrwx 1 root root 3 Dec 6 19:49 /bin/bsh -> ash*
lrwxrwxrwx 1 root root 4 Dec 6 19:48 /bin/csh -> tcsh*
-rwxr-xr-x 1 root root 168016 Jul 20 1999 /bin/ksh*
lrwxrwxrwx 1 root root 4 Dec 6 19:47 /bin/sh -> bash*
-rwxr-xr-x 1 root root 262152 Sep 25 01:01 /bin/tcsh*
-rwxr-xr-x 1 root root 340772 Sep 24 22:08 /bin/zsh*
[jon@frogbog jon]$
```

Here, the text of /etc/shells is included on the command line, so it is as if it read ls -l /bin/bash /bin/sh /bin/tcsh /bin/csh /bin/ash /bin/bsh /bin/bash2 /bin/ksh /bin/zsh. (Remember that the shell interprets line breaks simply as word breaks on a command line.)

We can use back quotes to emulate several of the backslash escape sequences that bash interprets as part of the PS1 prompt: \u can be replaced with `whoami`, \h can be replaced with `hostname|cut -d . -f 1`, and \W can be replaced with `basename $PWD`. Therefore, the command I use to set my default bash prompt, PS1='[\u@\h \W]\$ ', can be replaced with PS1='[`whoami`@`hostname|cut -d . -f 1` `basename $PWD`]$ '. One metacharacter I can't emulate is \$, which prints a dollar sign for all users except root, in which case it prints a pound sign (#).[1]

In most respects, back quotes are like the xargs command, with a pair of notable differences. First, xargs can only append information to the end of a command line. Second, xargs evades restrictions on the length of command lines, whereas back quotes do not. When a large amount of data is returned by an expression in back quotes, for example, a long list of files, there's a chance that the resulting command line will be too long for the shell to handle. In that case, it's best to find a solution that permits the use of xargs, despite its more limited flexibility.

---

1. Actually, I can emulate this; I just need a couple of things we haven't learned yet.

You may use most special shell characters within back quotes: This includes csh-style history commands, if your shell supports them; variables; and other quotes within the back-quoted expression. A careful user never deletes files with a wildcard before double-checking that it matches only the correct files.

```
[jon@frogbog jon]$ ls *.txt
meaningless.txt otherwise-engaged.txt worthless.txt
not-important.txt useless.txt
[jon@frogbog jon]$ rm `!!`
rm `ls *.txt`
[jon@frogbog jon]$ ls *.txt
[jon@frogbog jon]$ find . -name '*.old' -print
./bin/fixweb.old
./.gimp/gimprc.old
./.procmail/log.old
[jon@frogbog jon]$ rm `!!`
rm `find . -name '*.old' -print`
[jon@frogbog jon]$
```

Only after becoming certain that meaningless.txt and its cohorts are worthless do I delete them. Using back quotes and history commands saves typing and ensures that I know precisely what I'm deleting. In the second rm command, the history-expanded version contains single quotes, which work normally.

Double Quotes (")

Sometimes you don't want the shell to take *everything* literally. Sometimes you want to print the contents of a variable in the middle of a single argument, or you want to embed the output of a back-quoted command within a string. For these tasks, double quotes are the right tool for the job. Double quotes disable wild card substitution but leave history substitution, variable substitution, back quote substitution, and backslash escaping intact. Essentially, double quotes turn everything between them into a single element, disabling only a few crucial shell features.

Of course, it's easy to say that, but it's hard to see what it means in a practical sense. One way to think about it is to consider double quotes "weak quoting," while single quotes are "strong quoting": Single quotes make *everything* literal, while double quotes make only some things literal. (In this scheme of things, backslashes make only one thing—the next character—literal, and back quotes are something else entirely.) Perhaps it's best to see some examples of how quotes differ:

```
[jon@frogbog jon]$ echo *
arc bin Desktop docs gfx GNUstep include lib Mail mail man mediabits
News news nsmail private public_html queue scripts src thinkunix tmp
visor Xrootenv.0
 [jon@frogbog jon]$ echo '*'
*
[jon@frogbog jon]$ echo "*"
 *
```

In this case, there is no difference between single quotes and double quotes. Either variety prevents the shell from interpreting the asterisk.

```
[jon@frogbog jon]$ echo bin
bin
[jon@frogbog jon]$ ls `echo bin`
add* cyclebg* fixweb* loadxrdb* newbg* printwork*
adjustbase* decryptpw* fixweb.old* mgphtml* picker* start_taper*
backup_jon* diary* jukebox* mgprint* printhome* tarweb*
[jon@frogbog jon]$ ls "`echo bin`"
add* cyclebg* fixweb* loadxrdb* newbg* printwork*
adjustbase* decryptpw* fixweb.old* mgphtml* picker* start_taper*
backup_jon* diary* jukebox* mgprint* printhome* tarweb*
[jon@frogbog jon]$ ls '`echo bin`'
ls: `echo bin`: No such file or directory
```

In this case, the back quotes are executed in the double-quoted expression, resulting in the interpretation of echo bin as in the first back-quoted expression. When single quotes are used, however, the system looks for a file named `echo bin` and, not finding one, complains that it's not present.

Another example worth returning to is setting the PS1 prompt in ksh to an equivalent of bash's PS1='[\u@\h \W]\$ '. We've already seen that an excellent replacement for this is PS1='[`whoami`@`hostname|cut -d . -f 1` `basename $PWD`]$ ', but what happens when different types of quotes are used? Let's take a look:

```
[jon@frogbog jon]$ PS1='[`whoami`@`hostname|cut -d . -f 1` `basename $PWD`]$ '
[jon@frogbog jon]$ cd bin
[jon@frogbog bin]$ PS1="[`whoami`@`hostname|cut -d . -f 1` `basename $PWD`]$ "
[jon@frogbog bin]$ cd ..
[jon@frogbog bin]$ pwd
/home/jon
[jon@frogbog bin]$
```

When double quotes are used, the prompt doesn't change the last term inside the brackets to list the current directory, whereas it works fine with single quotes. What gives?

When single quotes are used, the back-quoted expressions within the prompt are not interpreted at the time the variable PS1 is set. That is, PS1 is set to [`whoami`@`hostname|cut -d . -f 1` `basename $PWD`]$. When the shell then sets the prompt, it sees the back quotes and interprets them at runtime. That way when you switch directories `basename $PWD` is run again, producing appropriate results based on the name of the current directory.

By contrast, when double quotes are used, the back-quoted expression is interpreted at the time the variable is set. Therefore, if I'm in the $HOME/tmp directory when I set my prompt, PS1 is set to [jon@frogbog tmp]$, and although the prompt is nominally reevaluated every time it is displayed, there is nothing to be interpreted.

If you're not entirely sure about when to use single quotes and when to use double quotes, my advice is to use single quotes unless you need to interpret a variable as part of your string. Cases such as the appropriate interpretation of prompt strings are relatively rare, and many users ignore them without too much peril. Users who actually like to understand their systems—you included—are better served with a full explanation, even when it might not be of much immediate practical use.

Practice Problems

8. Create a variable named `THIRDARM` that contains the number 4. Display the string `My third arm is number XYZ out of 1000`, where `XYZ` has been replaced by the contents of your `THIRDARM` variable.

9. Display the string `The serial number of my third arm is stored in the variable $THIRDARM`, where `$THIRDARM` is *not* replaced by the contents of that variable.

10. Display the string `Today's date is:`, followed by today's date.

11. Set a variable named `DATELINE` to `Today's date is:`, followed by today's date.

12. Set `DATELINE` to a value that will display the phrase `Today's date is:` followed by the current date *whenever* the command `eval echo "$DATELINE"` is run. (That command will interpret strings as they are displayed.)

HARD LINKS • SOFT LINKS • REDIRECTION AND F
REDIRECTING STDERR • NAME LOOKUP • ROUTIN
READING MAIL VIA POP3 • VI AND REGULAR EXF
FILENAME GLOBBING VERSUS REGEXPS • INTERA
COMMAND-LINE EDITING • HISTORY SUBSTITUTIC
CONTROL • VARIABLES AND QUOTING • CONDI
EXECUTION • WHILE AND UNTIL LOOPS • ALIASE
FUNCTIONS • THE X WINDOW CLIENT/SERVER N
WIDGETS AND TOOLKITS • CONFIGURING X • PE
AND OWNERSHIP • USERS AND GROUPS • HARI
SOFT LINKS • REDIRECTION AND PIPES • REDIRE(
STDERR NAME LOOKUP • ROUTING READING M/
• VI AND REGULAR EXPRESSIONS FILENAME GLC
VERSUS REGEXPS • INTERACTIVE COMMAND-LIN
HISTORY SUBSTITUTION • JOB CONTROL • VARIA
QUOTING CONDITIONAL EXECUTION • WHILE A

Conditional Execution and Loops

Another fundamental property of computers is *conditional execution*. Put simply, it means that computers can change what they do depending on the circumstances. That sounds completely obvious, but consider the implications: Without the capability to make decisions and act on input, a computer is just an expensive calculator. Without conditional execution, user input doesn't mean much of anything because there's no way to say, "If the user picks save, store the file on disk, but if the user picks load, ask what file to read off the disk." Conditional execution, broadly speaking, is the ability for a programmer to say, "If this is so, do this; otherwise, do this other thing."

Conditional execution also makes *loops* possible. A loop is exactly what it sounds like: It's a number of instructions that is repeated. It might do something for each item on a list. It might repeat itself a fixed number of times, or it might wait for a specific condition to be met, such as receiving a particular response from the user. In this chapter, we discuss how to use both conditional execution and loops to work more efficiently in the shell. As always, bash is our reference platform, although everything in this chapter should work equally well on ksh and most everything should function in sh. The tcsh and C Shells are different, and nothing in this chapter should work in either of those shells. (They do have syntax for equivalent functionality, but I do not cover it. Sufficient resources should be available on the Internet or in bookstores if you're interested in these shells.)

Sequential Execution

To understand conditional execution we must first understand the alternative, *sequential execution*. Sequential execution is just what it sounds like: one command run after another, regardless of the circumstances. This isn't quite the same as just typing in one command at a time because you might type different commands depending on what has already happened. For example:

```
[jon@frogbog jon]$ cd new_directory
bash: new_directory: No such file or directory
[jon@frogbog jon]$ mkdir new_directory
[jon@frogbog jon]$ cd new directory
bash: new: No such file or directory
[jon@frogbog jon]$ cd new_directory
[jon@frogbog new_directory]$
```

I make several mistakes in that sequence of commands. Because I'm using this shell interactively, I am able to correct those mistakes. That is a particular sort of conditional execution.

Unix uses the semicolon (;) to separate commands for sequential execution. Each command in that sequence, from left to right, is executed without regard for the success or failure of the previous command:

```
[jon@frogbog jon]$ mkdir the_flintstones ; cd the_flintsotnes ; touch barney
bash: the flintsotnes: no such file or directory
[jon@frogbog jon]$ pwd
```

```
/home/jon
[jon@frogbog jon]$ ls the_flintstones barney
barney

    the_flintstones:
```

In this case, the first command executed successfully, creating the directory the_flintstones, but the second command failed due to a typo. Nevertheless, the third command executed, creating barney in the current directory. This, of course, is not what we wanted to do.

Despite the many problems associated with sequential execution, it's convenient and easy to do, so many people use it. Heck, I use it sometimes. It's just a shortcut to type multiple commands on a single line, but it should be used carefully, for obvious reasons. Never rm files with sequential execution because a mistake in that circumstance could have drastic consequences.

Conditional Execution

Safer and more effective than sequential execution, *conditional execution* allows us to act differently as circumstances require. One very simple form of conditional execution allows us to run further commands on the basis of the success or failure of other commands.

Exit Status

For the idea of this to work, the computer must know whether the last command executed successfully. When a program exits, it returns a number. That is, it tells the shell, "my exit status is *N*," where *N* is a number. Zero usually means that the program finished executing successfully, whereas any other number usually indicates an error. Different numbers might mean different things, depending on how the program was written, but it almost always indicates some kind of error or failure to execute properly.

The shell makes the exit status of the last command executed available in the variable ?. You can simply echo $? to see the exit status of the previous command:

```
[jon@frogbog jon]$ cd tmp
[jon@frogbog tmp]$ echo $?
0
```

Simple enough: A successful cd returns a zero, as we would expect.

```
[jon@frogbog tmp]$ cd gargamels-castle
bash: gargamels-castle: No such file or directory
[jon@frogbog tmp]$ echo $?
1
```

```
[jon@frogbog tmp]$ echo $?
0
```

A failed cd returns nonzero. Specifically, it returns a 1. Why does the second echo command not return the same value? Because $? contains the return value of the first echo command, which was successful.

```
[jon@frogbog tmp]$ grep jon /etc/passwd
jon:x:500:500:Jon:/home/jon:/bin/bash2
[jon@frogbog tmp]$ echo $?
0
```

A grep that finds the regexp returns a 0, of course.

```
[jon@frogbog tmp]$ grep papasmurf /etc/passwd
[jon@frogbog tmp]$ echo $?
1
```

A grep that doesn't find the regexp returns a 1...

```
[jon@frogbog tmp]$ grep papasmurf smurf-village
grep: smurf-village: No such file or directory
[jon@frogbog tmp]$ echo $?
2
```

...but a grep that can't find the file returns a 2. Note that when cd couldn't find the directory, it returned a 1: the same error doesn't necessarily return the same error code between programs. grep always returns a 2 for file not found errors, but it's not guaranteed that a single other program will return the same value. Some programs, GNU's version of grep included, actually document the meanings of different exit status values on their man pages. If exit status values are not documented, don't assume that you can rely on them to be consistent among different versions of the program, except inasmuch as 0 is always success. (Sometimes nonzero can indicate success, but this is rare.)

Another way to think about exit status is that the shell is returning either *yes, this was successful* or *no, this was not successful*. If you shorten those responses to *yes* and *no*, you can see that these are equivalent to the Boolean values true and false, our good old friends 1 and 0 in a new guise. In this case, however, true is equal to 0 and false is equal to 1, a reversal of the traditional meanings. You can verify this through two executables present on the system: Unix actually has programs named true and false.

```
[jon@frogbog tmp]$ true
[jon@frogbog tmp]$ echo $?
0
[jon@frogbog tmp]$ false
[jon@frogbog tmp]$ echo $?
1
```

Finally, note that error codes aren't always low numbers. The command not found error in bash is 127:

```
[jon@frogbog tmp]$ smurfhunt
bash: smurfhunt: command not found
[jon@frogbog tmp]$ echo $?
127
[jon@frogbog tmp]$
```

&&, ||, and !

Unix provides a mechanism for executing subsequent commands based on the exit code of the previous command. Both work like sequential execution but replace the semicolon with a different symbol. To execute a command if the last command was successful, separate the two commands with a double ampersand (&&); to execute a command if the last command failed, use a double pipe (||). These are related to the Boolean operators AND and OR, respectively.

One important use for && is to put together a sequential string of commands that will halt when any of the commands fails. Let's retry our earlier example:

```
[jon@frogbog jon]$ mkdir the_flintstones && cd the_flintsotnes && touch barney
bash: the_flintsotnes: no such file or directory
[jon@frogbog jon]$ pwd
/home/jon
[jon@frogbog jon]$ ls the_flintstones barney
ls: barney: No such file or directory
[jon@frogbog jon$
```

Because the cd command failed, bash did not execute the touch command, and the file barney was never created. This has the effect of making it much safer to execute long strings of commands. The main use of || is to provide error detection and helpful error messages or even to correct errors:

```
[jon@frogbog jon]$ cd the_jetsons || mkdir the_jetsons && cd the_jetsons
bash: the_jetsons: No such file or directory
[jon@frogbog the_jetsons]$ cat george || echo "George isn't home right now."
cat: george: No such file or directory
George isn't home right now.
[jon@frogbog the_jetsons]$
```

In the first example, I attempt to cd into the directory the_jetsons and, if it's not present, create the directory and switch into it. The first cd reported the error, but the rest of the command acted on the failure of the first command and the directory was created. (There is a better way to do this that we'll talk about later in the chapter, but for now it's a good example.)

In the second example, I cat the text of the file george, but if it's not present I print an error message to that effect. (If the file was present but I didn't have permission to read it, the result would have been the same.) Both examples have a problem, although, in that the shell complains loudly about the failure of some of the commands. Better to send STDERR to /dev/null and keep the screen clean:

```
[jon@frogbog the_jetsons]$ cd .. && rm -rf the_jetsons
[jon@frogbog jon]$ cd the_jetsons 2>/dev/null || mkdir the_jetsons && cd\
the_jetsons
[jon@frogbog the_jetsons]$ cat george 2>/dev/null || echo "George isn't home\
right now."
George isn't home right now.
[jon@frogbog the_jetsons]$
```

There! No messy error messages to interfere with our nice, clean screen. You can think of the && operator as "If so, then …" and the || operator as "If not, then …" if doing so makes their use more clear.

The ! operator, not to be confused with the history recall command, is the equivalent of the Boolean NOT: It inverts the exit status of the command that follows it on the command line. You must have a space following the bang so that the system can distinguish between the use of the exclamation mark for history recall and for NOT.

```
[jon@frogbog jon]$ echo "Test"
Test
[jon@frogbog jon]$ echo $?
0 ·
[jon@frogbog jon]$ ! echo "Test"
Test
[jon@frogbog jon]$ echo $?
1
[jon@frogbog jon]$ ! cd nothing-to-see-here
bash: nothing-to-see-here: No such file or directory
[jon@frogbog jon]$ echo $?
0
[jon@frogbog jon]$ ! cd tmp
[jon@frogbog tmp]$ echo $?
1
```

In practice, most users tend to invert their use of && and || rather than to prepend ! to the command line, although the latter method makes clear the intention of the user. This should be important when writing shell scripts that others might eventually need to maintain, although in practice it hardly makes a difference. Also, any group of commands connected by ;, &&, or || is called a *list*.

If/Then/Else

The if, then, and else commands are probably the most frequently used control structure in the Bourne Shell family. if is followed by a command or list of commands that should return either true (0) or false (1). This is followed by a then, after which is the list of commands to be done if the if expression be evaluated as true. In the simplest case, this list of commands is terminated by fi, which marks the end of the construct:

```
[jon@frogbog jon]$ if cd tmp
> then
>     echo 'Fer sure, dude!'
>     echo "I've changed your directory."
> fi
Fer sure, dude!
I've changed your directory.
[jon@frogbog tmp]$
```

In this case, the command cd tmp is successful, thus the commands echo 'Fer sure, dude!' and echo "I've changed your directory." are run as well. Let's try this again from within tmp, so that the cd command will fail:

```
[jon@frogbog jon]$ if cd tmp
> then
>     echo 'Fer sure, dude!'
>     echo "I've changed your directory."
> fi
bash: tmp: No such file or directory
[jon@frogbog tmp]$ pwd
/home/jon/tmp
```

Now let's do this again, but both redirect STDERR for the cd command to /dev/null so that it won't clutter the screen, and add in an else clause to provide a stylistically consistent error message:

```
[jon@frogbog tmp]$ cd ..
[jon@frogbog jon]$ if cd tmp 2>/dev/null
> then
>     echo 'Fer sure, dude!'
>     echo "I've changed your directory."
> else
>     echo 'Bummer, Dude!'
>     echo "That directory isn't there."
> fi
Fer sure, dude!
I've changed your directory.
[jon@frogbog tmp]$
```

The else clause, obviously, executes the following commands if the if expression returned a nonzero exit status. Again, let's try this from within tmp so that it will fail:

```
[jon@frogbog tmp]$ if cd tmp 2>/dev/null
> then
>     echo 'Fer sure, dude!'
```

```
>     echo "I've changed your directory."
> else
>     echo 'Bummer, Dude!'
>     echo "That directory isn't there."
> fi
Bummer, Dude!
That directory isn't there.
[jon@frogbog tmp]$ pwd
/home/jon/tmp
```

The spaces before the echo commands are entirely optional. I've placed them there to make clear where *blocks* of commands begin and end. A block is simply several commands that, under a particular circumstance, would all be executed by the system.

The elif command is an abbreviation for "else if." If all previous if or elif commands in the if statement evaluated as false, then the current elif condition is tested and, if it evaluates as true, the block of commands up to the next elif, else, or fi are executed. All that sounds pretty confusing but should make more sense in practice:

```
[jon@frogbog jon]$ if false
> then
>     echo "The first statement is true"
> elif true
> then
>     echo "The second statement is true"
> else
>     echo "Neither the first nor the second statement is true."
> fi
The second statement is true
```

In this case, because the if statement evaluates to false but the elif statement evaluates to true, the program prints the second message, "The second statement is true." If the if statement evaluated to true, the first message would be printed but not the second or third statements. If neither the if nor the elif evaluated to true, the third message would be printed. Any number of elif statements might be used, but one is enough to demonstrate the principle.

The Test Command

The test command is one of the most frequently used commands in if or elif expressions. It provides a method for determining whether certain conditions involving files, directories, strings, and numbers are true. One use would be to determine whether a particular directory exists before trying to cd into it:

```
[jon@frogbog jon]$ if test -d tmp
> then
>     cd tmp
>     echo "I'm in tmp now, man."
```

```
> else
>     echo "where's tmp?"
> fi
I'm in tmp now, man.
[jon@frogbog tmp]$ pwd
/home/jon/tmp
```

The -d option for test returns 0 if the argument is a directory. (If it doesn't exist, it's not a directory.) The -f option tests whether the following argument is a regular file, -L indicates whether or not it's a symbolic link, -r indicates that the user has permission to read the file, -w indicates permission to write to the file, and -s indicates that the file is not empty. Many more options available for test deal with files, but these are the most common. If an exclamation mark and a space precede an option, the condition is inverted.

How would you test to see if a file exists but is empty? You might try to negate the -s option:

```
[jon@frogbog tmp]$ ls -l
total 8
drwxr-xr-x 5 jon jon 4096 Sep 9 20:30 Rollemup/
drwxr-xr-x 8 jon jon 4096 Feb 29 20:20 mozilla-M14/
[jon@frogbog tmp]$ touch testfile
[jon@frogbog tmp]$ if test ! -s testfile
> then
>     echo "The file is empty."
> else
>     echo "No file or file not empty"
> fi
The file is empty.
```

So far so good. Let's make sure it works correctly when the file has content:

```
[jon@frogbog tmp]$ echo "Text" > testfile
[jon@frogbog tmp]$ if test ! -s testfile; then echo\
"The file is empty" ; else echo "No file or file not empty"; fi
No file or file not empty
```

In the previous test, I've combined the various parts of the command onto a single line to save typing. This part also works correctly. Now let's try it with no file at all:

```
[jon@frogbog tmp]$ rm testfile
[jon@frogbog tmp]$ if test ! -s testfile; then echo\
"The file is empty" ; else echo "No file or file not empty"; fi
The file is empty
```

Unfortunately, this isn't what we want to do: The file is empty but it doesn't exist, so we would like to return the second message, not the first. There are two ways to solve this problem. The first is to nest a second if statement within the first if statement:

```
[jon@frogbog tmp]$ if test ! -s testfile
> then
>     if test -f testfile
```

```
>     then
>         echo "The file is empty"
>     else
>         echo "No file"
>     fi
> else
>     echo "File not empty"
> fi
No file
```

Of course, the original problem doesn't ask us to distinguish between files that don't exist and those that are full. Although we could simply put the same response for either case in the previous problem, that would be inelegant. Instead, we would like to test for the conjunction of two conditions. The -a option for test enables you to AND two other test conditions, one on either side of the -a:

```
[jon@frogbog tmp]$ if test -e testfile -a ! -s testfile
> then
>     echo "The file is empty"
> else
>     echo "No file or file not empty"
> fi
No file or file not empty
[jon@frogbog tmp]$ touch testfile
[jon@frogbog tmp]$ if test -e testfile -a ! -s testfile
> then
>     echo "The file is empty"
> else
>     echo "No file or file not empty"
> fi
The file is empty
[jon@frogbog tmp]$ echo "stuff" > testfile
[jon@frogbog tmp]$ if test -e testfile -a ! -s testfile
> then
>     echo "The file is empty"
> else
>     echo "No file or file not empty"
> fi
No file or file not empty
```

Finally, an elegant solution to the problem! Complementary to the -a option is the -o option, which is a logical OR of the conditions on either side of that option. For example, imagine that I wanted to know if a file was either a directory or a symbolic link. I could test with the condition -L testfile -o -d testfile to see whether either of these conditions was true.

A shortcut exists for the test command. Rather than spelling out the word *test*, the test condition can be enclosed in square brackets. Not only does this involve two fewer characters, but it helps make the condition being tested for more obvious.

(That, of course, assumes that you're comfortable with the short options used by the test command. man test for full details.)

```
[jon@frogbog jon]$ if [ ! -d tmp -a ! -e tmp ]
> then
>    mkdir tmp
> else
>    echo "Directory or file tmp exists"
> fi
Directory or file tmp exists
```

As long as I'm talking about shortcuts, it's worth noting that because test is a regular old-fashioned Unix command (even the square bracket version), you can use it in any control structure, not just as part of an if/then/else statement. For example, if we want to make a directory if it's not present and nothing's in the way, we can simply run the command [-d tmp -o -e tmp] || mkdir tmp. In English, that's "If there is a directory named tmp or any other file named tmp then don't make a directory with that name." It's not the most straightforward way to frame the problem, but it does save quite a bit of typing. And if you do it that way, people will just assume that you're a Unix guru. Of course, that will be well on the way to being the truth.

case Statements

The case statement is just a specialized form of the if/then/else construct designed to deal with the circumstance of many possible options, each requiring a different sequence of events to be handled properly. It works as follows:

```
[jon@frogbog thinkunix]$ FOOD=carrots
[jon@frogbog thinkunix]$ case $FOOD in
>
> corn)
>    echo "I like corn."
>    ;;
>
> peas)
>    echo "Peas are better than corn."
>    ;;
>
> carrots)
>    echo "Carrots are best of all."
>    ;;
>
> *)
>    echo "I don't even know what $FOOD is."
>    ;;
> esac
Carrots are best of all.
```

case matches a word with a list of terms. Each term is followed by a closing parenthesis, and the list of commands to be executed in that case is terminated with a pair of semicolons. Only after all specific terms and their related commands are listed can you have an asterisk instead of a term, indicating that this final case matches all others. If an asterisk is listed above another portion of the case statement, it will be executed. After a single portion of that case statement is executed the rest is ignored; therefore, if we listed two sections for peas above, only the first would ever be executed.

You can also list multiple terms, separated by a pipe:

```
[jon@frogbog thinkunix]$ FOOD=carrots
[jon@frogbog thinkunix]$ case $FOOD in
>
> peas|carrots)
>    echo "Peas and carrots go well together."
>    ;;
>
> *)
>    echo "Yuck, I hate $FOOD."
>    ;;
> esac
Peas and carrots go well together.
```

If you're not a programmer, and you're not writing menuing interfaces, you might not use case. If you want it, however, it's there.

Practice Problems

1. Make a directory named theoretical and cd into that directory if it has been successfully created.

2. touch a file named test within that directory and cd to theoretical's parent directory. Now try to remove that directory and print the message Theoretical is actual if you are unable to delete it.

   Make sure that rmdir doesn't display any error messages of its own.

3. Using the negation operator (!), cd into not-really-a-directory and print an error message if that command fails.

4. Using an if statement, append the contents of /etc/passwd to a file named passwordlists if that file exists and you have verified that you can write to it.

5. Add an error condition to your if statement if either of the previous conditions is not met.

6. Now add a clause to the previous statement to create the file if it does not exist, but do not add any data to it. Make sure that your error message is appropriate if the file cannot be written to.

7. Without using a formal `if` statement, print the message `That's not a mouse!` if `/dev/mouse` is a symbolic link.

8. Use a `case` statement to print the message `That's a great book!` if the variable `AUTHOR` is set to Lasser. If it is set to `Sterling` or `Stephenson`, print the message `That's a pretty good book`. If `AUTHOR` is set to anything else, print the message `I haven't read that book`.

Loops

Often it is useful to run several commands not just once but for every file in a group of files, until a condition is met, or for a specific number of times. *Loops* allow us to repeat tasks as desired, based on any number of criteria. The two basic types of loops available on Unix are `for` loops and `while` loops. We will also discuss two sorts of loops related to `while` loops, `until` loops, and loops that execute a predetermined number of times.

`for` Loops

My favorite type of loop is the `for` loop. Most often I use it to repeat an action for a group of files, although it can be used for any number of things. Let's say I wanted to work on several files in the `superheroes` directory, but I wanted to back up all the files before messing around with them just in case. (This is a particularly useful thing to want. I very strongly suggest that you should want to back up files before working on them.) Let's say I wanted all my superheroes to have backup files with a `.retired` extension appended to their names:

```
[jon@frogbog superheroes]$ ls
aqua-man green-lantern spider-man the-tick
batman robin superman wonder-woman
[jon@frogbog superheroes]$ for foo in *
> do
>    cp $foo $foo.retired
> done
[jon@frogbog superheroes]$ ls
aqua-man                robin              the-tick
aqua-man.retired        robin.retired      the-tick.retired
batman                  spider-man         wonder-woman
batman.retired          spider-man.retired wonder-woman.retired
green-lantern           superman
green-lantern.retired   superman.retired
[jon@frogbog superheroes]$
```

The for itself is followed by the name of a variable, in this case foo, the word in, and a list of items.[1] In this case, the asterisk expands to the list of files in the directory: This line could be expanded to read for foo in aqua-man batman green-lantern robin spider-man superman the-tick wonder-woman and it would have the same effect.

The commands listed between the do and done are executed, once for each of the terms in the for statement. In this case, the variable foo is set to every one of those filenames in turn and the block of statements executed. Because wildcards expand in alphabetical order, it is as though the shell sets foo=aqua-man, runs through the block of code, then sets foo=batman, runs through the block of code again, and so on.

Combined with sed and back quotes, for loops are also good for renaming files. Let's say I wanted to replace the hyphens in all those filenames with underscores:

```
[jon@frogbog superheroes]$ for foo in *
> do
>     mv $foo `echo $foo|sed 's/-/_/g'`
> done
mv: 'batman' and 'batman' are the same file
mv: 'batman.retired' and 'batman.retired' are the same file
mv: 'robin' and 'robin' are the same file
mv: 'robin.retired' and 'robin.retired' are the same file
mv: 'superman' and 'superman' are the same file
mv: 'superman.retired' and 'superman.retired' are the same file
[jon@frogbog superheroes]$ ls
aqua_man                robin               the_tick
aqua_man.retired        robin.retired       the_tick.retired
batman                  spider_man          wonder_woman
batman.retired          spider_man.retired  wonder_woman.retired
green_lantern           superman
green_lantern.retired   superman.retired
[jon@frogbog superheroes]$
```

Let's take apart the one line in our for loop that executes once for each file in the directory: mv $foo `echo $foo|sed 's/-/_/g'`.

In each iteration of the loop, foo is set to the name of a file in the directory. That file is then renamed using mv. The source filename is simply the contents of foo, and the destination filename is the output of the command echo $foo|sed 's/-/_/g'. That command feeds the name of the file into a sed program that applies the regular expression s/-/_/g, which replaces every occurrence (global) of the character - with _.

---

1. *foo* is one of the classic metasyntactic variables in Unix culture. That is to say, whenever one needs to use an arbitrary variable, foo is often used as a placeholder. After foo, bar and baz are most common, though local variations on tradition exist.

Of course, we've learned every one of these pieces already except for the `for` loop, but it is the way that the `for` loop brings them all together that is important. We're using flow control statements (the `for` loop), variables (`foo`), `mv`, back quotes, single quotes, pipes, and regular expressions all at once. If you're comfortable with this little renaming program, consider yourself a Unix power user.

`while` and `until` Loops

Whereas a `for` loop iterates once for each item in a list, a `while` loop executes while a particular condition is true. That condition, not surprisingly, is the exit status of a Unix command or series of commands. Let's say I had a series of nested subdirectories each named `tmp`, and I wanted to `cd` into the innermost subdirectory of that name. A `while` loop would be a convenient way to do this:

```
[jon@frogbog jon]$ while cd tmp
> do
>     pwd
> done
/home/jon/tmp
/home/jon/tmp/tmp
/home/jon/tmp/tmp/tmp
/home/jon/tmp/tmp/tmp/tmp
/home/jon/tmp/tmp/tmp/tmp/tmp
/home/jon/tmp/tmp/tmp/tmp/tmp/tmp
/home/jon/tmp/tmp/tmp/tmp/tmp/tmp/tmp
/home/jon/tmp/tmp/tmp/tmp/tmp/tmp/tmp/tmp
/home/jon/tmp/tmp/tmp/tmp/tmp/tmp/tmp/tmp/tmp
bash: tmp: No such file or directory
[jon@frogbog tmp]$
```

The general format is that the word `while` is followed by a list of Unix commands. If the exit status of the last command in that list is true (zero), the commands between the `do` and the `done` are executed. In the previous example, the `while` statement executes until `cd` returns an error, which happens when there are no more `tmp` directories into which it can `cd`.

I run the `pwd` command within the loop for two reasons. First, the list of commands between the `do` and the `done` can't be empty; second, it's nice at this stage of the game to see what's going on. If I absolutely positively didn't want to do anything within that loop, I could run a useless dummy command such as `NULLVALUE=0` or `echo "" > /dev/null`.

The `until` command is just like the `while` command, except that the `until` loop runs while the exit status of the first list of commands is not zero. That is, an endless `while` loop would be of the format

```
[jon@frogbog jon]$ while true
> do
```

```
>    echo "This just goes on and on and on..."
> done
This just goes on and on and on...
This just goes on and on and on...
This just goes on and on and on...
. . .
```

while an endless until loop would instead be

```
[jon@frogbog jon]$ until false
> do
>    echo "...no dna no dna no seog tsuj sihT"
> done
...no dna no dna no seog tsuj sihT
...no dna no dna no seog tsuj sihT
...no dna no dna no seog tsuj sihT
. . .
```

No, I'm not at all sure why two separate commands are necessary. Personally, I always use a while loop and will negate the exit status of the condition as desired.

Counting Loops

Sometimes you just want to run a set of commands a given number of times. For example, I might want a number of test directories created, each with a name followed by a number. If the number of items I want is small, I just use a for loop:

```
[jon@frogbog jon]$ cd tmp
[jon@frogbog tmp]$ mkdir testdirs
[jon@frogbog tmp]$ cd testdirs
[jon@frogbog testdirs]$ ls
[jon@frogbog testdirs]$ for foo in 1 2 3 4 5 6 7 8 9
> do
>   mkdir test-$foo
> done
[jon@frogbog testdirs]$ ls
test-1/ test-2/ test-3/ test-4/ test-5/ test-6/ test-7/ test-8/
test-9/
[jon@frogbog testdirs]$ rm -rf test-[0-9]
[jon@frogbog testdirs]$ ls
[jon@frogbog testdirs]$
```

That works great for a small number of items. If, however, I wanted 100 directories, it would be best to use a while loop:

```
[jon@frogbog testdirs]$ DIRCOUNT=0
[jon@frogbog testdirs]$ while [ $DIRCOUNT -ne 100 ]
> do
>   DIRCOUNT=`expr $DIRCOUNT + 1`
>   mkdir test-$DIRCOUNT
> done
```

```
[jon@frogbog testdirs]$ ls
test-1/     test-22/    test-36/    test-5/     test-63/    test-77/    test-90/
test-10/    test-23/    test-37/    test-50/    test-64/    test-78/    test-91/
test-100/   test-24/    test-38/    test-51/    test-65/    test-79/    test-92/
test-11/    test-25/    test-39/    test-52/    test-66/    test-8/     test-93/
test-12/    test-26/    test-4/     test-53/    test-67/    test-80/    test-94/
test-13/    test-27/    test-40/    test-54/    test-68/    test-81/    test-95/
test-14/    test-28/    test-41/    test-55/    test-69/    test-82/    test-96/
test-15/    test-29/    test-42/    test-56/    test-7/     test-83/    test-97/
test-16/    test-3/     test-43/    test-57/    test-70/    test-84/    test-98/
test-17/    test-30/    test-44/    test-58/    test-71/    test-85/    test-99/
test-18/    test-31/    test-45/    test-59/    test-72/    test-86/
test-19/    test-32/    test-46/    test-6/     test-73/    test-87/
test-2/     test-33/    test-47/    test-60/    test-74/    test-88/
test-20/    test-34/    test-48/    test-61/    test-75/    test-89/
test-21/    test-35/    test-49/    test-62/    test-76/    test-9/
[jon@frogbog testdirs]$
```

Simple enough. The one new element in this command is that in this example test takes two arguments in addition to the operator. [ARG1 -ne ARG2] is true if ARG1 is not equal to ARG2. There are similar numeric tests for "equal to" (-eq), "less than" (-lt), "greater than" (-gt), "less than or equal to" (-le), and "greater than or equal to" (-ge). test supports a large number of other tests we have not discussed; check your documentation to find more applications of this versatile command.

Unix being Unix, all sorts of things are possible. This is just a taste of how loops can be used to accomplish tasks. As you experiment with Unix, you will find dozens of other ways in which loops are useful.

Practice Problems

9. For every file in your home directory, print the message (filename) is a directory if the file (filename) is a directory.

10. For every letter of the alphabet, print the letter and a colon on one line, and then ls everything beginning with that letter in the directory. (Don't worry about uppercase versus lowercase; just stick to lowercase for now.)

11. Make a directory called signal. Then make a while loop that prints a message as long as that directory exists. Remove that directory in another terminal session, or after suspending the loop with Control-Z. Make sure the loop actually stops when the directory is removed.

12. Using an until loop, print a message until a directory named signal is removed.

REDIRECTING STDERR • NAME LOOKUP • ROUTIN
READING MAIL VIA POP3 • VI AND REGULAR EXF
FILENAME GLOBBING VERSUS REGEXPS • INTERA
COMMAND-LINE EDITING • HISTORY SUBSTITUTIC
CONTROL • VARIABLES AND QUOTING • CONDI
EXECUTION • WHILE AND UNTIL LOOPS • ALIASE
FUNCTIONS • THE X WINDOW CLIENT/SERVER M
WIDGETS AND TOOLKITS • CONFIGURING X • PE
AND OWNERSHIP • USERS AND GROUPS • HARI
SOFT LINKS • REDIRECTION AND PIPES • REDIREC
STDERR NAME LOOKUP • ROUTING READING MA
• VI AND REGULAR EXPRESSIONS FILENAME GLC
VERSUS REGEXPS • INTERACTIVE COMMAND-LIN
HISTORY SUBSTITUTION • JOB CONTROL • VARIA
QUOTING CONDITIONAL EXECUTION • WHILE A

Shell Scripts
and More

This chapter is here to sweep up all the bits and pieces of basic command-line Unix shell knowledge that I haven't already covered. After this chapter, we move on to the X Window System, the Unix GUI environment. This chapter covers grouping commands, which are used to (drum roll, please!) group commands. It also covers aliases, functions, and shell scripts, all of which can be used to automate complex interactions.

Grouping Commands

Grouping commands do exactly what their name implies: They group commands. Why would you want to do that? There are four basic reasons to group commands: First, to run a set of commands in a *subshell* so as not to alter the current environment; second, to redirect input and output from more than one command at a time; third, to execute a series of commands in the background; and fourth, to group commands to alter what occurs during conditional execution.

For these three purposes we have two different grouping commands, the curly braces ({ and }) and parentheses ((and)) . The difference between the two is that commands grouped with parentheses run in a subshell, whereas commands grouped with curly braces run in the current shell and have merely been grouped.

A *subshell*, as the term itself should make plain, is a shell that runs within the current shell. Although it inherits the environment from the current shell, including variables, the current directory, and the like, changes made from within that subshell do not affect the shell in which that subshell executes. Perhaps a simple example is in order:

```
[jon@frogbog jon]$ ( cd thinkunix ; pwd ; SOMETHING=nothing ; echo\
$SOMETHING ) ; pwd ; echo $SOMETHING
/home/jon/thinkunix
nothing
/home/jon

    [jon@frogbog jon]$
```

Clearly, changes to the subshell, in which the parenthesized list of commands is executed, do not affect the main shell being used in this case. When curly braces are used and no subshell is created, the outcome is different:

```
[jon@frogbog jon]$ { cd thinkunix ; pwd ; SOMETHING=nothing ; echo\
$SOMETHING } ; pwd ; echo $SOMETHING
/home/jon/thinkunix
nothing
/home/jon/thinkunix
nothing
[jon@frogbog thinkunix]$
```

In this case, no subshell is created, and any changes to the environment that occur within those braces persist in later commands.

The second use for grouping commands is to redirect I/O for that entire list of commands in one fell swoop. This works with either grouping command: We can `( cd /etc ; grep my-regexp * ; cd * ) 2> /dev/null` or `{ cd /etc ; grep my-regexp * ; cd * } 2> /dev/null`, and in either case STDERR will be redirected to `/dev/null`. Of course, redirecting STDIN and STDOUT both work as well.

Similarly, either type of grouping command can work to put an entire group of commands in the background. I could put long and automated commands in the background, such as `( cd /etc ; for foo in `find . -type d -print`; do ls -l $foo >> /tmp/my-data ; done ) 2>/dev/null &`. In this case, note that I would use parentheses so as not to affect my current shell. When a group of commands is put in the background, the shell immediately receives an exit status of zero, just as when a single command is backgrounded.

Sometimes, you want to alter what occurs when conditionally executing code. Most of the time this isn't necessary because the exit status for a group of commands is the status of the last command in that group, so `(true || false) && echo "true"` is equivalent to `true || false && echo "true"`. (Either of these statements will print the word "true" because the `false` command is never executed.) Sometimes, however, you might want to run the command `true || (false && echo "true")`, which will print the word "true" only if the first part of the statement is false and the second is true. (In this case, the word "true" is not printed because the whole subshell is never executed.) Although this is useful, in most of these cases it's better to rewrite your conditionals as a formal `if` statement.

Aliases and Functions

Using Unix sure would be inconvenient if you had to type long sequences of commands all the time. Fortunately, Unix provides several different features to save you typing. Or, if you prefer, you can type the same amount as you would otherwise but have the environment customized to work just the way you want it to work. The two basic ways of doing this are to tell the shell, "Whenever I type this thing, do all this other stuff," or to put everything you'd like to happen in a single file and let the shell execute that file. That first solution is, in Unix terms, to use aliases and functions; the other solution is to write a shell script, but one thing at a time!

Aliases

An *alias* is, not surprisingly, a command that stands in for another command. If you've been paying attention, you might have noticed that every time I run `ls`, it functions as `ls -F`, even when I use other options or arguments with the command.

That's because I have the following line in my `.bashrc`:

```
alias ls="ls -F"
```

The syntax is, you should note, remarkably similar to setting, or more precisely exporting, a variable. Consider the new, aliased command to be a variable that is being set to some existing command. Aliases are not interpreted recursively: You can't refer to other aliases within your aliased command. (If that was the case, the previous example would expand to `ls -F -F -F -F -F`, and so on, out to infinity. That wouldn't be very useful at all, and might even get in the way of productive work.) Anything typed after an alias on the command line is automatically appended to the expanded alias. Given my aliased `ls`, the command `ls -lR` would expand to `ls -F -lR`, an entirely satisfactory state of affairs.

As the previous example should make clear, the shell will execute an alias, when present, before executing a command stored on disk that possesses the same name. When I was busy switching my mail reader of choice from pine to the more powerful mutt, I found that I would nevertheless type `pine` instead of `mutt` due to long-standing habit. To help me switch mail readers, I added the line `alias pine="echo 'Run mutt instead!'"` to my shell startup scripts. Whenever I tried to run pine, I was instead presented with the message `Run mutt instead!`. Due to inertia, in fact, that command is still present in my `.bashrc`.

Getting rid of an alias is trivial. To remove my pine alias, I can simply run the command `unalias pine`. Just typing the command `alias` will display a list of all available aliases.

Functions

Functions are more powerful than aliases for two reasons. First, functions have access to *positional parameters*, variables that represent arguments typed on the command line. Second, functions can return an exit status to the programs that call them.

One simple function I have in my `.bashrc` is as follows:

```
function addtopath
{
[ -d $1 ] && export PATH=$1:$PATH
}
```

Clearly, the syntax for functions is more involved than that of aliases. Nevertheless, it's not too complex: The word *function* and the name of the function are followed by curly braces that contain any number of commands. The `$1` in the previous function is a positional parameter. It's a variable that cannot be altered by the user which contains the first argument to the command line. The second argument to the command line would be stored in `$2`, and so on. `addtopath` depends on one positional parameter, the name of a directory. If that directory exists ([-d $1]), it should be prepended to our current PATH.

Because the body of the function is enclosed in curly braces, that should suggest to you the fact that functions execute in the current shell environment, not a sub-shell. Any change made in the function persists after that function exits. This brings up the question as to how a function exits. The two basic ways that functions end are to simply reach the closing braces, as in the previous example, and to exit with the return command. By default, the return command exits the function with an exit status equal to that of the last command run, but any number can be appended to the command as an exit status.

Let's make up a function called lcd, short for loud cd, which will provide information when we try to change into a directory:

```
[jon@frogbog jon]$ function lcd
> {
> if[-z $1 ]
> then
>     echo 'You must provide a directory name!'
>     return 1
> elif [ ! -d $1 ]
> then
>     echo "$1 is not a directory."
>     return 2
> else
>     cd $1
>     return
> fi
> }
[jon@frogbog jon]$ lcd
You must provide a directory name!
[jon@frogbog jon]$ echo $?
1
[jon@frogbog jon]$ lcd tmp
[jon@frogbog tmp]$ echo $?
0
[jon@frogbog tmp]$ ls
Rollemup/ mozilla-M14/
[jon@frogbog tmp]$ lcd ..
[jon@frogbog jon]$ lcd tester
tester is not a directory.
[jon@frogbog jon]$ echo $?
2
[jon@frogbog jon]$
```

Note that, in the case where we cd into the directory, we don't explicitly return a status of zero. There are many cases in which cd might fail that we do not check for, such as inadequate permissions, and we should return that error code to our calling program.

Getting rid of functions is like getting rid of variables: Use the unset command. What if you have a function named test_thing and a variable of the same name? Use unset -f test_thing to unset the function and unset -v test_thing to unset the variable. unset test_thing will unset both the function and the variable of that name.

Practice Problems

1. Whenever I try to move files, I tend to type mc instead of mv. Create an alias so that this mistake won't slow me down.

2. Modify this alias so that it will warn me when I make this mistake.

3. Destroy this alias.

4. Create a function named mc that will move files after giving a warning. Assume that only one file will be moved.

5. Create a new function named vm that will move one file, but with the destination preceding the source.

6. Destroy both the function named mc and the function named vm. Take care not to destroy any variables of the same name.

Shell Scripts

Similar to aliases and functions, a shell script allows you to create a new Unix command out of shell commands and other existing Unix commands. Unlike aliases and functions, shell scripts are persistent across shell invocations: Because their contents reside in a file, they will not be lost on exit. To create persistent aliases and functions, you must place them in a shell script, probably one of the startup files I discussed in Chapter 7. If you were paying attention, you might have noticed that I actually called those startup files "scripts," and I even briefly discussed the source command, which I'll get back to in just a few moments.

Kinds of Shell Scripts

There are three basic ways in which you can run a bunch of commands stored in a file. Loosely speaking, all three could be termed *shell scripts*, although that term is usually applied only to the last of these three methods.

Sourcing Files

The first method is known as *sourcing* a file: You stick all the commands in a file and then tell the shell to read in that file, executing it one command per line, as though it were typed in at the prompt. To source a file in bash, csh, or tcsh, simply type *source my-file*. To source a file in ksh or bash, type *. my-file*: That's a single period, followed by a space and the name of the file to be sourced. Let's see how this works:

```
    [jon@frogbog jon]$ echo $MY_FAVORITE_BEER

[jon@frogbog jon]$ cat source-me
MY_FAVORITE_BEER="something special"
echo "Today we have $MY_FAVORITE_BEER on tap."
[jon@frogbog jon]$ . source-me
Today we have something special on tap.
[jon@frogbog jon]$ echo $MY_FAVORITE_BEER
something special
[jon@frogbog jon]$ cat source-me-too
echo "My favorite beer was $MY_FAVORITE_BEER"
echo "But I forgot what it was."
unset MY_FAVORITE_BEER
[jon@frogbog jon]$ source source-me-too
My favorite beer was something special
But I forgot what it was.
[jon@frogbog jon]$ echo $MY_FAVORITE_BEER

    [jon@frogbog jon]$
```

When you source a file, everything takes place within the current shell. Any variables set or unset will persist after the file is sourced. Sourcing a file is useful when you want to alter your current environment, as for example, in your shell startup scripts.

Using a File as an Argument to a Shell

If you run a shell on the command line, you may provide a filename on that command line. The shell will then read in that file and execute it, as shown previously. However, the script will be executed in a *subshell*: It will not be run in the current shell, but in another shell inside your shell. This means that variables set or unset in that script will not affect your current shell, unlike sourcing a script:

```
[jon@frogbog jon]$ cat dont-argue-with-me
MY_FAVORITE_BEER="a tasty Belgian-style red ale from Quebec"
export MY_FAVORITE_BEER
echo "My favorite beer is now $MY_FAVORITE_BEER"

[jon@frogbog jon]$ /bin/bash dont-argue-with-me
My favorite beer is now a tasty Belgian-style red ale from Quebec
[jon@frogbog jon]$ echo $MY_FAVORITE_BEER

    [jon@frogbog jon]$
```

This method is "cleaner" than sourcing files because any variables used by the script disappear automatically when you're finished. It is, however, somewhat less convenient than what most people mean when they use the term *shell script*.

Full-Blown Shell Scripts

This is what most people mean when they talk about shell scripts. It works identically to appending the script name as an argument to the shell but allows you to run your script exactly as you would any other program on the system. To do this, you prepend a line to the top of the script beginning with a pound sign, a bang, and the full path to the shell in which the script runs:

```
[jon@frogbog jon]$ cat bin/add
#!/bin/sh
# add adds a list of integers fed to it on STDIN one per line
# and prints the # result. Combine with awk or cut to achieve
# some useful functionality.

    SUM=0

while read THINGY
do
    SUM='expr $SUM + $THINGY'
done

echo $SUM
[jon@frogbog jon]$ add
3
5
7
11
Control-D
26
[jon@frogbog jon]$
```

The first line, `#!/bin/sh`, tells the system which program receives the rest of the script as input. This doesn't have to be a shell. Often, programming languages such as perl or tcl that run on Unix can execute programs fed to them in this manner. The next three lines are comments. When interpreting a script, any unquoted pound sign begins a comment, either at the beginning or in the middle of a line.[1] Always comment your scripts: Even a two- or three-line script might not be obvious six months after it's written. The rest of the script is a simple `while` loop, which reads input and adds numbers together, printing the result when no more input follows.

---

1. In bash, you can `set -o interactive-comments` to enable this feature when in a regular interactive shell; by default, the interactive-comments option is disabled.

This sort of shell script must be set executable. Remember to chmod +x these scripts before trying to run them. Because these scripts run in a subshell, you can't return a value. Instead, you must exit the shell and append an exit status to that, such as exit 1 to return an exit status of 1.

Reading Input

The read command is new for us. It's a pretty simple command. The word *read* is followed by any number of variable names. The shell reads in one line from standard input and assigns one word to each variable, in order. Any extra text is appended to the last variable, and if fewer words are input than there are variables requested, excess variables are set to null strings:

```
[jon@frogbog jon]$ TEST2=something
[jon@frogbog jon]$ read TEST1 TEST2
test1
[jon@frogbog jon]$ echo $TEST2

[jon@frogbog jon]$ read TEST1 TEST2
test1 test2 test3
[jon@frogbog jon]$ echo $TEST1
test1
[jon@frogbog jon]$ echo $TEST2
test2 test3
[jon@frogbog jon]$
```

The shell uses the IFS variable to determine what constitutes a word. IFS is short for Inter-Field Separator and is by default set to a space, a tab, and a newline, in that order. Any character contained in the IFS variable indicates a word break when present in a string. Therefore, tabs, spaces, and newlines all indicate a word boundary. (Newlines cannot separate words in the above example because the read command uses a newline to indicate the end of input.)

If you're interested in having the user pick an answer from a list, you can do this with the select command. Oddly enough, the select command is also a sort of loop command. You can look at it as a variant of the case command, if you want. This might be easier to see than to explain, so let's have a look:

```
[jon@frogbog jon]$ select FRUIT in apples pears cherries jellybeans
> do
>     if [ $FRUIT = "jellybeans" ]
>     then
>         echo "Jellybeans are not a fruit."
>         break 2
>     fi
>     echo "Your favorite fruit is $FRUIT, huh?"
>     [ -z $LASTFRUIT ] && LASTFRUIT=$FRUIT
>     if [ $FRUIT = $LASTFRUIT ]
>     then
```

```
>        echo "I like $FRUIT too."
>    else
>        echo "Myself, I prefer $LASTFRUIT."
>    fi
>    LASTFRUIT=$FRUIT
> done
1) apples
2) pears
3) cherries
4) jellybeans
#? 2
Your favorite fruit is pears, huh?
I like pears too.
1) apples
2) pears
3) cherries
4) jellybeans
#? 3
Your favorite fruit is cherries, huh?
Myself, I prefer pears.
1) apples
2) pears
3) cherries
4) jellybeans
#? 3
Your favorite fruit is cherries, huh?
I like cherries too.
1) apples
2) pears
3) cherries
4) jellybeans
#? 4
Jellybeans are not a fruit.
[ jon@frogbog jon ]$
```

What's going on here? The first word after the select is the name of a variable to be set to any of the words following in. After that, select functions like a while loop, requesting a number corresponding to one of the choices as input. When it receives a valid choice, it executes the block of commands between the do and the done, such as any other sort of loop. You can exit this loop with an EOF (a Control-D), or the program can break out of the loop with a break statement. The break statement will by default break out of the innermost control structure, the one most directly affecting the statement. In the above example, the break occurs within an if statement but we would like to break out of the select statement that contains the if statement. To do this, we need to tell break how many levels to break out of, which is two in this case. (If this doesn't make much sense to you, you're probably not a programmer and it probably doesn't matter. It's worth trying a few examples to figure out, though.)

Special Variables

When you are inside a shell script, there are several special variables at your disposal so that you can handle arguments on the command line. These variables are the positional parameters 0 through 9, which work identically in functions or shell scripts; @; and #. When you run a shell script, the variable # contains the number of arguments to the command line. @ contains all these arguments in a single string, separated by the first character of IFS, which is by default a space. The variable 0 contains the name of the script and 1 through 9 are the first nine arguments to the command line.

Let's look at a straightforward example:

```
[jon@frogbog bin]$ cat testthing
#!/bin/bash
echo "This script is named $0."
echo "Our full list of arguments is: "
echo $@
echo "And there are $# positional parameters."
echo "Our positional parameters are: "
echo "$1 $2 $3 $4 $5 $6 $7 $8 $9 $10 $11 $12 $13 $14 $15"
echo "Very interesting. Shifting by five."
shift 5
echo "$1 $2 $3 $4 $5 $6 $7 $8 $9"
echo "Does $@ change?"
[jon@frogbog bin]$ ./testthing one two three four five six seven eight
nine ten eleven twelve thirteen fourteen fifteen sixteen
This script is named ./testthing.
Our full list of arguments is:
one two three four five six seven eight nine ten eleven twelve thirteen
fourteen fifteen sixteen
And there are 16 positional parameters.
Our positional parameters are:
one two three four five six seven eight nine one0 one1 one2 one3 one4
one5
Very interesting. Shifting by five.
six seven eight nine ten eleven twelve thirteen fourteen
Does six seven eight nine ten eleven twelve thirteen fourteen fifteen
sixteen change?
[jon@frogbog bin]$
```

Note that when I try to echo $10 and above, it doesn't work. I can, however, use the shift command to renumber the variables. A single shift with no options will make 1 equal to what used to be 2, 2 what used to be 3, and so on. As you can see, this enables us to access more than the first nine parameters to the command.

Most often, positional parameters are used to specify filenames. More complex command-line interpretation might be best effected via the getopts command built into the shell. getopts is beyond the scope of this book, but quite worthwhile when writing shell scripts that require interpreting options on the command line.

Practice Problems

In many ways, this is the end of the book. Although there are still two chapters to go, those chapters are concerned with the GUI applied on top of Unix. Although we'll continue to work on the command line, we're just going to be adding individual commands to our knowledge. As far as basic Unix knowledge goes, this is where the train gets off. There's a lot more, to be sure, but most of it is obscure or undocumented, or more complex use of the tools we've discussed. In particular, we've barely scratched the surface of sed, awk, regular expressions, and shell globbing, but we've done quite a bit. Because this is the culmination of our command-line experience, some of these practice problems might be quite difficult. Mastery of these problems is indicative of very strong understanding of the system, and might take more than one try to get right.

Congratulations, in any case, on making it this far.

7. Create a script named act that takes the name of a single file as an argument. If that file does not exist or is not a regular file, print an error message and exit with an error status of 1. If that file does exist and is a regular file, feed it through both tac and rev, sending the output to STDOUT. Do not explicitly set an exit status in this case.

8. Modify act so that, if no filename is given or if the filename given is a single hyphen (-), accept input from standard input rather than a file.

9. Create a script named spaced-out that will read one line of text in from STDIN and echo it back to the user after replacing all spaces with underscores.

10. Modify spaced-out so that, if receiving input from a terminal, it will print a prompt before asking for a line of input. (Hint: Use the -t option for test and refer to our discussion of file handles in Chapter 3.)

11. Modify spaced-out so that it will continue to take new lines of input until it receives an end–of–file marker. It should only prompt for text one time, and the script need not read in all text before outputting modified text.

X Window System
Concepts

HARD LINKS • SOFT LINKS • REDIRECTION AND I
REDIRECTING STDERR • NAME LOOKUP • ROUTIN
READING MAIL VIA POP3 • VI AND REGULAR EXF
FILENAME GLOBBING VERSUS REGEXPS • INTERA
COMMAND-LINE EDITING • HISTORY SUBSTITUTIC
CONTROL • VARIABLES AND QUOTING • CONDI
EXECUTION • WHILE AND UNTIL LOOPS • ALIASE
FUNCTIONS • THE X WINDOW CLIENT/SERVER M
WIDGETS AND TOOLKITS • CONFIGURING X • PE
AND OWNERSHIP • USERS AND GROUPS • HARE
SOFT LINKS • REDIRECTION AND PIPES • REDIRE(
STDERR NAME LOOKUP • ROUTING READING MA
• VI AND REGULAR EXPRESSIONS FILENAME GLC
VERSUS REGEXPS • INTERACTIVE COMMAND-LIN
HISTORY SUBSTITUTION • JOB CONTROL • VARIA
QUOTING CONDITIONAL EXECUTION • WHILE A

10

Thinking
Like X

The standard graphics system for Unix is formally known as The X Window System and is known informally as X Windows (which for some strange reason really upsets some purists), and is known even less formally as X. I say it's a graphics system rather than a graphical user interface because in fact there isn't a single GUI built on top of X but many different GUIs that you can choose to use. No matter what GUI you choose, almost any X-based application will run just fine on it, though the look and feel might not be at all consistent with the rest of your environment.

This chapter is dedicated to helping you understand the design decisions that created this system and to giving you a quick look around the X Window System. Frankly, it's not worth the time it takes to teach most X applications because many are simply point-and-click menu-based interfaces. This chapter should get you comfortable with X, and the next chapter will teach you how to customize your environment.

What X Does Differently

If you're not already clear on the concept, you should know that X does things a little bit differently than either Windows or Macintosh. In particular, the X Window philosophy is "mechanism, not policy," and almost the entire design flows from that idea. Another idea is that X is *network transparent* and *client/server*. First we need a little bit of history, and then we can discuss what all of this means to you.

A Little Bit of History

The X Window System grew out of a 1980s MIT project known as Project Athena. There were two goals for the project: first, to discover how MIT should integrate computers into their curriculum; and second, to build a distributed computing environment for the MIT campus. Project Athena was started in 1983 and scheduled to run for five years. (Ultimately, the project was extended for another three years and finally shut down in 1991 after achieving many of its central goals.) What distributed computing environment really means is that anyone on the MIT campus should be able to get to any file, any machine, and any printer from anywhere. To do this, you needed a good network on campus, and software and hardware to support that network.

In 1984, the Macintosh was released, and, as part of Project Athena, the X Window System was created. Like Apple's Macintosh, X was designed to be a graphical system. Unlike Macintosh, the X design team was not staffed by a team of artists, and therefore it simply didn't look as nice. Furthermore, the Macintosh operating system was tightly coupled to the hardware, whereas the design of X was not.

Why wasn't the design of X closely tied to the computer for which it was designed? Simply, MIT didn't know what hardware would become available, or what hardware people at the university would design. Therefore, the X Window System needed to be designed to run on any graphical computer made available to the staff or student body of the university.

At first, of course, hardware support was rather limited. Nonetheless, the idea of a graphical terminal took hold. Rather than having one computer that both displayed CPU-intensive graphics and ran large, complex pieces of software, it might be more efficient to use one large, shared computer to do the calculations—our standard multitasking multiuser Unix server—and a separate machine to display the graphics. That separate machine wouldn't have to do much work. Like an old terminal, it would merely need to display whatever was sent to it by the main computer.

The X Window Client/Server Model

The division of tasks between two separate machines in this fashion is known as the *client/server model*, a now commonplace term in the computing industry. In the standard client/server model nomenclature, the *server* is the heavy-duty machine in the background, and the *client* is the machine responsible for display and possibly initial processing of data.

To illustrate the traditional client/server model, imagine a Web browser and a complex Web site, such as an e-commerce site. That site is the server, and your Web browser is the client. In fact, for many specialized applications the browser/server model has overtaken the traditional client/server model, which presupposes custom-written client software on a particular target platform (see Figure 10.1).

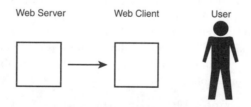

Web Server   Web Client   User

Figure 10.1

The traditional client/server model.

The X Window System reverses the traditional nomenclature of the client/server model: The *server* is the machine that displays the data (it serves the graphics), and the program that displays to said server is the *client* (see Figure 10.2). This means that on an X terminal or workstation, the big piece of software that runs to display stuff is called the X Server. This has been known to confuse professionals; just accept it and nod your head.

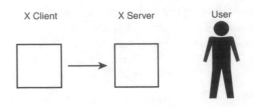

Figure 10.2

The X Window system client/server model.

It's very important to understand that the display you see might be of software running elsewhere or on the local machine: The X Window protocol is said to be *network transparent* because it acts the same regardless of how that data is conveyed. All of a sudden, though, we're talking about the X Window protocol. What does that mean?

The X Window protocol is a sort of language through which the client conveys what must be displayed to the server. It's a protocol in the same sense that SMTP, POP3, and HTTP are protocols: It's a set of rules and procedures through which the two systems communicate. In this case, that communication consists of instructions for drawing the screen.

Any machine that can interpret the X Window System protocol and draw the right things on a screen as a result is an X Server. That X Server can be a stand-alone machine that does nothing but draw windows (an X Terminal), a piece of software on a Unix box that does other things as well (an X workstation), or even a piece of software on a Windows or Macintosh computer. The client doesn't care what the server is, although it does know the resolution of the screen, number of colors, and so on. As with any piece of software that's more than 15 years old, X has evolved. The current version of the X Window System at the time of this writing is X11R6.4. That's X11, Revision 6.4. The revision is essentially a traditional software version number, and the X11 that precedes the revision means that it is version 11 of the X protocol.

Version 11 of the X protocol dates back to September 1987, making it well over 10 years old at the time of this writing. Because so many devices use the X11 protocol, it's probably never going to change again: Any change would create incompatibilities. As it stands now, any device created to support the X11 protocol over the last dozen or more years can serve graphics for any client created during the same time period. So if the core protocol doesn't change, how can new features be added to X? The X Window System was designed to be extensible, and one can load extensions on an X server. The client can discover what extensions are available and use them to improve performance or add features without breaking compatibility.

"Mechanism, Not Policy"

Extensibility, network transparency, and the client/server model are all crucial to the success of X, but few users will be immediately aware of any of these design decisions. One design decision most users recognize right away is "Mechanism, not policy." In short, X does not dictate appearance or functionality, only a method for getting stuff done. How everything looks and how everything works is up for grabs.

This has bad points and good points. First, the bad points. There is not a consistent look-and-feel across X applications in the same way that there is on the Macintosh and to a lesser extent on Windows machines. There isn't a consistent set of interface rules to follow or keys to press to achieve certain goals. There isn't even an entirely standard way to configure applications.

The good part about mechanism, not policy is that even as application interfaces change, the underlying system need not break compatibility: Even the oldest X Terminal can run newer software with whatever the new look is, although perhaps rather slowly. Furthermore, this strategy allows the system to evolve along with ideas about human-computer interaction in a way that other operating systems do not.

The Root Window

One piece of policy embedded in X is the idea of a window hierarchy: Windows are created and then owned by other windows. As with name servers and directories, the master window is the root window. The root window corresponds to the background of the screen. You can change some properties of the root window with the `xsetroot` command: `xsetroot -solid black` sets the root window to a solid black background, for example.

Window hierarchies are useful, as we'll see in the next chapter, because they make it possible to operate on groups of windows simultaneously. Keep this thought in the back of your mind for the time being because it might help to subtly illuminate certain concepts.

Nuts and Bolts

How does X sever mechanism from policy? First, the design of the X Window System enables programmers to use different widgets and toolkits to design their applications. Second, X enables the user to use any window manager to decorate and manage the root window and all subordinate windows.

Widgets and Toolkits

What's a widget? In the noncomputer world, the term *widget* refers to any little mechanical device or can be used in place of an actual device in a hypothetical situation. In a sense, it's a metasyntactic variable, like *foo*, for people who don't necessarily know what a metasyntactic variable is.[1]

In terms of the X Window System, widgets are all those little pieces that make up the GUI interface: scrollbars, menus, buttons, check boxes, text input fields, and so on. Even more easily than on Windows or Mac, developers on Unix can create their own widgets, although most will use any one of a number of prebuilt widget sets. Each widget set can have a completely different look, though in most cases all widgets in a given package of widgets are designed to look similar to each other.

The most common widget set is the *Athena widget set*. Created at MIT as part of Project Athena, these widgets are stark and utilitarian…that is to say, ugly. Nevertheless, because they're entirely standard, many X applications are designed to use this widget set. A slightly better looking variant on this set is the Athena 3D widgets, which provide a somewhat more modern look. Even these widgets are not too attractive. Several other drop-in replacement sets are available to make Athena widget applications look more like OpenStep, Windows 95, or other systems. Figure 10.3 shows xedit, an application that uses Athena widgets.

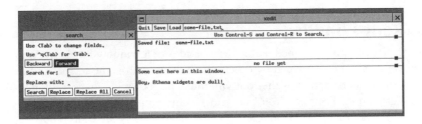

Figure 10.3

Another common widget set, available on almost all commercial Unix versions, ia the Motif widgets, which are similar in appearance to Windows 3.x controls. Because the Motif environment is distributed under a license that requires payment (that is, because Motif is commercial software), most Linux and free Unix versions don't include Motif. Some commercial vendors do sell these operating systems with Motif, but that's rather unusual. To compete with commercial Unix versions, a group of developers has created Lesstif, a Motif clone. Although it still needs work, Lesstif can replace Motif for many systems at present, with more support on the way. Because it is fairly standard, and because it looks better than the

---

1. There are, by the way, two actual devices called widgets: The first is that little plastic thing that holds razor blades, and the second is the thing inside a can of Guinness Stout that releases nitrogen into the beer when you open the can. Yum!

Athena widgets, many commercial Unix programs such as Netscape and WordPerfect are based on Motif.[2]

Widget sets often accompany or are accompanied by toolkits. Because X is such a massive and complicated environment, few programmers write applications for raw X. Instead, many toolkits are available that simplify the process of writing applications for the X Window System by handling much of the work. The X Toolkit is fairly standard, as it comes with X, but it's not the only solution: In addition to having custom widgets, Motif is a toolkit.

In fact, almost every widget set is paired with a toolkit, and vice versa. One of the newer toolkits that appears to be increasing in popularity is GTK, the GIMP toolkit. GTK goes a step further than most toolkits in that it's themable: you may install any number of themes that change the appearance of the widget set. Many themes are available for GTK, including themes that make GTK widgets look like Motif, MacOS, Windows, BeOS, and hundreds of themes just made to look good. Figure 10.4 shows *The GIMP*, an application that uses the GTK widget set's default appearance.

Figure 10.4

The GIMP, an application that uses GTK widgets.

These are far from the only toolkits and widget sets available for X, but they are the most common. The diversity of these components and the ease of creating additional such components are one of X's major strengths. Mechanism, not policy means that the system can evolve over time. After more than a decade and a half, people are finally writing X applications that look as good or better than those for other operating systems. Had the X Window System not been designed with this flexibility in mind, it would have been discarded years ago.

---

2. At the time of this writing, many of these applications are beginning to migrate away from Motif in favor of newer alternatives. This transition will probably take several years, however, and the Lesstif project ensures that Motif-based applications will run for the foreseeable future.

Window Managers

While widgets and toolkits vary between applications, window managers vary on a per-user or per-login basis, although most systems have a default configuration. Unlike Windows or Macintosh, the X Window System doesn't have a single way to iconify, move, resize, close, or even decorate individual windows. Window managers decorate windows, create menus, handle standard functions for managing windows, and manage virtual desktops. The first three functions are common to most if not all windowing systems, and the last of those is alien to the Windows and Macintosh worlds.

When you look at the windows on your system, it might not occur to you that they've been decorated. In Figure 10.5, we have two xterm windows running without any window manager at all. (The xterms are the white areas with the text in them; the stippled bars to the left of the windows are standard Athena widget scrollbars.) Without a window manager running, windows can't be moved, resized, iconified, or closed (except when they close themselves). On top of that, it's pretty ugly.

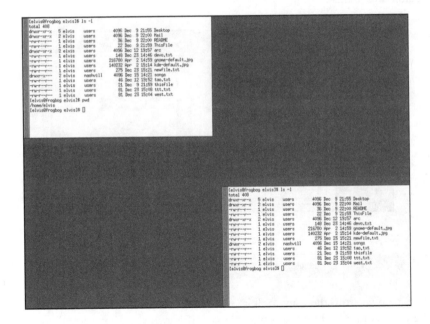

Figure 10.5

X Running without a window manager.

Most window managers also allow you to have a customized menu when you click on the desktop. Which button brings up the menu, if indeed a menu is available, varies according to your window manager; read your documentation for details. This menu is generally known as the *root menu*, although your window manager might have a different name for this menu.

At this point, it's worth mentioning (although you've probably already noticed) that X uses three mouse buttons, not the two of Windows or the one of MacOS. If your mouse has only two buttons, you might be able to emulate the middle button by clicking both buttons on your mouse simultaneously. If your mouse has only one button, you might be able to emulate the second and third buttons with key combinations; check your documentation for more details.

One feature not present on Windows or Macintosh systems, although it might be available with system enhancements, is virtual desktops. Virtual desktops allow you to keep several windows on one "screen" and allow you to switch between these screens. Not all window managers support virtual desktops, nor do any two window managers necessarily support virtual desktops in the same way. I'll be sure to note what sort of virtual desktops are supported in each window manager as I discuss it.

I will certainly not be able to discuss every window manager available: Dozens of different window managers exist. I will briefly discuss some standard window managers, some popular ones, and a few that have a claim to being particularly "Unix-like" in some way. Although most Unix distributions ship with only one or two window managers, many more are available on the Internet. Some pointers exist in Appendix B, "Glossary and References."

Standard Window Managers

Some window managers are more standard than others. In particular, *twm* and *mwm* are on almost every Unix system on the planet. twm is the Tab Window Manager, which accompanies the X Window System by default, and mwm is the Motif Window Manager, which accompanies that toolkit and is thus present on virtually every commercial Unix system. (Lesstif also includes a clone of mwm, so it is available on many Linux distributions as well.)

twm

twm, the Tab Window Manager, is the one window manager included in the standard X11 distribution. When a new window is created in twm, an outline of that window is displayed on the screen. That skeleton can be moved around and can be placed with a click of the first button, at which point the window will be placed on the screen. twm also allows you to create and edit menus by editing a `.twmrc` in your home directory. twm also allows you to iconify windows. Although twm does not support virtual desktops, a (nonstandard) variant named tvtwm supports them.

Unlike Windows and Macintosh, twm selects any window under the mouse pointer. That is, you must move the mouse pointer into a window to set the keyboard *focus*. This is known as *focus-follows-mouse* among people who care about differences between window managers. See Figure 10.6 for a picture of twm.

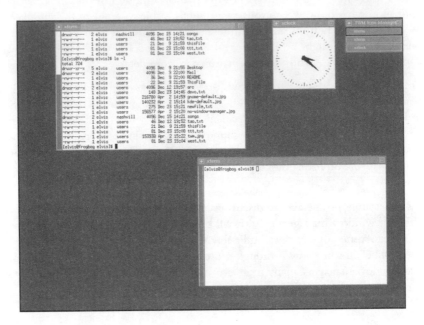

Figure 10.6

X running with twm.

mwm

The Motif Window Manager accompanies the Motif toolkit and widget set. Like Macintosh and Microsoft Windows, upon which its look and feel was based, it is a standard click-to-focus system. Similar to those systems, windows are placed automatically upon their creation. The appearance, including menu options, can be configured via a `.mwmrc` file in your home directory. mwm supports virtual desktops and displays a *pager* in one corner. To switch to a different desktop, click on the miniature view of it in the pager. Figure 10.7 shows Lesstif's version of mwm running.

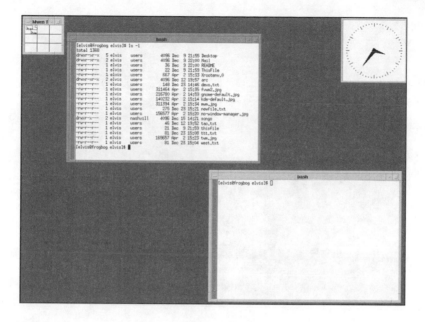

Figure 10.7

X running with mwm.

Popular Window Managers

For reasons involving history, taste, and any number of other hard-to-pin-down qualities, certain window managers have become enormously popular among that group of users who care enough to switch window managers in the first place. Two of these popular window managers are fvwm and Window Maker. In this section, we'll take a quick look at these window managers and try to note some of their special qualities.

fvwm

fvwm's name is shrouded in mystery: The man page says that the name is fvwm— F(?) Virtual Window Manager for X11, not exactly a particularly meaningful name. Originally based on the twm code, early versions were designed to look similar to mwm but with a more flexible configuration file. (Bringing this full circle is the fact that Lesstif's mwm is based on the fvwm code.) Its default look is similar to that of mwm, as can be seen in Figure 10.8.

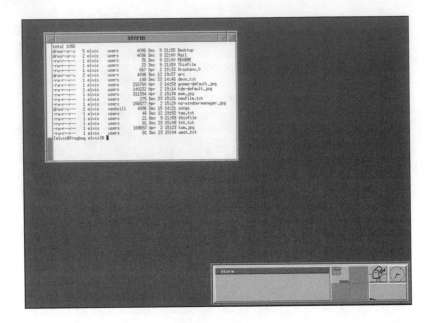

Figure 10.8

X running with fvwm, version 2.

fvwm achieved great popularity with early Linux distributions because it was one of the first full-featured window managers available for free. (The other contenders were twm and Sun's Open Look Window Manager [olwm], which has since fallen by the wayside. Lesstif had not yet been written, nor had the other window managers we shall discuss shortly.) The first version was relatively simple, quite small, and is still in use. Version two is more popular today due to many modular features available and an optional new look quite similar to that of Windows 95. This new appearance is known as fvwm95 and can be seen in Figure 10.9. fvwm95 is simply an alternative set of configuration files running on top of standard fvwm version 2.

fvwm offers one additional focus mode. *Sloppy focus* selects a window when the mouse pointer enters that window but does not deselect it until the mouse pointer enters another window besides the root window. This allows the user to select windows quickly and efficiently and then hide the pointer.

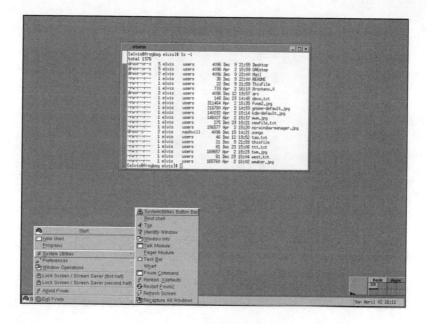

Figure 10.9

X running with fvwm95.

Window Maker

Window Maker (also known as WindowMaker and wmaker, the name of the executable) is a popular window manager that emulates the look and feel of the NextStep/OpenStep environment. (Another window manager, AfterStep, also emulates OpenStep and is based on the fvwm version 1 code.) Window Maker is fast and flexible, it looks good, and it supports just about everything that fvwm does. It can be configured either with a series of configuration files in the ~/GNUstep directory or with an included GUI-based application. The GUI-based configuration is simpler but somewhat less powerful than manual configuration. See Figure 10.10 for a picture of a default Window Maker configuration. (Window Maker supports themes that make it simple to significantly change its appearance.) Window Maker supports workspaces, which are essentially identical to virtual desktops, albeit with a different pager tool.

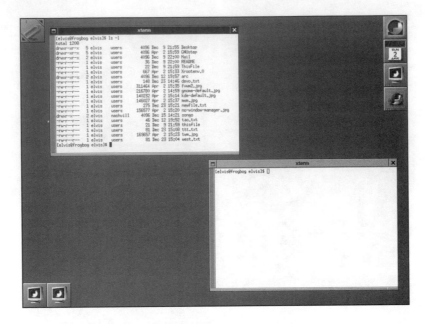

Figure 10.10

X running with Window Maker.

Unix-Like Window Managers

Some window managers seem particularly "Unix-like" for one reason or another. Some are incredibly flexible, and some are incredibly sparse. We're going to look ever so briefly at three of these window managers: Enlightenment, SawMill, and wmx, each of which has something noteworthy about it.

Enlightenment

Enlightenment, also known simply as E, is particularly Unix-like in its almost infinite flexibility: Almost every single aspect of the window manager is subject to alteration. Advanced users can create themes that mimic just about every other window manager or operating system down to the littlest detail. Much of it can be configured using a small GUI-based application, although writing themes is rather more work. Showing a running copy of Enlightenment doesn't do much good because it can look like almost anything; nevertheless, in the section on GNOME, shown later in Figure 10.15, a copy of Enlightenment is running.

SawMill

SawMill is a window manager that is similar to Enlightenment in its incredible flexibility. Not only can its appearance be altered with themes, but different windows on the same screen can run different themes. The whole shebang is configurable in Scheme, a variant of LISP, the same programming language through which Emacs can be configured. Figure 10.11 shows a fairly simple SawMill configuration.

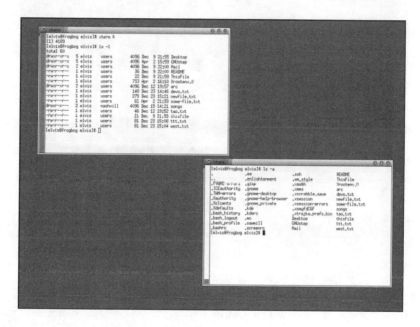

Figure 10.11

X running with SawMill's default configuration.

wmx

wmx is a very fast, very small window manager with a slightly unusual appearance: Window titles are displayed rotated 90 degrees along the left edge of each window, like file folders held sideways (see for yourself in Figure 10.12). Except for a simple menu, all aspects of wmx's configuration are done using a configuration file at compile time: All configuration information is built directly into the binary, and to reconfigure it the software must be rebuilt from source. If this sounds extreme, you might be surprised to discover that wmx is an enhanced version of wm2, which has neither a menu nor support for *channels*, wmx's virtual desktop feature. wmx is not especially popular, although if you're comfortable building software it might be worth a look.

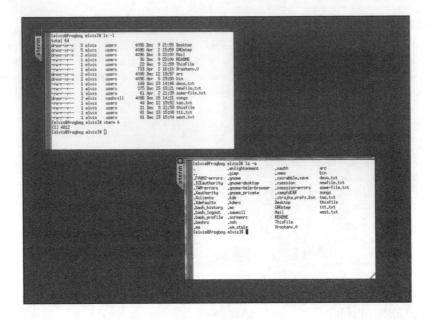

Figure 10.12

X running with wmx's spartan default configuration.

Desktop Environments

For some people, a window manager isn't enough: Some people prefer fully integrated environments that offer a more consistent user experience. The three most popular of these are CDE, KDE, and GNOME. We'll look briefly at each of these in turn.

CDE

CDE stands for Common Desktop Environment. It is built upon Motif and, like Motif, is only available commercially. Sun and Compaq (formerly Digital) ship CDE as the default graphical environment with their flavors of Unix, as do several other Unix vendors. Several companies offer versions of CDE for Linux as well.

CDE uses Motif for its window manager and adds an applications bar similar to that of Windows 95 along the bottom of the screen. This bar has some application buttons and menus available. Four different desktops can be accessed via the labeled buttons on the application bar. CDE also offers a calendar program, among other custom applications. Figure 10.13 shows CDE running.

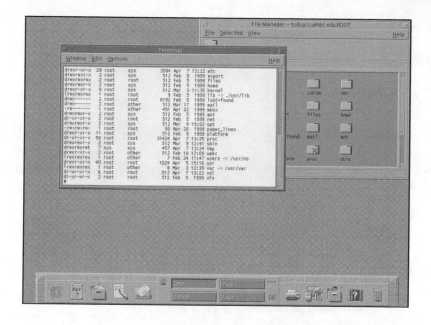

Figure 10.13

The Common Desktop Environment running on Solaris 2.6.

KDE

The *K* in KDE doesn't stand for anything, only a reminder that CDE served as something of an inspiration for this desktop environment. KDE offers the same basic features as CDE, along with dozens of applications that can be configured through the KDE control panel. KDE has its own custom window manager and can be seen in operation in Figure 10.14.

Although it is available for free, KDE is based on the semicommercial qt toolkit. Because qt's software license is controversial in certain open-source software circles, a number of users have kept their distance from this environment. Version 2.0 of qt has a less restrictive license that has eased this controversy, though the presence of another free desktop environment, GNOME, has kept KDE from becoming a de facto standard.

KDE offers many games and tools. In fact, a free office suite named KOffice is under development and promised for the end of the year 2000. Only time will tell if this deadline can be met, although, if it can it would be cause for some excitement.[3]

---

3. Other office suites available for X include Sun's StarOffice, Corel's WordPerfect Suite, and ApplixWare.

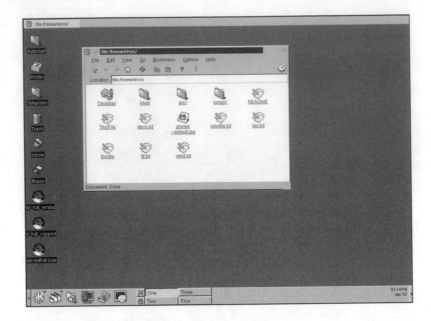

Figure 10.14

The K desktop environment.

GNOME

GNOME is another freely available desktop environment and is built upon the GTK toolkit. It lags behind KDE in some areas and leads it in others. If your system has both environments preinstalled, you might want to try both. (If neither is installed on your system, I note simply that building these large desktop environments is perhaps left to more experienced users and system administrators due to the size of the packages and the complexity of the process.) In general, applications from either environment will run fine in the other environment or in plain old X, though some features will probably not work right. Those features include drag-and-drop between applications and onto the desktop, but it seems that few applications support those features at present anyway.

GNOME offers a full-featured spreadsheet, gnumeric, and can use any one of several GNOME-enabled window managers, including Enlightenment, Window Maker, SawMill, and BlackBox. Over time, KDE and GNOME should offer better compatibility with one another, although it seems unlikely that they will ever become a single project. GNOME can be seen with the Enlightenment window manager in Figure 10.15.

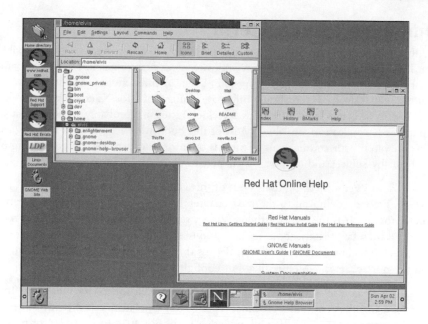

Figure 10.15

The GNOME desktop environment.

Why Many Users Avoid Desktop Environments

Many users, myself included, generally steer clear of desktop environments. They offer few benefits but take up vast amounts of memory and slow the system down. Mostly, the applications included with these environments run fine without all the extra weight of the massive infrastructure those environments depend upon. Furthermore, each of these environments has its own configuration method, which is generally less powerful and less flexible than the standard methods for configuration.

In short, many power users feel hobbled by desktop environments and feel that sufficient enhancement to the ease of use provided by the environment does not outweigh the loss of power and control. One measure of this brain damage is that each environment provides its own terminal program to replace the venerable xterm. None of these replacements is as configurable, stable, or functional as the original, although they may be simpler for novices to configure. Finally, many users feel that desktop environments are a waste of all-too-limited screen space.

Something Useful: xterm

All of this brings us to xterm, the one application that saw great use for probably at least the first 10 years of the X Window System's existence. For years, the standard X environment probably consisted of two or three xterms running in twm along with xclock, which simply offers an analog clock for X. (xclock can be seen in Figure 10.6 and Figure 10.7. It's the clock.) xterm is probably still the most popular X application available. (Most of this book was written in vi running in an xterm, often with another pair of xterms open on another desktop containing my subject-by-subject and chapter-by-chapter outlines of this book.)

So that you get something useful out of this chapter, I'll cover basic features of xterm before moving on to the next chapter. I will discuss some general xterm behaviors, such as the use of Athena Widget scrollbars and X's cut-and-paste mode, and I'll then talk briefly about menu options available in xterms. Although xterm is incredibly configurable, I will not discuss that now: Instead, I will talk about that in the next chapter, which is all about configuring X.

xterm is, of course, a terminal that runs in X, but what sort of terminal is it? In fact, xterm offers two basic terminal types: It can emulate a vt102 (with some vt220 enhancements), and it can emulate a Tektronix 4014 terminal. Most people use the first option because it's the default. The vt102 is probably the world's most emulated terminal, so most programs are written to take advantage of its feature set. The Tektronix 4014 was an older graphics terminal, but most graphics programs these days are written directly for X rather than for any particular graphics terminal.

The Athena Widget Scrollbar

X's scrollbar is by default along the left side of the screen rather than the right side of the screen as on MacOS and Windows. When the cursor is over the scrollbar, the left mouse button moves the scrollbar down toward the bottom of the screen, the right mouse button moves the scrollbar up toward the top of the screen, and the middle mouse button moves the scrollbar to the cursor's position. You need not grab the highlighted indicator on the scrollbar to move it, unlike many other operating systems. This is the behavior of any standard Athena widget scrollbar. Motif and GTK applications, among others, have more traditional PC or Mac style scrollbars.

Copy-and-Paste

Copy-and-paste is quite different in xterm and all standard X applications from the cut-and-paste familiar to PC or Macintosh users. To select text to be copied, simply hold down the left mouse button and select whatever text you want to copy. Next, move to the window where you would like that text to be copied and position the cursor. Finally, click on the middle mouse button and—voila!—your text has been copied.

Other features are available for selecting text to copy. To select one word at a time rather than a visual block, move your cursor over the word you would like to copy, and double-click with the left mouse button; to select the entire line, triple-click with that button. If you find that you would like to reduce or expand whatever text has been selected, use the right mouse button. To add text before or after your selection, simply move the cursor to the precise location outside your current selection and single-click the right mouse button. To remove text from your selection, it must be at either the beginning or end of your selection: There's no way to deselect text in the middle of your selection. Simply move the cursor to the point at which you would like the text to be removed and click the right mouse button. If the cursor is in the first half of the text that has been selected, X will deselect from the beginning of the block to your cursor location. If the cursor is in the second half, X will deselect from your cursor to the end of the selected block of text. Although it may take some getting used to, X's copy-and-paste feature is quick and powerful.

The Three Menus

xterm has three menus available. This is not surprising because the number of available menus in any given application seems to correspond rather closely to the number of available mouse buttons. Each menu is available by holding down the control key and clicking one of the buttons while the pointer is inside the xterm. Hold the mouse button down until you're finished. When the button is released, the menu disappears.

The menu I find most useful is the right-button menu, which allows you to change the size of the xterm font. Seven sizes are available, ranging from invisibly small to indisputably huge. Simply continue to hold down the control key and the right mouse button, move the pointer to your selection, and release the mouse button. All of a sudden, your font is a different size. Doing this may allow you to make your window larger to hold more text, or to make a smaller window more visible. Be careful. X will allow you to have a window larger than the screen, which can make things hard to handle.

The middle mouse button provides access to many features that can be either on or off. To switch the state of a feature, select it with the pointer and release the mouse button. The only features I tend to play with are Scroll to Bottom on Key Press and Scroll to Bottom on tty Output, both of which are rather self-explanatory. There are also terminal reset features available, in hard and soft varieties. The hard variety is particularly useful when one application or another has messed with your screen and you'd like to reset it to behave normally: Perhaps your text is constantly inverted or

Enter doesn't take you to a new line. In either case, a hard reset of the terminal might be your answer. (This is the equivalent of turning an old terminal off and on again.)

The left mouse button has several useful features, including options to redraw the window and switch between Sun and standard function keys. It also enables you to send several signals to the window and to secure the keyboard. Only this last option requires any special discussion.

Because X is network transparent, it's entirely possible for users to connect to your system and redirect your input elsewhere. The Secure Keyboard option makes sure that your input goes only to whatever is running inside that xterm. It will invert the text that you are typing while you're in this mode. In general, most systems now ship with X in a relatively secure state and few users ever switch into this mode. Nevertheless, it's there if you're interested. Read the xterm man page if you'd like further details.

There! You've (finally) learned something useful in this chapter and I can go on to the next with a clear conscience.

Suggested Exercises

1. Using the xsetroot command, try changing the background on your display to another color.

2. Figure out what window manager or desktop environment your system runs. There should be one or more processes with names that should give it away if it's not immediately apparent. If you still can't figure it out, read your documentation. Ask your system administrator or local guru only as a last resort.

3. Find out how to add menu options, if possible, in your window manager. Add something, just to prove you can do it.

4. See if you can switch to a different window manager or desktop environment. If you can't figure out how, don't worry: We'll discuss this in the next chapter.

5. Open two xterms. Change the font size and make sure that they both fit on the same screen. Open vi in each of them. Practice the copy and paste features, selecting different blocks of text and altering those selections.

HARD LINKS • SOFT LINKS • REDIRECTION AND I
REDIRECTING STDERR • NAME LOOKUP • ROUTIN
READING MAIL VIA POP3 • VI AND REGULAR EXF
FILENAME GLOBBING VERSUS REGEXPS • INTERA
COMMAND-LINE EDITING • HISTORY SUBSTITUTIC
CONTROL • VARIABLES AND QUOTING • CONDI
EXECUTION • WHILE AND UNTIL LOOPS • ALIASE
FUNCTIONS • THE X WINDOW CLIENT/SERVER M
WIDGETS AND TOOLKITS • CONFIGURING X • PE
AND OWNERSHIP • USERS AND GROUPS • HARL
SOFT LINKS • REDIRECTION AND PIPES • REDIRE(
STDERR NAME LOOKUP • ROUTING READING M/
• VI AND REGULAR EXPRESSIONS FILENAME GLC
VERSUS REGEXPS • INTERACTIVE COMMAND-LIN
HISTORY SUBSTITUTION • JOB CONTROL • VARIA
QUOTING CONDITIONAL EXECUTION • WHILE A

Configuring X

Now that you're familiar with the basics of the only X program that really matters, xterm, it's time to discuss why the X Window System is really better than anything available for Windows or Macintosh: Unlike those systems, X is almost infinitely flexible. Every aspect of X's behavior can be configured. As always, there is a learning curve involved. Most X programs can be thoroughly configured only after significant effort has been put into the process. There are two general ways to customize the X Window System: first, to customize what begins when you start X or log in, and second, to configure particular X applications. Although some recent X applications have graphical configuration tools, I won't talk about that because they explain themselves for the most part. What I will talk about are *X resources*, the configuration method used by applications based on the standard X toolkit and Athena widgets, as well as by other applications that choose to follow this standard.

X resources are notoriously difficult for users to understand and edit, although they really are much simpler than most users believe. Several tools exist to help use X resources, and I will discuss some of these briefly. I will also pay special attention to configuring colors and fonts, two of the most commonly altered resources, each of which requires a little bit of extra understanding.

Starting X

These days, most systems already have X started when you sit down at the machine and you log on through a graphical login program, such as xdm. On some systems, however, X does not start by default, and you must start it after you log in. In either case, X usually has a large number of defaults that are set for you by the system and a list of programs that are run for you by the system. Usually, you can override these defaults with dotfiles in your home directory, although exactly what files contain these defaults can vary depending on how you start X.

Login Using xdm

xdm is the *X Display Manager*. Although it can manage remote logins and complex environments, it is most often used to manage one display, usually the system console. xdm is also quite configurable, so anything I say about it might be different in your installation. Check your documentation or ask your system administrator for details. (I bet you're sick of my repeating that phrase by now. Don't worry, this is the last chapter, so you won't hear it too many more times!)

xdm starts by asking you for your username and password. After you've entered this information, the system might load some default X resources, on top of which it will probably install any X resources you've configured. Finally, the system will run a script that includes default programs to run, including your window manager. By default, that script will look for a script named .xsession in your home directory and run that instead, if it's present. This allows you to override system defaults and do things your own way.

X will log you out after the last command in your .xsession file has run. There-fore, if you create a .xsession file, the last thing you should do is exec your window manager, if you want to log out when you quit your window manager. Some peo-ple prefer to have a particular xterm that, when closed, will cause the system to log you out, but personally I find that confusing and dangerous. (If I have 10 or 12 xterm windows open, trying to figure out which one I can't safely close is a bad idea.) The reason you exec this window manager or xterm is simply because exec will exit the shell that runs through your .xsession file. This will save a process and its associated memory, although in reality it's no big deal.

Using exec to execute your window manager has other benefits as well. The bot-tom of my .xsession reads as follows:

```
# And run our window manager of choice
[ -x /usr/X11R6/bin/RunWM ] && exec /usr/X11R6/bin/RunWM
[ -x /usr/local/bin/wmaker ] && exec /usr/local/bin/wmaker
[ -x /usr/bin/X11/wmaker ] && exec /usr/bin/X11/wmaker
[ -x $HOME/bin/wmx ] && exec $HOME/bin/wmx
[ -x /usr/local/bin/wmx ] && exec /usr/local/bin/wmx
[ -x /usr/bin/X11/4Dwm ] && exec /usr/bin/X11/4Dwm
[ -x /usr/bin/X11/twm ] && exec /usr/bin/X11/twm
```

Because whatever command is run via exec will not return to the script afterward, I include a list of preferred window managers that, if present, are executed. Only the first present window manager is run, and when it exits, I am logged out of X rather than dropped into the next window manager. In this case, my first choice, /usr/X11R6/bin/RunWM, is a script included in Red Hat Linux that uses a file in your home directory to determine your preferred window manager. If that script isn't present, I look for a localized version of Window Maker, followed by a system default version. If neither of those is present and I have installed a copy of wmx in my home directory, I run that, followed by a systemwide version of that window manager. If neither of those is present, I will run 4Dwm, SGI's modified version of mwm, and if even that is absent, I will run twm, which is almost certainly present wherever I may be.

The other side of this coin is that any programs that you want to start in addition to your window manager must be started in the background so that the startup script will continue to run up through to the window manager. In my case, the portion of my .xsession file above my window manager selection code is as follows:

```
 # Things to run

# If we've got our background cycling program, run that.
if [ -x $HOME/bin/cyclebg ]
then
$HOME/bin/cyclebg &
# Otherwise, set up a pretty background, if it's there:
elif [ -e $HOME/mediabits/Irridescent-Slate-5.JPG ]
```

```
then
xloadimage -onroot $HOME/mediabits/Irridescent-Slate-5.JPG
else
# If we don't have that, just set up a nice plain background
xsetroot -solid black
fi
```

Except for my background-cycling script, which must run in the background, the
rest of this code doesn't execute in the background. It doesn't need to, because it
exits almost immediately. This allows the script to continue running:

```
# Set up screensaver
xset s off
xscreensaver -install -lock-mode -no-splash &

# Install some apps
(sleep 1; xdaliclock)&
xload &
[ -x /usr/local/bin/xfortune ] && /usr/local/bin/xfortune &
```

xset also exits immediately, and so it doesn't need to run in the background. In this
case, I use xset to turn off X's built-in screen saver, after which I run the xscreen-
saver program, which provides lots of nice eye candy and is highly configurable.

Finally, I run some additional programs in the background before moving on to
the window manager selection. Note that on some systems, I had problems running xdaliclock in the background right away and found it started better if I
delayed running it. To effect this without slowing down the rest of my startup procedure, I run it in a subshell along with a sleep command, and I run all this in the
background so that it doesn't slow down the rest of my X startup procedure. I
found that it solved my problem with relatively little effort. Although this problem
doesn't exist on most systems, and can even be fixed, I still haven't changed this. It's
no big deal, and everything runs fast enough that there seems to be no benefit to
risking the reappearance of the original bug.

Some systems have replaced xdm with a different display manager. CDE, GNOME,
and KDE each have a different display manager available at the system administrator's option. Most of the time, these programs obey user defaults in the same fashion as xdm does, though you should check your system's documentation for more
details. At any rate, many if not most sites choose to run the standard xdm instead
of these replacements, and xdm is the standard to which its replacements must
compare. Nevertheless, my remarks toward the end of the previous chapter about
desktop environment brain-damage still stand, and you might find yourself banging
your head against a wall trying to customize your X environment.

Starting X After Login

In contrast to starting via xdm, which works pretty much the same way across all
Unix versions, every version of the X Window System has a different way of starting

X from the command line.[1] X itself includes a program called xinit, which allows you to specify an X server and a client program. Generally, the default X server is correct, and you can put all the commands you want to run in a file in your home directory named .xinitrc. Because I always want to run the same programs no matter how X is started, I generally make .xinitrc a link to my .xsession file.

Because xinit is so bare, many systems provide a different program that starts X more nicely. These programs are generally named x11, xstart, or startx. The last of those is especially popular and is provided with all systems that use XFree86. It, too, uses the .xinitrc file as the user-provided startup script, though it has more sensible defaults if no such file is present. Some other systems use a .xclients or .Xclients file to provide the default startup script. I make this file a link to .xsession as well. I highly recommend having a single startup file for X, unless you actually want X to behave differently, depending on how you start it.

Many security issues are related to X applications' access to the display, and several technologies are used to manage these issues. Most modern X systems have sensible defaults with regard to security mechanisms, so we will not discuss this extensively. X Security is a particularly arcane topic and one few users ever need to deal with. I might mention particular details as we proceed, but as always, check the documentation if you have questions.

Command-Line Options

X programs, especially those based on the X Toolkit (known as *Xt* for short), generally have a more complex set of command-line options than most other Unix programs. Almost every one of these options has a counterpart X resource that can be used to provide a default behavior, but the command-line option will always override the X resource. We will examine options and resources for xterm, although most of these options will apply equally well to other programs using the X Toolkit. (All the programs included with X itself use Xt, and other X programs do so as well, including those based on Motif but not those based on GTK.)

The first thing you probably want to do to customize xterm is to change its colors. To start an xterm with green text on a black background, you can simply type xterm -fg green -bg black & in an extant xterm. We run xterm in the background so that it can run while we use the current terminal for other tasks. -fg allows us to

---

1. This seems as good a time as any to note that X is made available for free by a consortium and that each vendor is free to do as it wishes to that version. Each vendor must, at a minimum, create an X server customized for the video hardware in its workstation and alter the software so that it will build cleanly with that vendor's compilers. Many vendors, however, will change file locations, add additional software, change defaults, and so on. This includes changing how to start X using the command line, although in all fairness, the X Consortium version of X does not include a good way to do this. On the free Unix versions, there is somewhat more regularity because virtually all these install XFree86. XFree86 is a port of X originally intended to support all sorts of PC hardware, although it now supports several other architectures as well. Because XFree86 is available free of charge and builds easily on most systems, it sees wide use.

select the foreground color. We could use `-foreground` instead if we wanted to be clear about the meaning and type a whole lot more. Similarly, we could use `-background` instead of `-bg` to set the background color. To start an xterm with blue text on a yellow background (Ouch! The very thought hurts my eyes!), I could run `xterm -background yellow -foreground blue &`.

The second thing you probably want to change is the size of your window. You can do this using the `-geom` or `-geometry` option. To start an xterm 90 characters wide by 10 characters high, you would run `xterm -geom 90x10`. Because X is a character-based application, those measurements are in characters, but most X applications' geometry is measured in pixels: `xload -geometry 200x100 &` would run xload in a window 200 pixels across and 100 pixels high.

In addition to specifying the size of a window, the `-geometry` option allows you to specify the window's location, too. `xterm -geom +100-50 &` would start an xterm of the default size with its left edge 100 pixels from the left side of the screen and with the bottom of the window 50 pixels from the bottom of the screen. To start an xterm with the right edge of the window 75 pixels from the right side of the screen and with the top 45 pixels from the top of the screen, I would use a geometry of `-75+45`. These values are known as location offsets, and you can combine window size and location. To start a 40×10 xterm 20 pixels from the left side of the screen and 30 pixels from the bottom, I would run the command `xterm -geometry 40x10+20-30 &`.

The third thing you probably want to change is the default font. The `-fn` or `-font` option allows you to specify this. We'll talk more about fonts later in the chapter, but for now I will use the 6x10 and 7x14 fixed-width fonts included with X. To use the 6x10 font with xterm, you would simply run `xterm -fn 6x10`. For xterm, this controls the size of the font used for the terminal itself. Most other X programs use this font for the menu bar or informational displays because they don't have large quantities of text to display.

The `-title` option, for which no short name is available, allows you to specify the window title used on the window's title bar by most window managers. If I run `xterm -title "Jon's Special Window"`, the title bar on my xterm will read `Jon's Special Window`. This is useful if you have many login windows opened to different machines and want to distinguish them easily. One option of which I'm not especially fond, although some people are, is `-iconic`, which starts the program up minimized rather than as a window. After you de-minimize the window in your window manager, it will appear in its default location at its default size.

One option specific to xterm is `-sb`, which turns on a scrollbar. This is the default for xterm on most systems, which raises the question of how to turn off the scrollbar. The answer is rather counterintuitive: The `+sb` option turns off the scrollbar. Because the hyphen is used for normal options, the developers of X wanted to distinguish options to turn off features and chose to prepend those with a plus sign. They might have chosen to prefix the option name with a `no`, but they didn't. This is strange, and it will take some getting used to, but in the long term it makes no real difference.

The Display Option

One final option worthy of discussion is the `-display` option, which is common to most X programs. This is the implementation of network transparency, and you'll soon see that it's not all that transparent. `-display` allows you to specify the name of the display upon which the window with the program should appear.

On a machine with only one display, that display is usually `:0.0`, which means the first display and the first screen of that display. Each keyboard and monitor combination is typically one display, and if additional monitors are hooked up to a particular keyboard/monitor combination, those are considered additional screens. If the program displays its output on a different machine than the current one, place the machine name before the colon. If I were logged on to `razorback` from a window on `frogbog` and wanted to run an X program from `razorback` but have it display on `frogbog` so that I could use it, I would run it with the option `-display frogbog:0`. It's legal to omit the screen number if it's zero, the default.

Rather than run each program with the `-display` option, you can set an environment variable named `DISPLAY` to the correct default display. When you start X, the default is usually set to the name of the current display. The command-line option always takes precedence over the environment variable, so you can have a default that is easy to override.

Because the display can be any other machine on the network, there are clear security issues. It would be bad for anyone to be able to display their client on your X server because they could capture your keystrokes and get information from you that you'd rather keep private. To solve this problem, some sort of authorization is required for a client to get access to a given server. The less good solution is `xhost`, which simply gives all clients on a given host access to your server. `xhost frogbog` would give all X clients running on `frogbog` access to the current server.

`xhost` reverses X's already reversed conventions: If you specify a plus sign before the host name, that host gets access to the current display, and if you specify a minus sign, that host is denied access. Therefore, `xhost -frogbog` would deny frogbog's access to this display, whereas `xhost +frogbog` would grant access. If you're living dangerously, you can grant every host access to your display by running `xhost +`. *This is not recommended under any circumstances whatsoever,* but people always ask how to do it. Similarly, to deny from all hosts, you can run `xhost -`. This is more acceptable. After running this command, you can add particular hosts from which you would be willing to accept connections.

Even so, `xhost` is a bad solution. Because Unix is a multiuser operating system, it's difficult to guarantee that you want to grant every user on a particular system access to your X server. Instead, the `xauth` command gives you a way to grant access on a more particular basis, using authority files and magic cookies.

The bad news is that almost nobody, myself included, can be bothered with the complexity of xauth on a daily basis. Fortunately, X gives you access to the display from your default session. To run X programs remotely, the best solution is probably to use the X forwarding built into ssh. When you ssh into a remote host, ssh automagically sets the DISPLAY variable on the remote host correctly in such a way as to send all the X information through ssh's encrypted channel so that it can display properly on your local machine. For many users, this feature alone is worth switching to ssh from telnet or rsh and is how I recommend you run X programs remotely. All other methods are fraught with doubt and danger. Score one for network transparency![2]

Suggested Exercises

1. Figure out what startup scripts X uses on your system. If default startup scripts exist in your home directory, back up a copy of each of these scripts with a .dist extension so that you can restore the default configuration at any time.

2. Alter your personal X startup scripts to add a clock to your desktop. If a clock is present by default and xdaliclock is installed, switch your clock program to xdaliclock instead. If you don't have X startup scripts in your home directory, make them. Make sure you edit the right files for your system.

3. Alter your startup scripts to use a different window manager than the default, if more than one window manager is installed. If you don't like your new choice of window manager, switch back.

4. In your startup scripts, change the color of your background. If xloadimage or xv is installed on your system, try to put a picture in your background rather than just a color.

5. Start xterm with different foreground and background colors until you find a comfortable configuration.

X Resources

Often you want a given program to start the same way every time unless you override it with a command-line option; that is, you want a sensible default behavior. The standard method of setting these behaviors is to set some X resources.

Just as directories and domain names form a hierarchy, there is a hierarchy of X resources. This hierarchy mirrors the widget hierarchy. In fact, many resources are bound to particular widgets and can thus be configured on a widget-by-widget basis. Many applications don't create all their widgets at once, but only as necessary. Figure 11.1 displays an xterm widget hierarchy where the only widgets created beyond the startup values are in the font selection menu. Each widget listed in that hierarchy has resources associated with it. You can think of this as though each

---

2. Please read the note in Chapter 4 regarding the legal issues surrounding ssh before switching to it.

widget were a physical object, with various attributes or qualities. Unlike a physical object, there are a limited number of such attributes, and they can often be modified. *editres*, the tool used to display the widget hierarchy in Figure 11.1, allows you to change the resources for a widget while the window is live. Figure 11.2 shows the resources available for that widget.

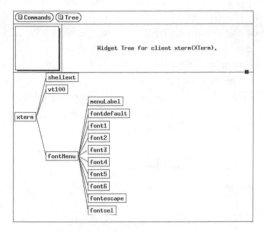

Figure 11.1

A partial widget hierarchy for xterm, displayed via editres.

Figure 11.2

The resources available for xterm's font menu, via editres.

If you set the background resource for the xterm font menu, that would change the background color only for that font menu.

Specificity and Order of Evaluation

To fully specify a particular resource, you would start with the top widget name and progress down the tree, ending with the name of the particular resource. That is, the full name of the resource that represents the background for the font menu is xterm.fontMenu.background. Sometimes, however, you might want to change more than one resource at a time. If you wanted to change the background not only for the font menu but for all menus and for the VT100 window, which is the terminal itself, you could change the resource xterm*background. In this case, the background resource for any widget in the xterm widget tree would be set whenever you changed the value of the resource.

Customized values for X resources are stored in the file .Xdefaults in your home directory. Entries in that file look like this:

```
xterm*background: WAYDARKBLUE
xterm*foreground: Green
xterm*scrollBar: true
xterm*reverseWrap: true
```

Here I set the foreground and background colors for all widgets in the xterm tree, turn on the scrollbar wherever necessary, and set the reverseWrap option, which is documented on the xterm man page. However, to change the default font for only the VT100 window but not menus, I need to be more specific in my resource setting:

```
xterm*SimpleMenu*font: -b&h-lucida-medium-r-normal-sans-*-120-*-*-p-*-*-*
xterm*VT100*font: 7x14
```

In this case, the VT100 font is set separately from the SimpleMenu font. The SimpleMenu widget is a widget that doesn't refer to any object on the screen but from which the different menus are derived. Any of the other menus will take on properties assigned to xterm's SimpleMenu widget.

SimpleMenu is a standard widget in the Athena Widget set. If I wanted to set the SimpleMenu font for all menus derived from this widget in all applications, I could set

```
 *SimpleMenu*font: fixed
```

In this case, the asterisk stands in not only for intermediate widgets in the hierarchy, but for top-level widgets (that is, windows or applications) as well. What if I had an application whose top-level resource was named SimpleMenu and I wanted to set its default font differently from the other SimpleMenu widget fonts? I could specify that SimpleMenu was a top-level widget by prepending a period:

```
 .SimpleMenu*font: 6x10
```

There is, of course, a notional root widget specified by an empty string before this period. That way, there's a whole tree of widgets, just like directories or domain names, and it has a root, just like both of them. In practice, the root widget hardly matters because it has no properties of its own: Setting .background would have no effect.

I could have specified xterm.VT100.font because there are no other widgets in the tree that can be substituted, but I tend to set widgets as generally as possible. In fact, in the previous example, I could set xterm*SimpleMenu*font to one value and xterm*font to another value. The menus would always use the correct font, from the SimpleMenu*font resource. How does the system know to do this? It knows because *the most specific resource setting always takes precedence.*

What's the most specific setting? It's simply the setting with the first period in the name closest to the beginning, or with a more precise widget name than other apparently applicable widgets. For example, *background is as nonspecific as a resource can get and will be overridden by anything with a widget name to the left of the asterisk, such as xterm*background. This resource, in turn, can be overridden either by xterm.VT100*background or by xterm*SimpleMenu*background, and so on. Whatever is most precise will take precedence. This allows you to have very vague general defaults: *font: fixed simply means "Use the fixed font unless I say otherwise," and xterm*font: 7x14 means "Use the 7x14 font for xterm unless I say otherwise." By this measure, xterm.VT100.font and xterm.FontMenu.font are saying otherwise.

Another way to measure specificity is to imagine how far to the right that resource would appear in the widget tree. What actually happens is that the tree sets the resources, and the resource manager traverses the tree. Each time a widget is used, the resource manager starts at the top of the tree and resets the resource to the given value each time it moves to another branch of that tree. When it finally reaches the end, the value of the resource is whatever the last thing that was interpreted in the tree.

Where do you find what resources are good to set? Somewhere in your system's installation of X is an app-defaults directory that contains some default resources for different applications. (On my Red Hat system, this directory is /usr/X11R6/lib/X11/app-defaults.) These resources all begin with an asterisk; the system prepends the top-level widget name. In most cases, the top-level name is that of the executable, although that might be set differently in a given application. (You can override the default name with the -name command-line option.)

Certain widget names are common to all widgets of a given type from a given widget set. All buttons or text boxes in the Athena widget set have a .label resource that specifies the text label for that widget. The simplest, and often the best, way to discover good resources to set is to read the man page for the given application. Most X application man pages have a Resources section that describes

X resources specific to the application. (Few, if any, man pages list all the standard Athena widget resources. Some of those can be found on the man page for X itself, along with the standard X Toolkit command-line options.) The editres tool is also invaluable for these situations, though it takes some getting used to.

xrdb

xrdb is the program that is used to interpret X resources. (Its name is short for *X Resource DataBase*.) The normal use of xrdb is to specify a filename that contains a list of X resources. By default, all X resources are overwritten by the contents of that file. (If no filename is specified, the data is taken from STDIN.)

The default is equivalent to the `-load` option. If the `-override` option is used instead, resources from the given file will replace extant resources. `-merge` is a little bit scary, in that it does its best to merge current resources with extant resources. To me it seems somewhat unpredictable, so I recommend sticking with `-override` instead. Finally, `-remove` will remove the resources listed in the file.

xrdb and cpp

Earlier, you might have noticed that I had the following resource set:

```
xterm*background: WAYDARKBLUE
```

In fact, WAYDARKBLUE is not an actual color supported by X. (I'll talk more about colors later in the chapter, but for now just take my word on this.) Because I want to use a nonstandard color as a background in many situations, I found that the easiest way to set this color was to put the following command up near the top of my .Xdefaults file:

```
#define WAYDARKBLUE #000033
```

This line means that whenever xrdb encounters the word *WAYDARKBLUE*, it's replaced with #000033, which represents the particular color I like using. (Again, you'll have to take my word on this for now.) This define statement is interpreted by the C Preprocessor (cpp). Whenever xrdb loads X resources, it passes them through cpp unless told to do otherwise.

What's the C Preprocessor? Put simply, it's a simple language, like a shell programming language but even simpler. It allows you to define symbols and act upon those definitions. The preceding #define statement defined WAYDARKBLUE to be equal to the value #000033. cpp doesn't care what that value represents, nor does it care what the program eventually does with that information. It simply takes input, processes it according to a small number of rules, and produces output: It's a filter.

Besides #define, there are a few other commands that we care about. Up near the top of my .Xdefaults file, I have the following command:

```
#ifdef COLOR
*customization: -color
#endif
```

What this statement means is that, if COLOR is defined, set the resources listed between that #if and the #endif. Just as every sh if statement must end with an fi, every #if, #ifdef, and #ifndef statement must end with an #endif.

#ifdef processes the text if that parameter is defined at all; it doesn't care whether it's set to something specific or merely set. (You can define a variable with a #define whatever, without providing a particular value for that define.) #ifndef processes the text if that particular variable is not defined. Finally, #if lets you do numerical comparisons. In my .Xdefaults, I have the following code:

```
#if HEIGHT == 768
xterm*font: 7x14
xterm*font1: 5x7
xterm*font2: 6x10
xterm*font3: 7x13
xterm*font4: 8x16
xterm*font5: 10x20
xterm*font6: 12x24
#elif HEIGHT == 600
xterm*font: 6x10
xterm*font1: 5x7
xterm*font2: 5x8
xterm*font3: 6x9
xterm*font4: 7x14
xterm*font5: 8x16
xterm*font6: 10x20
#elif HEIGHT == 1024
xterm*font: 7x14
xterm*font1: 5x7
xterm*font2: 6x10
xterm*font3: 7x13
xterm*font4: 8x16
xterm*font5: 10x20
xterm*font6: 12x24
#endif
```

xterm supports seven different fonts through the font menu we mentioned in the previous chapter. font is the default font, and font1 through font6 are the fonts available on the menu from top to bottom. xrdb automatically defines the HEIGHT variable to be equal to the vertical resolution of the screen. (That is, the number of pixels from top to bottom on the screen.) I like to set my font sizes based on the resolution of my screen.

In this case, I have different fonts selected for various common screen resolutions (1024×768, 800×600, and 1,280×1,024), separated with `#elif` statements, the equivalent of the Bourne Shell's `elif` statement. If none of these resolutions is correct, the default values provided by the system are accepted. Similarly, I like to define the size of my window based on the size of the display:

```
#if HEIGHT == 768
xterm*VT100*geometry: 80x35
#elif HEIGHT == 600
xterm*VT100*geometry: 80x25
#elif HEIGHT == 1024
xterm*VT100*geometry: 80x45
#endif
```

Note that, in this case, I must specify that the geometry is for the `VT100` widget hierarchy. Had I specified merely `xterm*geometry`, I would have defined the size of all three menus to be 80 by however many pixels because the menu widget geometry is measured in pixels, but the menu widget can inherit the `xterm`'s geometry, which is measured in characters. (In fact, when I was new to X resources, I made just this mistake. It took me weeks to discover what I'd done wrong.)

`COLOR` and `HEIGHT` are far from the only symbols defined by xrdb and cpp. (In fact, xrdb specifies a large number of definitions on the cpp command line, in which they're actually defined. If you think about it for a few minutes, it will make sense.) To see all the values defined by xrdb, simply run the command `xrdb -symbols`.

Because I want to define some additional values when I run xrdb, I use the following command in my `.xsession` to run xrdb:

```
xrdb -load $HOME/.Xdefaults -DHOSTNAME=`hostname | \
cut -d . -f 1` -DUSERNAME=$USER
```

This defines `HOSTNAME` to be equal to the short hostname of the machine and `USERNAME` to be equal to my username. All this allows me to have useful defaults for my xterm title bar and icon name, even as I move my `.Xdefaults` from system to system:

```
xterm*title: USERNAME@HOSTNAME
xterm*iconName: HOSTNAME
```

I'm a big fan of having the same configuration files everywhere, and xrdb allows me to do this, especially with a handful of extra definitions.

Unfortunately, cpp is quite simple, and you can't compare strings. It would be dreadfully convenient to say, "If this is my hostname, do this other stuff, but if it's that, do that other stuff instead." You can rig this by running xrdb using a shell script that sets variable definitions based on those conditions, but you can't test them directly. This is quite unfortunate, in my opinion, but it's probably never going to change: cpp has remained more or less constant for years.

Suggested Exercises

6. Change your default xterm colors to the color combination you favored in exercise 5 earlier in this chapter.

7. Change the number of lines in your xterm scroll buffer. (Hint: Read xterm's man page to find the name of the appropriate resource.)

8. Change the colors for xcalc to match your default xterm color scheme.

9. Use editres to examine the available resources for an xterm. Change the foreground color of an active xterm using editres.

10. Look at the editres `app-defaults` file. Customize the appearance of editres to make it look nicer.

11. Add the `*customization: -color` resource if COLOR is defined. See how this affects the appearance of editres and other X applications.

12. Change the size of your xcalc window based on the *horizontal* resolution of your display.

Color Names and Numbers

Because X is a framework for graphical environments, color is important. We like to color-code displays of information so that we can have important information simply jump out at us. To work with colors, we must be able to specify particular colors. To work with realistic tones, we must be able to specify shades of colors more specific than blue or green. In X, there are several standard ways to specify colors, including device-independent color specifications that are used by few, if any, users. The most common scheme to specify colors is to use the RGB color model, which we will look at in more detail.

The RGB Color Model

Most people who use computers know that every pixel on the computer screen is made up of three elements: a red element, a green element, and a blue element. Any color that can be displayed on a CRT or LCD must be expressed as a value for the red portion, the blue portion, and the green portion of the pixel. The brightest, purest blue would be the blue pixel at 100% brightness and the green and red pixels at 0%. (Actually, the red, green, and blue portions of each pixel are really subpixels, but I may refer to them as pixels in this discussion for convenience.)

With 100% defined as 1.0 and 0% defined as 0.0, you can specify an RGB intensity specification as `rgbi:red/green/blue`. A pure red would be specified as `rgbi:1.0/0.0/0.0` and a medium gray would be `rgbi:0.5/0.5/0.5`.

The intensity model is only one of the options. More common are *scaled* colors. Because computers are digital, there is not the infinite gradation implied by the use of intensity numbers. Instead, each of those percentages must be turned into a number. Generally, colors in X are 24-bit values, which implies an 8-bit (one byte) value for each of the elements.[3] These 8-bit subvalues range from 0 to 255, as do all 8-bit values, but are expressed in hexadecimal. Pure green, therefore, would be expressed as `rgb:00/FF/00`, and that same medium gray expressed earlier is `rgb:80/80/80`. The RGB color model allows you to specify each scaled value from one to four hexadecimal digits, as long as each of the red/green/blue values for a given color share the same number of bits.

Old-Style Color Numbers

Back in the old days, before the presence of multiple color models in X, a color was simply specified as a hexadecimal number preceded by a hash sign. You can see this in my color definition from the previous example:

```
#define WAYDARKBLUE #000033
```

The pairs of hex digits in this 24-bit value are in the same order as in the above; only the notation differs. These values can also be from 12 to 48 bits, in multiples of 12, as in the newer RGB notation. This color, `#000033`, has no red or green in it, and only a little blue. How much blue? 33 out of FF. Converted to decimal, this is 51 out of 255, which is equal to 0.2, or 20%. In the new color model, this could be expressed as `rgb:00/00/33`, and in the color intensity model, it would be `rgbi:0.0/0.0/0.2`. I'm too lazy to update this, and I am somewhat wary about how older machines would deal or fail to deal with this, so I leave the number in the old-style scheme, at least for the moment.

Color Names: `rgb.txt`

Fortunately, we don't have to think of colors as numbers alone: The X Window System gives us a simple method of converting color numbers to names. Somewhere on your system is a file named `rgb.txt` (this file should be in the directory `lib/X11` relative to X's top-level directory). On my Red Hat system, this file's absolute path is `/usr/X11R6/lib/X11/rgb.txt`, although this might well differ on your system.

Let's take a look at a small portion of this file:

```
255 218 185 peach puff
255 218 185 PeachPuff
255 222 173 navajo white
```

---

3. In fact, many, if not most, displays are not 24-bit displays. More common are 8-bit displays, which use colormaps that use a palette—a specified subset of colors—in a given window. Also common are 32-bit displays, which generally comprise a 24-bit display and an 8-bit "alpha channel," which is displayed on top of or which somehow modifies the underlying 24-bit display.

```
255 222 173 NavajoWhite
255 228 181 moccasin
255 248 220 cornsilk
255 255 240 ivory
255 250 205 lemon chiffon
255 250 205 LemonChiffon
255 245 238 seashell
240 255 240 honeydew
245 255 250 mint cream
245 255 250 MintCream
240 255 255 azure
240 248 255 alice blue
240 248 255 AliceBlue
```

Several things are worth noting here. First, color names translate to 24-bit colors. Second, these color numbers are described in base 10 rather than base 16—why colors, which are represented in hexadecimal everywhere else in X, should be represented in decimal here is a mystery to me—in a format not quite identical to any other color description. Third, one color can possess multiple names. Note that colors whose names are one word have names that appear all in lowercase; colors whose names are two words have two names each. One name is each word lowercase, separated by a space. The other is a compacted form wherein the first letter in each word of the name is capitalized and all spaces have been removed.

There's not a whole lot more to say about color names. I highly recommend looking through the rgb.txt file to see what colors are available. Pay special attention to the shades of gray because it's convenient to refer to percentage grays.

Fonts

The font situation in X is even more complicated than the color situation. Many font formats are available, and X supports quite a few of them. Much of this support is on the administrator's side of things, so we won't cover it. What you must understand is how fonts are named, how to find the fonts available on your system, and how best to access particular fonts.

X makes working with fonts difficult because the available fonts must be installed on the server, not on the client: They must reside on the machine displaying the text rather than on the machine that is running the given program. One of the solutions to this problem is to run a *font server* on the network, from which all servers that require a given font may acquire it. This has led to no end of security problems, and the most common solution these days is to install fonts everywhere, and often to run a font server on every machine. From a user perspective, this is usually transparent. Sometimes, however, fonts aren't present where they should be.

Another problem is that different X distributions all seem to include different font sets. This too causes no end of headaches when trying to run clients on a machine other than the server and while sharing X defaults among different systems.

Listing Fonts

The simple way to list fonts is to run the program xlsfonts, which displays all fonts installed on the system when run without any options or arguments. Fonts can be named several different ways. Let's examine some output from xlsfonts. (This output is not necessarily in the order in which it would appear but as it is convenient for us to learn.)

```
[jon@frogbog jon]$ xlsfonts
. . .
10x20
12x24
5x7
5x8
6x10
6x12
6x13
6x13bold
6x9
7x13
7x13bold
7x14
7x14bold
8x13
8x13bold
8x16
9x15
9x15bold
. . .
```

These particular fonts are all monospaced fonts at a particular pixel size. 10x20 is 10 pixels wide by 20 pixels high, 5x7 is five pixels wide by seven high, and so on. Some of these fonts also have bold variants. All fonts used for display by xterm must be monospace fonts. These fonts are not only monospace fonts, but *bitmapped*: They are stored in the system on a pixel-by-pixel basis. If requested, the system will try to *scale* the fonts and use them at a size other than their physical resolution, but these fonts look blocky and jagged and are quite ugly as a result at any size other than their default.

Not all bitmapped fonts are monospace fonts. Some are *proportional* or *variable width* fonts:

```
[jon@frogbog jon]$ xlsfonts
. . .
lucidasans-10
lucidasans-12
lucidasans-14
lucidasans-18
lucidasans-24
```

```
lucidasans-8
lucidasans-bold-10
lucidasans-bold-12
lucidasans-bold-14
lucidasans-bold-18
lucidasans-bold-24
lucidasans-bold-8
lucidasans-bolditalic-10
lucidasans-bolditalic-12
lucidasans-bolditalic-14
. . .
```

These fonts are a particular number of pixels high, but each character in the font might be a different number of pixels wide. Most books are produced in proportional fonts because they are nicer for reading.

All these are short names for fonts; most fonts also have long names. Long names for X fonts look like this:

```
-adobe-times-medium-i-normal-12-120-75-75-p-63-iso8859-1
-b&h-lucida-medium-i-normal-sans-10-100-75-75-p-59-iso8859-1
-schumacher-clean-bold-r-normal-10-100-75-75-c-60-iso8859-1
-urw-palatino-bold-r-normal-0-0-0-0-p-0-iso8859-1
```

The hyphen at the beginning of a long font name is not optional. This hyphen is followed by the name of the font foundry, the company that produced this font. In these examples, the font foundries are adobe, b&h, schumacher, and urw. After another hyphen, the name of the typeface follows. In the examples, the typefaces are times, lucida, clean, and palatino. After another hyphen is the *weight* of the font, which in all the previous fonts is either medium or bold, although font weights can also be light or another value.

After another hyphen comes the *slant* of the font, which is usually r, which stands for *regular*, or i, which stands for *italic*. Next is the width, which is almost always normal, and an additional style, which is almost never used. Next come several values representing the size of the font. First is the size in pixels and then the size in points (one point is 1/72 of an inch). Pixel sizes are generally more useful because point sizes are not necessarily calibrated how one might expect. In theory, pixel size is device dependent, and point size is device independent. Don't ask me what this really means; I'm not sure anyone knows.

Next are the horizontal and vertical resolutions. These resolutions are for the display and are usually 72, 75, or 100 dots per inch. Few if any fonts have different horizontal and vertical resolutions, so the inclusion of both is at least somewhat surprising. After this is the spacing, which is P for *proportional*, M for *monospaced*, or C for *cell*. The difference between cell and monospaced fonts is that the latter theoretically have no restrictions other than fixed width. In practice there's no difference. This field is really just informational because few if any fonts are available in more than one of these flavors.

Next is the average width of the font, in points—another virtually useless field—and finally are the registry and encoding. The registry should tell the system what kinds of characters are included in the font, and the encoding is a sort of subregistry that tells the system what particular characters are included. This allows you to have a generalized encoding and a more specific encoding.

Outline fonts are stored not as a series of pixels but as a set of instructions on how to draw them. These fonts can be displayed at any size, but are more likely to look odd at particularly small sizes and low resolutions. Fonts in which all the size and resolution numbers are zero are outline fonts, such as urw palatino, shown earlier.

Finally, X font strings support wildcards. You can fill in with an asterisk any field for which you choose not to supply information. For example, if you have the Palatino typeface supplied by only one foundry, an asterisk in the foundry field is irrelevant because it can be replaced by only one foundry name. If, however, you have this typeface supplied by more than one foundry, an asterisk in this field is the equivalent of saying "I don't care," which is rather unlikely to produce ideal results. For example, an asterisk in the slant field means that, if the font exists in italic and upright variants, the italic variant will be selected. Also, any font name using wildcards should be quoted in most circumstances, to inhibit interpretation of the wildcard by the shell or other applications.

All this is rather complicated. The quick route to enlightenment is probably to start xfontsel, pictured in Figure 11.3, and to alter values until you get an intuitive feel for what's going on. xfontsel allows you one additional useful feature: If you want to use a font string for the font displayed, you can click the select button and use the middle mouse button to paste the font name in another window.

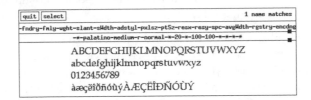

Figure 11.3

xfontsel, displaying a particular font.

A Few Final Words

It's late at night, and my deadline is fast approaching. It feels wrong to leave you with the suggestion that "fonts are complicated, so play around until you understand them," but in some sense that's what Unix is all about. The strategy of many little programs means that the behavior of each program should be easily comprehensible—predictable, or available by trial and error when not easily predictable. Each word in a sentence is, while not definite, limited in some sense, but the conceptual space of possible sentences is unlimited, and we can read whole books in a constant state of wonder at the use of language.

I started thinking about this book nearly two years ago, when I realized that I had nothing to recommend to smart, capable friends when they asked what book they could use to learn Unix. It seemed to me that no book took an approach in the spirit of the system, and I have tried to do that in this book. I have indeed learned quite a bit about the nooks and crannies of Unix while writing this, and I hope you have learned at least the basics. While I tried to write a book useful for people who have never used Unix before, I also wanted to write a book that would reward rereading. Only time will tell if I have met these goals.

Thank you for sticking with me through these 200 plus pages. I hope the experience is as rewarding for you as it has been for me.

HARD LINKS • SOFT LINKS • REDIRECTION AND F
REDIRECTING STDERR • NAME LOOKUP • ROUTIN
READING MAIL VIA POP3 • VI AND REGULAR EXF
FILENAME GLOBBING VERSUS REGEXPS • INTERA
COMMAND-LINE EDITING • HISTORY SUBSTITUTIC
CONTROL • VARIABLES AND QUOTING • CONDI
EXECUTION • WHILE AND UNTIL LOOPS • ALIASE
FUNCTIONS • THE X WINDOW CLIENT/SERVER M
WIDGETS AND TOOLKITS • CONFIGURING X • PE
AND OWNERSHIP • USERS AND GROUPS • HARI
SOFT LINKS • REDIRECTION AND PIPES • REDIREC
STDERR NAME LOOKUP • ROUTING READING M/
• VI AND REGULAR EXPRESSIONS FILENAME GLC
VERSUS REGEXPS • INTERACTIVE COMMAND-LIN
HISTORY SUBSTITUTION • JOB CONTROL • VARIA
QUOTING CONDITIONAL EXECUTION • WHILE A

IV

Appendixes

Answers to Practice Problems

Here are answers to the practice problems included throughout the book. This being Unix, there's often more than one correct answer, even though only one answer will be listed here.

Single command lines may occasionally be broken up over several lines. Generally, the context should make clear whether these are single or multiple commands.

Answers to Chapter 1 Problems

1. Dinner requires at least two arguments, a host and a hostess; any number of guests may be added.

2. In and out are mutually exclusive, and optional. Cuisine is mandatory and requires a type of cuisine. Count isn't an option; it's an argument.

3. `television [-off|-on]`

4. `icecream [-u|-o] flavor [...]`

5. `telephone [-h|-s] [[1][-]NNN[-]]NNN[-]NNNN`

Answers to Chapter 2 Problems

1. `first/file` is not a valid filename. The slash is not a valid character in filenames because Unix uses it to separate directories. `first!file` and `first file` are perhaps bad filenames, but Unix often gives you enough rope to hang yourself, and another couple feet for good measure.

2. `cat stupid_answer.txt`

3. `ls [ghp]*`

4. `ls g???tly.txt`

5. `Going.nxt` and `AGing.txt` are the only files listed that are matched by `[A-G]*ing.?xt`.

6. `mkdir chapter-2`

7. `cd chapter-2`

8. `mkdir test-1`
   `mkdir test-2`

9. `cd test-2`

10. `rmdir ../test-1`

11. On my Linux box, `rmdir .` works and leaves me sitting in that (now imaginary) directory. Remember what I said about Unix giving you enough rope to hang yourself?

12. `cd ~`

13. `rmdir chapter-2/test-2` (If `test-2` still exists)
    `rmdir chapter-2`

14. `chown trinity not-possible.txt`

15. `chgrp matrix no-spoon.txt`

16. Others can only read this file.

17. `chmod g-w too-many-hyphens`
    `-rw-r--r-- 1 jon jon 0 Dec 28 20:56 too-many-hyphens`

18. `chmod 000 too-many-hyphens`
    `---------- too-many-hyphens`

19. My system lets me delete it after asking me if I'm certain that I want to remove a write-protected file. If your system does not let you remove `too-many-hyphens`, `chmod 600 too-many-hyphens`, and then `rm too-many-hyphens`.

20. `ln here there`

21. Hard links are co-equal: They exist as though they are separate files that always share the same contents. Permissions on one do not affect permissions on the other.

22. You can still look at the contents of there because hard links persist even after the original file is deleted due to their co-equal status: A hard link points to the file stored on the disk.

23. `ln -s there everywhere`

24. You can't still look at the contents of everywhere because symbolic links only point to the target file's name. If that file isn't there, the symbolic link points nowhere at all. (If you did give a new file in the same directory the name there, everywhere would point at the new file.)

Answers to Chapter 3 Problems

1. The contents of something.txt are identical to those of /etc/passwd.

2. `cat < /etc/group`

3. `cat < /etc/group > something.txt`

4. `cat < /dev/null > null.txt`

    null.txt should be an empty (zero-length) file.

5. `cd zip 2> null.txt`

    null.txt should contain the error message telling you that you can't change into the directory named zip.

6. `cat > something.txt << NOTHINGATALL`
   ```
   > This file is named something.
   >
   > Presumably, that means something should be in it.
   >
   > All I see here is a whole bunch of nothing.
   >
   > How can that possibly be?
   > NOTHINGATALL
   ```

7. `cat /etc/passwd | wc -l`

8. `cat /etc/passwd | tail -5`

9. `cat /etc/passwd | tail -5 | sort`

10. `cat /etc/passwd | sort | tail -5`

11. `cat /etc/passwd|sort|tail -5|cut -d : -f 1`

12. `cat /etc/passwd|sort|tail -5|cut -d : -f 1,3`

13. `cat /etc/passwd|sort|tail -5|cut -d : -f 1,3 >`
    `last-users-on-system.txt`

14. In this answer, replace `jon` with your own username. If your username has `cat` in it, these won't work: They'll try to kill all your processes. Also note that these might complain about not being able to kill a certain process that doesn't exist; that process is generally the `grep` you're running to find processes named `cat`. Finally, note that you might have to type the command `fg` for `cat` to realize that it has been killed. All this complexity in the service of a practice problem; can you believe it?

    For SYSV systems' ps: `ps -ef | grep ^jon | grep cat | awk '{ print $2}'|`
    `xargs kill`

    For BSD's version of ps: `ps aux | grep ^jon | grep cat|awk '{ print $2}'`
    `|xargs kill`

Answers to Chapter 5 Problems

1. `:set number`

2. `:set wrapmargin=12`

3. `:map <F7> :q!`

4. `:map! <F7> ^[:wq!` (To enter the escape that precedes the colon, type Control-V and then hit Esc.)

5. `:map <F8> 1G!Gsort^M` (To enter the Control-M, type Control-V, and then hit Enter.)

6. `:map <F9> 1G!Gsort^M!Guniq^M`

7. `grep '!$'`

8. `grep 'n?t'`

9. `grep '[ ^]n?t[ $]'` should work in any regular expression engine. Other reg-exps may work equivalently.

10. `grep '(kitten|puppy)'`

11. `grep '^[ ]*[tT]he'` (There is both a tab and a space within the seemingly empty square brackets.)

12. `sed 's/yes/no/gi'`

13. `sed 's/\(Yes\).*\(No\)/\3\2\1/gi'`

14. `sed 's/\(No .*\)No/\1Yes/'`

15. `sed 's#/#///#g'` (Any character besides the forward slash can substitute for the #.)

16. `sed 's/[0-9]\{3\}/know/'` (Other expressions may achieve the same effect.)

17. `:s/whale/monster/`

18. `:s/whale/Jonah/g`

19. `:g/whale/s//krill/g` or `:1,$s/whale/krill/g`

20. `:g/start$/s//finish/gi`

Answers to Chapter 6 Problems

1. The answer is the value returned by `history | wc -l`

2. `echo !!`

3. `echo !-4`

4. `echo !?cat?`

5. `^cat^dog^`

6. `[ jon@razorback ]$ `**`rev`**
   `Control-Z`
   `[ jon@razorback ]$ `**`Enter`**
   `[1]+ Stopped rev`
   `[ jon@razorback ]$ `**`tac`**
   `Control-Z`
   `[ jon@razorback ]$ `**`Enter`**
   `[2]+ Stopped tac`
   `[ jon@razorback ]$ `**`jobs`**
   `[1]- Stopped rev`
   `[2]+ Stopped tac`

7. `bg %1` (All answers in this section assume that you had no other jobs running or suspended before answering these questions.)

8. `kill -STOP %1` or `kill -19 %1`

9. `kill %1 %2`

10. `[ jon@razorback ]$ `**`cat &`**

    `[1] 1414`
    `[ jon@razorback ]$ `**`fg`**
    `Control-C`
    `cat`
    `[ jon@razorback ]$`

Answers to Chapter 7 Problems

1. EXTRAPATH=$PATH

2. [jon@frogbog jon]$ **mkdir bin**
   [jon@frogbog jon]$ **PATH=$PATH:$HOME/bin**

3. [jon@frogbog jon]$ **THIRDARM=$PATH**
   [jon@frogbog jon]$ **export THIRDARM**

4. PATH=$EXTRAPATH

5. [jon@frogbog jon]$ **unset EXTRAPATH THIRDARM**
   [jon@frogbog jon]$ **export THIRDARM**

6. PS1='\n\n) '

7. PS1='\W [\!]$ '

8. [jon@frogbog jon]$ **THIRDARM=4**
   [jon@frogbog jon]$ **echo "My third arm is number $THIRDARM out of 1000"**
   My third arm is number 4 out of 1000
   [jon@frogbog jon]$

9. echo 'The serial number of my third arm is stored in the variable
   $THIRDARM'

10. echo "Today's date is: \`date\`"

11. DATELINE="Today's date is: \`date\`"

12. DATELINE='Todays date is: \`date\`'

Answers to Chapter 8 Problems

1. mkdir theoretical && cd theoretical

2. touch test ; cd .. ; rmdir theoretical 2>/dev/null || echo 'Theoretical is
   actual'

3. ! cd not-really-a-directory 2>/dev/null && echo "not really a directory"

4. if [-f passwordlists -a -w passwordlists]
   then
       cat /etc/passwd » passwordlists
   fi

5. if [-f passwordlists -a -w passwordlists]
   then
       cat /etc/passwd » passwordlists
   else
       echo "No file passwordlists or file not writable"
   fi

6. ```
if [-f passwordlists -a -w passwordlists]
then
    cat /etc/passwd >> passwordlists
elif [! -f passwordlists]
then
    touch passwordlists
else
    echo "File not writable"
fi
```

7. ```
[ -L /dev/mouse ] && echo "That's not a mouse!"
```

8. ```
case $AUTHOR in
Lasser)
    echo "That's a great book!"
    ;;
Sterling|Stephenson)
    echo "That's a pretty good book."
    ;;
*)
    echo "I haven't read that book."
    ;;
esac
```

9. ```
for foo in $HOME/*
do
    [ -d $foo ] && echo "$foo is a directory"
done
```

10. ```
for foo in a b c d e f g h i j k l m\
n o p q r s t u v w x y z
do
    echo $foo:
    ls -d $foo*
done
```

11. ```
[jon@frogbog jon]$ mkdir signal
[jon@frogbog jon]$ while [ -d signal ]
> do
>     echo "Signal exists"
> done
```

12.
```
[jon@frogbog jon]$ mkdir signal

[jon@frogbog jon]$ until [ ! -d signal ]
> do
>     echo "Signal exists"
> done
```

Answers to Chapter 9 Problems

1. `alias mc="mv"`

2. `alias mc="echo 'I think you mean mv.' ; mv"`

3. `unalias mc`

4.
```
function mc
{
echo "I think you mean mv.";
mv $1 $2
}
```

5.
```
function vm
{
mv $2 $1
}
```

6. `unset -f mc vm`

7.
```
[jon@frogbog jon]$ cat act
#!/bin/sh
if[!-f$1 ]
then
echo "$1 is not a regular file."
exit 1
fi
cat $1 | tac | rev
[jon@frogbog jon]$ chmod +x act
[jon@frogbog jon]$
```

8.
```
[jon@frogbog jon]$ cat act
#!/bin/sh
if [ -z "$1" -o "$1" = "-" ]
then
cat | tac | rev
```

```
elif [ ! -f $1 ]
then
echo "$1 is not a regular file."
exit 1
else
cat $1 | tac | rev
fi
[jon@frogbog jon]$
```

9.
```
[jon@frogbog jon]$ cat spaced-out
#!/bin/sh
read FOO
echo $FOO|sed 's/ /_/g'
[jon@frogbog jon]$ chmod +x spaced-out
[jon@frogbog jon]$
```

10.
```
[jon@frogbog jon]$ cat spaced-out
#!/bin/sh
[ -t 0 ] && echo "Please input a line of text: "
read FOO
echo $FOO|sed 's/ /_/g'
[jon@frogbog jon]$
```

11.
```
[jon@frogbog jon]$ cat spaced-out
#!/bin/sh
[ -t 0 ] && echo "Please input text: "
while read FOO
do
echo $FOO|sed 's/ /_/g'
done
[jon@frogbog jon]$
```

Appendix B

Glossary and References

An entirely comprehensive glossary is impossible to create, and frankly not of much value. Instead, I have tried to list only computer terms not explained adequately in the text, terms used far in advance of their full explanation, and terms about which I have strong opinions or that have strong cultural reference in the Unix world. In other words, this is my chance to both enlighten and inflame, a collection of big ideas and petty disputes.

Because a separate references section would need to be organized by topic, it seemed to make more sense to combine these sections. As with glossaries, comprehensiveness of a references section is not indicative of its value. I have stuck to particularly useful sources on topics that need expansion and were not mentioned elsewhere in the text.

The most comprehensive, yet useful, glossary of terms used in Unix culture is the Jargon File, available online at `http://www.tuxedo.org/~esr/jargon/html/`, also available in book form as

> Raymond, Eric S. (compiler)
>
> *The New Hacker's Dictionary, 3rd Edition*
>
> MIT Press. 1996.

Unfortunately, the World Wide Web is a whole lot more fluid than traditional print references. Any changes to these URLs that I know about will be included in my errata for this book, available on my Web page at `http://www.tux.org/~lasser/think-unix/errata.html`, which should be a relatively permanent address.

I hope that this section meets your needs.

admin   The System Administrator, owner of the fabled root account. See also *system administrator, root*

ASCII   Acronym for American Standard Code for Information Interchange, ASCII is the standard method for storing letters as numbers, due to the incapability of computers to work directly with letters. A useful ASCII chart is available online at `http://www.asciitable.com/`. If you want to ponder the deep structure of the arrangement of the ASCII code, convert all the numbers to binary and look at the bit boundaries.

awk   awk is a small programming language named after its three main instigators: Alfred V. Aho, Brian W. Kernigham, and Peter J. Weinberger. It is particularly well-suited to database-style manipulation tasks. The awk FAQ is available online at `http://www.faqs.org/faqs/computer-lang/awk/faq/`. The rather expensive manual written by the authors of the language is

> Aho, Alfred V., et al.
>
> *The Awk Programming Language*
>
> Addison-Wesley Pub. Co. 1988

The other popular guide to the language is

> Dougherty, Dale, et al.
>
> *Sed & Awk, 2nd edition*
>
> O'Reilly & Associates. 1997.

See also *sed*

bar   The second metasyntactic variable, after foo. See also *foo*

bash   The Bourne Again Shell is the GNU project's enhanced version of the original Bourne Shell. The bash home page is at
`http://www.gnu.org/software/bash/bash.html`. See also *csh, GNU, sh, zsh*

beer   The favored beverage of many a sysadmin. Many sysadmins prefer porters, stouts, and various Belgian–style brews. My favorite beers, at this point in time, are the various Belgian–style beers available at The Brewer's Art, a Baltimore-area microbrewery and restaurant, and La Maudite, a red ale brewed in Quebec in a style reminiscent of Belgian beers.

binary   The base-two numbering system, or anything dependent upon that base-two numbering system. Virtually all modern digital computers are based on binary numbers and Boolean algebra. See also *Boolean, decimal, hexadecimal, octal*

A computer program that has been translated into machine language. See also *compile, machine language*

bit   A single digit in a base-two numbering system: a binary digit. Represented by either a one or a zero, those states also correspond to true and false, respectively. See also *binary, byte, nybble, word*

block   The smallest unit of a disk or a tape that can be written to, usually 512 bytes.

A section of a computer program that forms a logical unit, sharing conditions of execution. Generally distinguished by a common level of indentation, forming a visual block on the screen or page.

Boolean   A Boolean variable is one whose status is either true or false. Named after George Boole, eminent logician, who developed the mathematical system that is the basis of digital computers. One very simple introduction to Boolean logic is available at `http://www.newsbank.com/whatsnew/boolean/`. A more in-depth explanation is available in

Feynman, Richard P.

Feynman Lectures on Computation

Addison-Wesley Pub. Co. 1996.

BSD   The Berkeley Software Distribution, a major deviation from the Unix distribution made available by Bell Labs. BSD contributed greatly to the development of Unix, and several free versions are available. The two most popular BSD flavors are probably FreeBSD, available at `http://www.freebsd.org/`, and OpenBSD, available at `http://www.openbsd.org/`. See also *SysV*

byte   Eight bits, also equal to two nybbles, a standard word size on early home computers. One byte is also equal to two hexadecimal digits. When octal was popular, some systems had nine-bit bytes, equal to three octal digits, but modern use refers almost exclusively to eight-bit values. See also *bit, nybble, hexadecimal, word*

C   The standard language for most complex, large tasks, although a newer, object-oriented variation named C++ is important as well. The Unix kernel is written almost entirely in C.

compile   To turn source code into a binary. See also *binary, source code*

csh   The C Shell. Although it once offered some advantages over then-current shells, programming in csh should be avoided at all costs. See the article "CSH Programming Considered Harmful," available at `http://www.faqs.org/faqs/unix-faq/shell/csh-whynot/`.

The way I see it, if you can't program with it, why learn its whole syntax just for interactive use?

decimal   Base-ten mathematics, what we use every day. Computers hate working with base-ten because it doesn't break up into an integral number of bits. That is to say, X bits can never precisely represent Y decimal digits, and vice-versa, where X and Y are integers and the ratio X/Y is an integer that remains constant for given X and Y. See also *binary, bit, hexadecimal, octal*

delimiter   A marker that separates two fields or records in a database. More data can be treated as databases than you might think. For example, the `/etc/passwd` file can be considered a database whose record delimiter is a newline (each line of the file is a record in the database) and whose field delimiter is a colon (each field in a record is separated from the other fields by a colon). Knowing your delimiter is a prerequisite to effective use of either cut or awk.

elm   elm is a seriously outdated mail reader for Unix. At some point, the development team stopped working effectively. At any rate, it occupies a very narrow middle ground between the simple PINE mail reader and the more advanced Mutt. The elm Web page is at `http://www.myxa.com/old/elm.html`. See also *PINE, Mutt*

Emacs   The Other Editor. Thoroughly programmable in LISP, it gobbles up all your system's memory and takes over your life. Some people love it, however, so if you want to try it, you might want to try the built-in tutorial. If you are interested, you might want to look at

Cameron, Debra, et al.

Learning GNU Emacs, 2nd Edition

O'Reilly & Associates. 1996.

It's worth noting that the ascendancy of Unix in the 1980s coincided with the fall into disuse of LISP machines and computers based entirely on that language. It's my suspicion that Emacs was created so that those users could emulate their LISP machines on faster, less expensive and arguably less elegant Unix machines. See also *LISP*, *vi*

Enlightenment   Enlightenment is a thoroughly customizable window manager. Although it's rather heavy on memory usage and wastes bazillions of CPU cycles, most machines are powerful enough that some users will run it. It can be very, very pretty looking, and it can be very, very difficult to use if the theme designer chooses to make things tough. The Enlightenment home page is at http://www.enlightenment.org/.

FAQ   Frequently Asked Questions. Most newsgroups and many informative Web sites maintain a list of frequently asked questions. It is considered polite to check this list to see whether your question is answered there before sending mail to any person, list, or newsgroup. A large, though far from complete, set of FAQs is maintained at http://www.faqs.org/.

foo   The first metasyntactic variable. When you want to discuss an arbitrary variable or if you need a placeholder to substitute for a variable, use foo. See also *bar*

free software   The "free" in "free software" does not refer to price, but to freedom. (The standard explanation is "Think Free Speech, not Free Beer.") Free software can be given away, modified, shared, sold, fixed, or broken by anyone. Most importantly, the source code is shared, not just binaries. Free software is distinguished from open source software by an ideological commitment to the principle that it's immoral to hoard code. The FSF and their GNU Project are the foremost exponents of free software. See also *binary*, *source code*, *open source*, *FSF*, *GNU*

FSF   The Free Software Foundation is committed to the principle of free software. They're the people behind the GNU project. Many people are fully committed to the ideals of free software, but many others are not, and they often deplore the tactics or goals of the FSF. Some of these people believe in open source software, and others are committed to commercial software. The FSF Web site is at http://www.fsf.org/. See also *free software*, *GNU*, *open source*

FVWM   F Virtual Window Manager. Once the most popular window managers in the Linux world, this stalwart is still in use by the faithful. Its configuration files can be customized using the C Preprocessor and other macro languages, making it extremely flexible. The FVWM Web site is at http://www.fvwm.org/.

GNU   GNU, a recursive acronym meaning "GNU's Not Unix," is an attempt to create an entirely free (in the sense of free software) Unix distribution. Having completed a large proportion of the work but not yet developed a kernel, Linux stepped in to complete the system. Partisans of the FSF often refer to Linux as GNU/Linux, to indicate that many of the tools come from the GNU project; others claim the GNU is responsible for a lesser proportion of the system than it claims. See also *free software*, *FSF*, *Linux*, *open source*

hexadecimal   Base-sixteen mathematics. Used by most modern computers because one hexadecimal digit is equal to precisely four bits. Hexadecimal used to compete with octal for popularity, and very definitely won that contest. See also *bit, octal*

ksh   The Korn Shell is the official AT&T follow-up to the original Bourne shell. It differs from bash in several ways, but these two shells compete on essentially equal footing. Some people prefer one, some people prefer the other, and many contemporary systems have both. See also *bash, sh*

Linux   Begun by Linus Torvalds in the early 1990s, at the time of this writing there are more users of Linux than any other Unix flavor. Not technically Unix, but a thorough reimplementation of the standards that make up Unix, Linux is developed by a loosely knit group of developers over the Internet. It is either free software or open source, depending on your point of view, and competes in the desktop Unix arena with the many flavors of BSD. See also *BSD, free software, open source*

LISP   A popular language among certain computing types, the LISP (List Processor) language is renowned for its elegance and purity. For most people, that means it's impractical and difficult, though its following is devoted. So devoted, in fact, that Emacs and the SawMill window manager are based almost entirely on LISP. The whole LISP culture that existed for decades is fanatical; many were forced to switch to Unix when their LISP machines were decommissioned. They grumbled so much about it that a number of them got together and wrote a book:

> Garfinkel, Simson L., et al.
>
> *The Unix Hater's Handbook*

These days, the book is outdated, but it always missed the point. This disagreement between LISP users and other Unix people suggests that there may be more than one sort of elegance. But we won, so why gloat? Besides, their book is out of print. See also *Emacs, SawMill*

Lynx   A terminal-based Web browser. Small, fast, fairly complete, and without distracting graphics. Lynx can be used when you don't have X running. Lynx's Web site is at `http://lynx.browser.org/`.

machine language   The ones and zeros that the computer actually executes, the final form of a computer program. Nobody writes machine code any more. The only people who ever did were those guys flipping toggle switches at the console to enter programs.

Mutt   The premier mail reader for text-based terminals, Mutt is small, fast, and highly configurable. It takes some getting used to but is heir to elm in everything but name. Mutt's Web site is at `http://www.mutt.org/`.

node   Imagine a graph of a computer network, or of pages on the World Wide Web. Imagine the links as lines, and the pages or systems as dots where the lines meet. Those dots are nodes. Terminals are nodes, computers are nodes, Web pages are nodes. You're a node, too, but what's the line, and what's on the other end of it?

An entry in the GNU Info hypertext system.

nybble   Four bits, equal to one hexadecimal digit. One byte is made up of two nybbles, hence the name. See also *bit, byte, hexadecimal*

octal   The base-eight numbering system. One octal digit is equal to three bits. In the 1970s, there was debate as to whether octal or hexadecimal was better for use in computer systems. The argument for octal was that it was more human-readable, and it didn't require the use of letters as digits. The argument for hex was that all hex words were powers of two bits long and that it was more compact. Hexadecimal won, decisively. See also *bit, hexadecimal, word*

open source   A new name for free software that emphasizes the practical rather than ethical or political aspects of the movement. Advocates of open source don't claim that open source is morally superior, but rather that it is technically superior, more secure, and provides for a greater level of control than closed-source counterparts. The Open Source Initiative home page is at `http://www.opensource.org/`. See also *free software*

perl   When people graduate from shell scripts and require more power and control, perl is the language they turn to. A sort of mishmash of C, sh, sed, awk, and regular expressions, it is a highly flexible and powerful combination. If you want to learn perl, the place to start is

> Schwartz, Randal L., et al.
>
> *Learning Perl, 2nd edition*
>
> O'Reilly & Associates. 1997.

The standard reference work on the topic is

> Wall, Larry, et al.
>
> *Programming Perl, 2nd edition*
>
> O'Reilly & Associates. 1996.

See also *awk, C, sed, sh*

PINE   PINE is the standard terminal-based mail program for users new to Unix. More like a typical PC application than a Unix application, PINE makes it difficult to make dangerous mistakes. It's slow, relatively large, and full of pretty menus and help screens. Choice of mailers, like choice of editors, is a religious war, and I'm sad to say that God is not on the side of PINE. The name, by the way, stands for "PINE Is Not ELM." The PINE home page is at `http://www.washington.edu/pine/`. See also *elm, Mutt*

procmail   procmail is a mail filtering system that separates mail into different folders based on regular expression matching. procmail is truly Byzantine in its syntax and complexity, but inordinately powerful as well. The man pages are comprehensive and yet somehow thoroughly unhelpful. The procmail Web site is `http://www.procmail.org/`; from there you might try to find a helpful tutorial. procmail and Mutt make a particularly powerful combination. See also *Mutt*

regex   See *regular expression*

regexp   See *regular expression*

regular expression   The pattern-matching and substitution language almost standard across Unix applications. More powerful than it needs to be for most applications, but powerful enough to do things you can hardly imagine. If you become obsessed with regexps, you might want to read a book about them:

> Friedl, Jeffrey E., editor.
>
> *Mastering Regular Expressions*
>
> O'Reilly & Associates. 1997.

root   The top entity in any hierarchy. The root directory is the top-level directory on a Unix system, the root window is the top window in X's window hierarchy, the root server is the top domain name server, and the root account is the system administrator's account. See also *system administrator*

SawMill   A window manager that is thoroughly customizable in LISP. The SawMill Web page is at `http://sawmill.sourceforge.net/`. See also *LISP*

sed   sed is a "stream editor" that applies regular expressions as a filter. It has a small programming language and can be combined in very powerful ways with awk, though the combination of sed and awk is losing ground to perl. See also *awk, perl, regular expression*

sh   The original Bourne Shell, still the standard for shell language programming. Highly portable among Unix systems, it nevertheless lacks many handy features for interactive use. All shell scripts should run in the Bourne Shell, no matter what you use for interactive use, but good interactive shells that largely share sh syntax are bash, ksh, and zsh. See also *bash, ksh, zsh*

shell   Any program that enables you to interact with the system and execute commands. A shell is a program like any other, but which acts as your interface and provides your command line. Many shells are highly programmable and contain tons of features to simplify your life, or improve it, at any rate. At least, that's what their authors tell us.

One can "shell out" to a command line from various applications. This simply means that the program executes a shell and gives the user access to the system. This is not often more useful than suspending the program, but sometimes you have no choice. See also *bash, csh, ksh, tcsh, zsh*

source code   The program as the programmer writes it. The source code is the most human-readable version of what is compiled by the compiler into a binary. Source code contains much more information about the programmer's thought process and is thus much more useful than just having binaries when debugging somebody else's program. Having the source code gives you technical opportunity to fix bugs, make improvements, and port code to different platforms. See also *binary, compile*

spool   A file that receives some sort of data for later use. The file that contains all your current email is your mail spool, the file that contains a list of things to send to the printer is your print spool, and so on.

ssh   The most popular way to protect your password and other private information when logging on to a remote host. Please read my footnote (#11) in Chapter 4 before using ssh, but also please don't telnet or rlogin to other systems.

sysadmin   See *system administrator*

system administrator   The person who maintains and manages a computer or group of computers. It's a tough job, and I get to do it. The system administrator creates and manages accounts, allocates system resources, and makes sure it's all running smoothly. Nobody notices a system administrator who is doing a good job, and everyone notices the system administrator when there's a problem. As a result, many system administrators have taken an interest in tea, coffee, chocolate, or beer.

If for some reason this sounds interesting to you, one rant on the topic is available at http://www.adminspotting.org/. If even this does not dissuade you, there are three books on the subject worth reading:

Carling, M., et al.

Linux System Administration

New Riders. 1999.

Frisch, Aeleen.

Essential System Administration, 2nd Edition

O'Reilly & Associates. 1995.

Nemeth, Evi, et al.

UNIX System Administration Handbook, 2nd Edition

Prentice Hall. 1995.

You should also buy the following book if you use Unix extensively, and refer to it *before* bothering your admin with redundant questions:

Mui, Linda

What You Need To Know When You Can't Find Your UNIX System Administrator

O'Reilly & Associates. 1995.

See also *beer*

SysV   System V Unix, the standard AT&T release of Unix. Heavily influenced by BSD Unix, SysV Unix was a step above previous AT&T releases, and System V, Release 4 (SVR4) is the standard to which most commercial Unix flavors claim to resemble. See also *BSD*

tcsh   An enhancement of csh that nevertheless contains the same systematic flaws as the original. It's much better for interactive use than anything other than bash, ksh, and zsh. If you're addicted to csh, this is what you should be running.

tty   An abbreviation for teletype, it has become shorthand for any and all character-based terminals hooked up to a Unix box. Every user on the system is attached to a notional tty whenever a shell window is open.

Unix   If you don't have an idea of what Unix is by this point, I'm not sure I can help you. Instead, let me point you at some useful resources:

If your question is "Why Unix?" Neal Stephenson has written an essay entitled "In the Beginning... Was the Command Line." It is available online, though in less-than-convenient formats, at `http://www.cryptonomicon.com/beginning.html`, and in print:

Stephenson, Neal

In the Beginning... Was the Command Line

Avon Books. 1999.

If instead you'd like a glimpse at the history of Unix, the book to read is

Salus, Peter H.

A Quarter Century of UNIX

Addison-Wesley Pub. Co. 1995.

If you'd like a reference to sit on your desk, I recommend going to the bookstore and looking at these two books. Pick one; owning both is probably excessive:

Abrahams, Paul W., et al.

UNIX For the Impatient, 2nd Edition

Addison-Wesley Pub. Co. 1997.

Robbins, Arnold, et al.

Unix in a Nutshell, 3rd Edition

O'Reilly & Associates. 1999.

If you actually have a Linux box on your desk, you might want *Linux in a Nutshell* instead:

Siever, Ellen, et al.

Linux in a Nutshell, 2nd Edition

O'Reilly & Associates. 1999.

Finally, if this whole book went by too fast for you and you need a gentler introduction to Unix, there's nothing better than

Hahn, Harley.

The UNIX Companion

Osborne McGraw-Hill. 1995.

vi   The premier editor for Unix. My favorite update is vim, available online at `http://www.vim.org/`. vi is so admired that there is a "vi Lover's Home Page" available at `http://www.thomer.com/thomer/vi/vi.html`. Admittedly, vi has a lot to remember. The best reference card around is

vi Reference.

Specialized Systems Consultants, Inc. (SSC). 1990.

ISBN 1-57831-005-9

If you'd rather have an online reference, the best one I've seen is `http://www.cs.wustl.edu/~jxh/vi.html`.

Window Maker   A window manager based on the look and feel of the NeXT interface. Relatively configurable and sometimes even lightweight, Window Maker is a popular choice among users who bother to change their default window manager. It's not perfect at anything, but it's pretty good about everything. Its Web page is at `http://www.windowmaker.org/`.

wmx   An almost pathologically small and fast window manager, its configurability suffers as a result. Still, for the small-is-beautiful crowd, it's a wonderful choice. And it looks really cool, too. Its home page is at `http://www.all-day-breakfast.com/wmx/`.

word   The quantity of data a CPU can process most conveniently. Usually a number of bits corresponding to a multiple of the byte. On octal machines, 36-bit words were common because they were four octal bytes long. On more modern machines, 32-bit words are the most common, with 64-bit machines becoming more common by the day.

X   See *X Window System*

X Window System   One of the largest, most often used, and most poorly understood tools on Unix. Although O'Reilly & Associates publishes the official manuals, they're not of much use. Nor is the official X Consortium Web site at `http://www.x.org/` much use, for that matter. I've never seen a book about X at the user level that was worth reading, unfortunately. One Web site with many links to useful technical information is `http://www.rahul.net/kenton/xsites.html`.

If you're interested in different window managers and want to find out about several before trying them out, the best place to look is `http://www.plig.org/xwinman/`, a large and very comprehensive list of window managers, along with sample screen shots and configuration files. Very classy, and very useful.

zsh   The ultimate kitchen-sink Bourne shell enhancement. It has tons of stuff that the author just liked. I'm not really sure who runs zsh, but somebody must like it. The zsh home page is `http://www.zsh.org/`.

Index